INNOCENT
WHILE INCARCERATED
THE DIARY OF JUSTIN LUNSFORD

JUSTIN W. LUNSFORD

‹

For information about this title or to order other books and/or electronic media, contact the publisher:
    Justin Lunsford
    Email: joy@riddlelawaz.com

Printed in the United States of America
Cover and interior design: 1106 Design, Phoenix, Arizona

▌▌ Table of Contents

Table of Contents

▮▮ Introduction By Gary L. Stuart

On July 8, 2008 at approximately 2:00 p.m. someone set fire to a white truck owned by 29-year old Mary Elizabeth Hermann in Cave Creek Arizona. A witness to the truck fire saw a six-foot tall man, weighing approximately 200 pounds, with reddish blond hair driving away from the truck fire in a 1990s model green and silver truck. Three and a half hours later, someone set fire to a house on Seven Palms Lane in Cave Creek, a short distance away from the white truck fire. Ms. Hermann had rented a room in the house. Once the house fire was extinguished, firemen and sheriff's deputies found Ms. Hermann's nude body. She was in a bed in an unburned part of the house. There were two used condoms on the floor beside the bed.

The Maricopa County medical examiner reported at autopsy that she'd been partially decapitated and had forty-five stab wounds in her groin, head, neck, abdomen and back. Someone stabbed her to death. At the time, no one knew who set her car or her house on fire and then massacred her.

Justin Lunsford was arrested and charged with her murder and the arson of her house. He told them he was innocent. He has maintained his innocence to this day. He pled no contest to a second-degree murder charge. The court sentenced him to twenty-three years in prison. He is still in prison and still maintains his innocence. He is actually innocent. The real killer is incarcerated in Arizona but has not yet been charged with Ms. Hermann's murder. This is Justin's story in his own words.

Cave Creek Arizona

••

Summers in the Sonoran Desert are known for their intense yet therapeutic dry heat and golden sunsets. Out-of-towners from colder climates flock to places like Arizona to create a more active and enjoyable winter lifestyle for themselves.

But it is not just the climate that people appreciate; it is also the culture. Arizona is replete with historic small towns turned tourist attractions, such as Prescott with its "whiskey row" and the epic old west town of Tombstone, where Wyatt Earp and Doc Holliday shot it out, guns a blazin' at the O.K. corral putting an end to Arizona's first known criminal gang—"The Cowboys," known for their red sashes and their inclination towards violence.

Even today, the deeper layers of small town Arizona lawmen, and citizens alike, are proud and embrace the straightforward nature of the old west mentality. Aside from the modern veneer, really things haven't changed that much. Common folks are working to provide for themselves and their families, lawmen are still working to enforce the law, and the outlaws, well, they're still doing outlaw things.

Arizona is dotted with countless small towns that are just like Tombstone. The only difference between Tombstone and some of these other towns, isn't that there was no Wyatt Earp or Doc Holliday-like characters, as much as there simply wasn't anyone left standing around to write about them.

I know this because I grew up in one of these small towns—Cave Creek. We were just common people, a sprawling working class family, but it wasn't hard for me to connect the dots as a kid, watching old westerns on the living room floor of the modest house my dad had built. I knew he could turn into Wyatt Earp if he needed to, and it was obvious to me, and all of my cousins, that John Wayne didn't have anything on our granddad.

To this day, I consider it an honor and a privilege to have been born into a little-known family full of such outstanding people, raised by honest, warm, hardworking men and women, in a town like Cave Creek.

We loved our fellow Cave Creekers. What a special town, what a special community. It was full of families just like ours, and some of them would become part of our family.

But just like the old west town of Tombstone, Cave Creek would experience challenges as it grew. After being number one on the list of fastest growing places almost every year for close to 20 years, Maricopa county was getting too big for its britches, and the small-town ruling classes were playing catch-up.

The Phoenix sprawl had now spilled over into the Cave Creek area, attaching the metropolis to the desert foothills and mountains 35 miles from downtown. There was now a new Cave Creek and an old Cave Creek, divided almost literally by carefree highway, the line of demarcation between the historic town and the newer development and subdivisions to the south of it. This was where the suburbs and the country held hands, and they actually made a pretty good couple.

MCSO—The Maricopa County Sheriff's Office

One of the most significant changes we noticed as the population grew was that the Maricopa county sheriff's office established a substation in Cave Creek. Led by sheriff Joe Arpaio, self-proclaimed "toughest sheriff in America," these substations were present in droves. It seemed he had allocated an enormous amount of money to have all the patrol cars painted black in order to help them blend in with regular traffic, but when combined with the condescending disposition his office seemed to have in general, it just made them seem more menacing. Perhaps that's what he was going for, similar to Wyatt Earp adjoining himself to Doc Holliday, a known outlaw, the whole entourage dressed in black, certainly Arpaio's Sun City voters liked it, loved his to-hell-with-procedure, shoot from the hip, political grand-standing lifestyle.

But to us simple folks, working class people, always in the middle of a busy day, it all just seemed like an annoyance. In my early mid 20s I was in the prime of my life; invincible, excited for the future, everything was simple. Due to the growth in the county, our homebuilding company was thriving with no end in sight. My brother and some of our cousins now had children, Granny and Grandad were healthy, so we enjoyed four generations of relatives, and every one of us lived in or around Cave Creek.

After living outside of Cave Creek for about a year I was glad to be back. I had gone from living in a large house of my own in a very brief and young marriage that we both knew was never going to work, with too many bills to pay, to being back at my dad's with him and my brother, (it was like we got the band back together). And I had no bills, a good income and was single. It was perfect.

I reconnected with Jill, the one that got away. We had the time of our lives together every weekend, in between our respective work weeks. We esteemed ourselves as soul-mates, best friends, and would always love each other. But my nonchalant approach to our relationship and life in general, drove her absolutely crazy every now and then. And as a result we would take a "break" from time to time. It was during one such break that I lost my life and everything I loved, on a warm southwest night, in my hometown of Cave Creek, and I never could have seen it coming.

Monday, July 7th, 2008

I had taken over payments from Garnett, my best friend on his motorcycle, a 2006 Honda cbr 600 crotch rocket. It was all black, flat black, no decals, and lighting fast. Riding it had become my favorite hobby, and favorite excuse to go run errands.

I was running one such errand on the evening of July 7th 2008, heading to Target to get a new cell phone. After insisting on having the nicest, newest, cell phone and sunglasses in my younger years, and breaking, cumming-up, or dropping it from the roof of a house I was working on countless versions of both, I had become more frugal. I bought prepaid flip phone from Target, 30 bucks out the door, ready to go.

Riding east on carefree highway, the threshold between civilization's future and its past, and in a symbolic way my own, it was a hot, beautiful summer evening. When the desert sun starts to sink in July, the air temperature stays well over 100 degrees but the lack of direct sunlight can make it feel more like a warm bath, of easy-to-breath dry desert air, which was the actual reason Doc Holliday had moved to Arizona all those years ago, to cope with his health condition, as many still do.

At the east end of carefree highway, after going in to Target, purchasing the phone and pulling out, I only had one tough decision to make—would I go straight back home, or dip north of carefree highway for the four or five mile loop through Cave Creek itself, maybe stroll slowly past the restaurant patios and old west style store fronts, maybe stop in on an old friend.

Yep, I was sold, talked myself into it. Riding through Cave Creek had some thera-peutic value. The whole world just slowed down once you entered "the creek." It was like its own world. Town ordinances created when the city was pushing in on us had dictated, and done it well, that no fast-food restaurant, Walmarts or car dealerships could ever be built north of Carefree Highway.

As a result, the wooden stone fronts would remain and remain forever, leaving some parts of town to look exactly like Mayberry, or a scene from Bonanza. That's exactly what frontier town was, a 10-12-acre tourist attraction in the center of town. Plus, the twenty-five mph limit made you go slow and take it all in.

I pulled into a western style restaurant and bar at the east end of the drag, called *Harold's Corral*. My ex from the afore-mentioned brief marriage held a second job there, and we remained amicable. I thought I'd get an ice tea and say hello, but it was a busy happy hour. Not a single open stool at the huge horseshoe-shaped bar, so she said she'd come by after her shift, and I carried on westward.

I still wasn't ready to go home; I was looking for a reason to stop again, so I figured I'd stop in and see an old friend of mine, Sam Parker. Sam lived in a new condo complex on the west end of town. I hadn't seen Sam in a couple of months, and that was kind of on purpose. The last time I'd seen him, my friend Marvin and I were almost run over by him in the parking lot of the *Buffalo Chip Saloon*, a restaurant and bar of the strangest kind. Owned by retired MCSO Chief Deputy Larry Wendt, and a personal friend of the toughest sheriff in America himself, Joe Arpaio. The *Buffalo Chip* was frequented by MCSO personnel, especially on the night of Arpaio's retirement party; a lot of western folks, especially on Friday nights when bull riding took place in the small arena out back, and even the Hell's Angels. Especially during bike week when they'd station their tent at the *Buffalo Chip*, and every year for their founder Sonny Barger's birthday party, also held at the *Buffalo Chip*. Sonny, like so many others, had moved to the Cave Creek area in recent decades.

Mary Elizabeth Hermann—"Liz"

A young woman named Liz Hermann, who I'd never met or heard of, had also moved to Cave Creek, just a couple months prior after moving out of the north Phoenix house she shared with her estranged husband. She'd taken up bartending for Larry Wendt at the Buffalo Chip. I would meet her on this night.

As I pulled into Sam's small complex, my mind brimmed with curiosity. That last time I'd seen him, he appeared to either be in the middle of some kind of drug-induced paranoia, or literally losing his mind. There wasn't really a third option. After he'd almost run us over, he skidded to a dusty halt in the dirt parking lot, jumped out of his silver Cadillac STS, punched Marvin in the stomach, accused him of being a "cop" and in a panic told us to get in the car.

I have no idea why we got in the car. On the one-mile drive to his condo he told us he had a "kilo of heroin" in the trunk and continued to rant. When we pulled up to his condo he went straight into the bathroom and Marvin and I tiptoed out the door and back to the Buffalo Chip. That was the last time I'd see him.

Pulling up on my bike I wanted to know if his "crazy" was real. As I made the automatic right and then the elbow-turn left I saw Sam standing in his driveway with a young woman and two other guys, one of them Joey Paradise. Yes, that is his real name.

Joey lived in the condo across from Sam's, was my realtor at one point, and was a responsible adult. The young woman with them looked healthy; Sam looked fine, so I found the whole scene to be disarming. I got off my bike and they offered me a beer, I didn't want to be rude so I quickly accepted. I wasn't planning on drinking that night, it was a Monday, but we did have a rare break in work that week. We weren't starting the next house until the following week. I knew that if I had more than two beers I was probably staying.

By the time it got dark we'd finished every beer in his fridge, and we were drunk. I was happy to see that my friend Sam seemed fine. I had really only known him for a couple of years but I was sentimental in nature. We'd gone to high school together but had never hung out socially until I was 24 and he was 23.

I never asked him about the episode he had the last time I'd seen him. Guys in their twenties don't really bring up uncomfortable topics, and I was too young to understand the context anyway. We both were.

At that point all we were trying to figure out was how to solve the riddle of the fridge with no more beer in it. Just Sam, Ashley Madison and I began the half-mile walk to the Circle K.

After getting thereand buying a case of beer, and me paying for it because Sam had forgotten his wallet, Sam opined that we should walk another half mile east and go to the bar. We were already halfway there.

We left the case of beer behind the Circle K, taking a handfull with us, drinking them as we walked alongside the main thoroughfare—the only thoroughfare—Cave Creek Road, toward the amber lights of the dilapidated *Hideaway Bar*.

The *Hideaway Bar* was a run-down looking biker bar. It wasn't the type of bar you went to at two o'clock in the afternoon when it was still early enough to feel shame, or see how dirty the walls really were. It was the place you went to when you were already drunk and didn't care about frivolous things such as aesthetics or biohazards.

It was also the first bar you encountered when approaching the area from that direction. Almost directly across from the *Buffalo Chip* it was the farthest west of the

Harold's, Buffalo Chip, Hideaway trifecta. There was a fourth called *Hammerhead Jacks* at the time, owned by retired Phoenix Sun Tom Chambers, but it did not yet count. There is an unspoken rule in Cave Creek that a bar has to keep the same name for over a year before it is worthy.

Anyway, the *Hammerhead*, as they called it wasn't a "real" Cave Creek establishment yet. My good friend Garrett Bischoff was a bartender there, and a great guy, so I knew they had a chance. Also some transplant from Michigan worked there, a guy named Nathan Noble, whom I didn't know nor would know for another ten years. I had no idea on this fateful night how impactful both of these individuals would eventually be in my life, in two totally different ways.

It had to be after 9 o'clock, p.m., when Sam Parker, Ashley Madison, and I stumbled up the wooden steps of the *Hideaway*. It was actually a trailer. That's why it required steps to get up into it. They'd dressed it up with a wooden patio on the front and a small room added to the left, as you approached. Mark Bradsway, the short, squat, biker-looking owner with a big frizzly beard showed his customers there was no structural deficiency that could not be covered up with enough *Coors Light* ribbons and *Budweiser* posters. The west end opens up like a garage door, so as you approach you can see right through the umbrella-tables on the patio, into the establishment, all the way to the bar.

Right away I recognized family friend Mark Lofgren, a plumbing contractor who I'd worked with, standing at the bar waving to me. Mark was married to my cousin's best friend. They had all "grown up" together; some grew up more than others did. As a result I usually saw him and his wife and kids at our family gatherings, him sitting on a lawn chair across from me "shushing" me about whatever bar I'd seen him in the week before. He was in his 30s, a dad, and his wife wasn't supposed to know.

Sam and Ashley grabbed a patio table, and I went inside to get the drinks. I was the only one with a wallet. I gave a warm greeting to Mark, who had a young lady under his arm. He introduced her to me, telling her that I was "the guy" a couple of times. "This is the guy, this is the guy,

He told her.

Her name was Liz. She had dark hair, a white dress, was every bit as drunk as I was, and really wanted to find some cocaine.

"Oh," now I know what he meant. Do I have any? She wanted to know.

"No, no I do not, I am not the guy."

"Can you get us some, can you please get some? We know you can get it."

It was true. I could get it. About two years earlier, the first time I caught my ex cheating, I deviated from my wholesome roots. My lifelong best friend, who was present for the whole ordeal, saw how dumbfounded and hurt I was and offered to cheer me up.

"Trust me, bro," Isaac had said, in his soft-spoken 32016 Mexican demeanor.

Isaac had driven me a half hour south, into north Phoenix where he introduced me to a Mexican national from Sinaloa named Leo. Leo and his brother Freddy, as it turned out, were kind of a big deal in that world. Isaac and I sat down with Leo in his apartment, drank Cervezas, and did lines of premium Sinaloa cocaine.

I found out right away why Johnny Cash liked it so much, and why Robin Williams always talked so fast during his stand-up comedy bits. I couldn't shut up. But I guess all that self-disclosure endeared him to me because Leo told me I could come back whenever I wanted. And I kind of liked him too.

But there was literally no chance that I was getting on my crotch rocket, already drunk, and driving all the way down into Phoenix for any reason.

I told Liz, "sorry, not tonight."

But she would not relent. She was pushy, not rude, but pushy. I had objective reasons for not going. I was too drunk to drive; I didn't want to spend the money. She had objective reasons why it didn't matter. She would drive us. She would pay for it. And she would not take no for an answer. I lost the debate. I left Sam and Ashley a couple of twenty-dollar bills and told them I'd be back in an hour.

Worst decision I ever made.

Sinaloan Drug Dealers

Liz and I left the *Hideaway* and walked down and across the street into the dirt parking lot that the *Buffalo Chip* shared with *Harold's Corral*, got into her truck, and headed south. Apparently she had gotten off from her shift earlier that evening at the *Buffalo Chip* and went to the *Hideaway* to socialize, getting drunk in the process.

Since Leo had gone back to Mexico for the time being, I called his brother Freddy to let him to know I was headed that way. Since I still had not gone through the long and boring automated process of turning my new flip phone on, I called Freddy from Liz's phone.

She seemed to understand everything I said to him, even though it was almost all in Spanish. She explained that she had some experience somewhere south of the border with something related to drugs. I leaned much later that Liz had an aunt in Paraguay with a Hispanic last name.

When we pulled up into Freddy's apartment complex I said I'd be right back, but she said she was going to come in with me.

"Nope," I said.

But again, she would not relent. So, with my nonchalant disposition and current intoxication, I said "Okay, but let's act like we actually know each other."

We agreed on a back-story and went in. Freddy was not there, which was often the case. But one of his guys, Jesus, welcomed us at the door. We went in, made the purchase, and hung out for about a half hour. We each did a line, Jesus and another henchman did a line. Of course, spirited conversations began.

I couldn't hear what Liz was talking to *Hydo* about, but I could tell that she was talking a lot. I was in the kitchen talking to *Jesus*. Liz and Hydo were in the living room area, when he got up and approached me, re-asking the same background questions we'd already discussed, making everyone uncomfortable. So I initiated goodbyes and we left.

The One-Night Stand

When we headed back north on *Cave Creek Road*, back toward the *Hideaway*, Liz told me her roommate was out of town and asked if I'd like to just go back to her place instead. We stopped at the Chevron gas station at the intersection of Cave Creek Road and Carefree highway, picked up a case of beer, and went to her house right around the corner, about three-quarters of a mile southeast. My own house was three-quarters of a mile northwest of the Chevron, so it turned out that we actually lived pretty close to each other. But then again, in the small town of Cave Creek, everyone lived pretty close to each other.

We went east. I had driven though the same stretch of road hours earlier on my motorcycle, having no idea I'd be doing it again later with someone I'd just met. We turned south on 56th street, and after a couple of blocks slowed down and eased right, onto a gravel road called *Seven Palms Lane,* where she stopped in the middle of the road. She was staring at two sedans parked on the left shoulder, empty.

Apparently her house was the first one on the right, so the cars were parked directly across from her house. Next to the cars were mailboxes, but no one was standing there checking their mail, and the headlights shining through the cabs showed the cars to be empty. There were no streetlights or sidewalks, no house across from hers, just desert landscape everywhere, and it was almost midnight at this point, so it was kind of suspicious.

She reluctantly pulled into her driveway on the right, and then careened left to a stop, directly in front of the front door. There was no garage or carport, just a modest Cave Creek home, not dissimilar from my own.

I followed her in. She immediately stopped, this time staring at the back door, which was wide open. Someone had been, or still was, in her house. Before she took another step she pulled out her cell phone and called Allen, her roommate, three times. She told him about the situation and asked if he'd happened to come home and leave the backdoor open.

No" he said, "he hadn't been there for two weeks."

I should've known at that point that something wasn't right, but I was twenty-six, naïve, and easy going.

We spent the next little while checking all the rooms and searching for the dog and the cat, which were both nearby. A half hour after we resumed recreational activities, and a couple hours after we did what grown-ups who leave bars together do.

Sometime before sun-up, Liz drove me back to Sam's where my motorcycle was. He was gonna be pissed. He probably waited all night for me to come back to the bar. At least I'd left him forty bucks, enough for him and Ashley to enjoy themselves, so he shouldn't have that much to complain about.

Unfortunately, or fortunately, Sam never answered the door. My keys were inside, Liz had already driven off, and my phone wasn't activated yet. So I was stuck on the porch. What a wild night. Recognizing defeat, I slouched down on his porch and got comfortable. It would not be the first time I'd slept in a strange place after a wild night, and it definitely would not be the last.

Gerald Coco—Tuesday, July 8, 2008

Gerald Coco was sitting in front of his computer Tuesday July 8th, at about noon working on his online classes when I called him, asking for a ride. He said he'd could really use a break from his online schooling anyway, so he got in his white Monte Carlo and drove five minutes north, into Cave Creek, to pick me up at the *Circle K* on Basin road, near Sam Parker's condo. As I got in his car I told him Gerald about my wild night with a girl I met while drinking with Sam *Hideaway Bar*. Gerald did not like Sam. Gerald's little brother Kellen had taken recreational drug use about 100 miles per hour into mastication, then addiction, and had ended up on the bad list of several drug dealers, including Sam, which ended one night in a car accident/fist fight.

Cave Creek was just like Tombstone in the 1800s, when that golden southwest sun sank down behind the saguaro-spotted desert hills, and darkness often gave way to dysfunction.

It was this dysfunctional element Gerald and I talked about driving past the *Rancho Manana* golf course, on the Cave Creek curve, heading south past the MCSO substation, towards my house and Gerald's. At the time, we were still young and naïve enough to believe that there really was fun in dysfunction, as long as we kept it recreational—an idea we shared with many American youths.

I told Gerald that I left the Hideaway Bar with a girl had a one-night stand with her, but couldn't quite remember her name. I didn't know then that Liz would become a household name in Cave Creek. I told Gerald she had basically dragged me out of the Hideaway Bar that night insisting that I help her get some powder cocaine and not relenting until I finally agreed. Mark Lofgren had introduced us and put me on the spot, telling her that I was "the guy" who could help her achieve the goal that she had apparently already set—finding coke.

I told Gerald I took her to "Freddy's" apartment. Technically she took me there, and that I had become so comfortable with her on the half-hour drive down there that when she insisted that I go inside their apartment with me I reluctantly greed.

Gerald's eyes bulged. He knew these Sinaloan drug dealers, and knew despite their kind demeanors and polo tee shirts; they were connected to the Sinaloan cartel, and thus dangerous. More specifically, his little brother Kellen had peddled coke for Freddy and his brother, Leo. Kellen, due to his usual lack of self-control and disillusions had snorted it all up and never paid them, putting himself in danger. Gerald didn't have to remind me about that. His deliberate eye-bulge said it all.

"Don't worry" I retorted, This young lady and I made up a back-story that we had been dating for 6 months. I vouched for her. She jumped right into character, initiating handholding and a kiss while inside their apartment. It seemed to be going fine, we made the purchase, hung out with the two henchmen for a bit—Jesus and Hydo—did a couple of lines each, chatted, and when Hydo began re-asking the same background questions I quickly initiated good-byes and we left. It was fine.

On the way back to the Cave Creek bar, she told me that her roommate was out of town, asked me if I wanted to just go back to her place and so we did. A one-night stand. Then she drove me back to Sam's condo where my bike was. Sam didn't answer the door. My keys locked inside. Liz had already driven off, and so I was stuck on the porch.

I also told Gerald that we'd seen two suspicious cars in front of Liz's house, that Liz was spooked by their presence, and that when we stepped into her house she panicked at finding the back door open. as if sowmeone had just fled out the back. She called her roommate three times, even though it was midnight to ask if he had been at the house and he said he had not, for two weeks and knew nothing about it. We checked the rooms, found the dog and the cat, calmed and went about the night.

Gerald in his charming Boston accent suggested that she must have had something going on her personal life.

"Yeah, doesn't everybody," I said, in my easygoing demeanor.

Gerald and his mom and dad, and brother, had moved to Cave Creek from Boston about ten years earlier. Gerald was thin but not frail, a poor man's Ben Afflack, fluent with young women but nervous, anxiety-plagued, and always had his prescription Xanax close by. If the Xanax didn't do it, he would chase the pills with booze; if it did, he would chase it with booze anyway and when he got really comfortable, he liked his coke.

Murder & Arson

. . . .

Unbeknownst to Gerald, or me, the small town of Cave Creek had become engulfed in the most horrific and eventually controversial murder and arson in its history. It had taken place while we were stumbling around north Phoenix. It happened to the girl I'd had the one-night stand with the day before. Liz.

As he drove me into Cave Creek, her house crawled with first responders and emergency personnel. They said her nude, badly brutalized body lay on the gravel driveway inw plain sight of onlookers. Much later, I learned that police reports confirmed the initial 911 callout was at 8:30pm, and that detectives, after a brief stop at the house fire, went directly into the Cave Creek bar scene. That was at the direction of private citizen Joy Gorski, Liz's friend and coworker.

Gerald and I stopped at my house to grab some money and then we headed to his apartment at *Azure Creek*, where his mom Cindy fed us a homemade *Macaroni* for lunch, which she had prepared the day before her own birthday. *Azure Creek* was a very tasteful apartment complex, about five minutes south of my house, and Carefree Highway, on Cave Creek road. I had actually lived at *Azure Creek* two years earlier, when and where my first, brief marriage began circling the drain. My roommate, Isaac and had good times there. Perhaps too many. But I didn't miss it, and Kelly, the property manager, who lived directly above my apartment, didn't miss us either. Eventually my ex trespassed the property by smashing her stiletto high-heel shoe through my dining room window, foot, leg and all, in the middle of the night, to wake me, and our neighbors up. She insisted on finishing an argument she'd started the day before. She was a peach, but I'm sure I didn't help. Eventually she talked Kelly into letting her come back by faking a pregnancy.

While Gerald and I sat at the dining room table, shoveling macaroni and beer down our gullets, his sweetheart of a mom, Cindy, accommodated us. She treated all of us guys like her sons. However, something strange, bizarre, and disturbing had begun to take place five miles away, totally unbeknownst to us.

As Gerald, Cindy and I casually ate lunch and visited, from 1 pm to 3 pm, Kenneth Martinez, a Maricopa County sheriff's deputy, deputy, stood on the side of Cave Creek road near Liz Hermann's house, taking a statement from a man named Jimmie Larson. Larson explained to Martinez that at 2:15 p.m., he witnessed a tall, light-skinned man with red, bushy hair, wearing white and tan clothes ignite a white Chevrolet truck on fire, and then get in a "green colored vehicle" and driving off as fast as he could. While the deputy was interviewing Larson, the charred, white Chevrolet truck sat ominous and grey behind them. Wisps of smoke lingered from an orange gas can in the cab.

Gerald and I had been at his apartment with mama Coco for over an hour at this point. At about 3:15 p.m. I walked out to the parking lot. My black hair was buzzed short. My skin was very tanned. I wore a black tee -shirt and dark grey shorts. I drove Gerald's white Monte Carlo with him. Neither of us were aware of the sequence of events that had been set in motion a ways down the road. We drove to one of our favorite sports bars, *Gallagher's*. It was on Carefree Highway near my dad's house, where I lived. Surveillance video showed us entering the bar at 3:35 p.m., me in dark clothes, with black hair, and us sitting at a cocktail table where we had some drinks.

MCSO Investigation

∙∙

While we were still at Gallagher's, at exactly 4:15 p.m., deputy Kenneth Martinez was pulling up to the house of the registered owner of the torched Chevy truck which he had found a half burnt plastic gas can in the cab, with 2 to 3 inches liquid gasoline still in the bottom. An obvious arson. Bizarrely, deputy Martinez made no attempt to locate the victim of the arson, twenty-nine year-old Liz Hermann. If he had, he may have saved two lives. Hers and mine.

Surveillance video from Gallagher's shows us sitting at Gallagher's, just two young guys, friends, having some drinks and watching ESPN, while deputy Martinez is knocking on Ms. Hermann's door. After getting no response he leaves, and goes about finishing his shift.

Gerald and I finished our beers and are seen on video walking out of Gallagher's at 4:25 p.m., where we got in his white Monte Carlo and headed south. Who knows where the light-complected red-haired arsonist in the green vehicle was then. MCSO was not even looking for him, or Liz Hermann.

Gerald and I went to Phoenix, and didn't come back to Cave Creek until he dropped me back off at my home at 9 p.m. Had it been up to me I would've gone from Gallaghers. I was tired, I had not yet showered, and had gotten most or all socializing out of my system the night before. But by now Gerald had had enough drinks and Xanax to inspire ambition and was really in the mood for some powder cocaine. Since he couldn't get it from his brother, or the people that his brother burned out of about a thousand dollars, Freddy and Leo, he needed me to get it for him. Ergo, just like Liz the night before, Gerald was now asking me to get it for him. Was I the only person who had not stiffed them?

How did I end up in this position, how did I end up being "the guy"? I was anti-drug until I was twenty-four. I always told my friends and my ex back then there were absolutely no drugs allowed at my apartment or my dad's house, except the occasional bag of reefer. They'd say, after all, if Topher, Grace, and Ashton Kutcher smoked it on the "70s show" it must be safe, right?

We were "beer-only" partiers, and it was important to have an abundance and share, if at all possible. Unfortunately, I the "yes-man," applied that same generosity to all Cave Creek cokeheads after Isaac plugged me into Freddy and Leo. I was just being generous; after all, they were people too. And I didn't see any harm in it, yet. I knew successful contractors who I looked up to in the work environment who recreated that way occasionally. It was common knowledge within the context of American history that President Franklin Delano Roosevelt, "FDR," had used powder cocaine the day he entered the United States into WW II.

At any rate, by 2008, as Gerald and I headed south into Phoenix, I began to realize that it wasn't so much the cocaine that was bad, as much as it was all the "new friends" it came with. Gerald was terrified of being anywhere near Freddy. So, we went to the apartment of Max Piper and Andrew Phillips, a couple of low-level party boys who usually had coke, weed, and all kinds of pills. Drew and Max lived in north Phoenix, about five minutes from Freddy's apartment locations; they had several. Sam Parker's best friend, Hunter Anacker, had introduced me to Phillips a year earlier at a Cave Creek house party, where Garett Bischoff almost beat him up for selling coke in the garage.

Cave Creek is a thirty-minute drive from Phoenix. There are socioeconomic and cultural differences between Cave Creek and the part of Phoenix we were headed that day. Drew and Max lived in "the square," an area known for drugs and crime. No one drove into the square with good intentions; no one drove out of the square in compliance with the law.

Trap and trace cell phone data would later show Gerald and me arriving in north Phoenix by 5:30 p.m., then moving around the area within "the square" until 7:30 p.m. We could not fathom what was happening in Cave Creek while we were in Phoenix, or how it would unfairly change both of our lives forever. Unfortunately, the cell phone data would be buried by the MCSO for over 10 years before I figured out how to break the codes on the call logs.

Just before 5:30 p.m., Gerald and I arrived at Drew and Max's apartment, to find Drew at home with a friend inside, Ryan Milhoff, whom we did not know. Max wasn't home, and that was unfortunate because he was basically in charge of their low-level dealing. For the one year that that I'd known them, neither ever had a job, until about a week before our visit that day. Max had gotten a job at a temp-agency and was at work when Gerald and I stopped by.

Drew did not have what Gerald wanted, so we weighed our options. Drew stood in the doorway, bloodshot eyes sunk into the pale backdrop of his light complected freckled face, lined by his scruffy red hair, with that thousand-yard stare, waiting for an answer. One thing you could always count on was that Max would take enough downers to have himself in a coma by 9 p.m., unless there was coke. Drew would ingest any drug that was placed in front of him, except meth or heroin. None of us did those two drugs. Those were for "losers." Yes, I see the irony.

I told Gerald if he wanted coke that bad he would just have to pull his bootstraps up and drive me to Freddy's. He could wait in the parking lot. That's what we did, except, to stay away from Freddy, Gerald dropped me off and drove over to the Safeway and Walgreens' parking lot next door to wait for me.

I walked up to Freddy's door, knocked, no answer. Knocked harder, no answer. Toe-kicked the door. Nothing. So, I left. I walked fifty yards through the complex and popped out next to the Walgreens, didn't see Gerald, or his white Monte anywhere. But I did see a payphone, so I used it to call Gerald. He didn't answer, so I called him again. Both times it went straight to voicemail. Great.

Then I thought 'what the heck' and called Freddy's cell phone from the payphone. Freddy answered the phone and was yelling at me, screaming actually. He said that "the girl" I had brought to his apartment the night before was a "C.I." He meant "confidential informant." So, he said Jesus and Hydo had to vacate the apartment immediately, and our relationship was over.

"Damn," I thought. That's the last time I'll ever talk to them.

Then I called Gerald again. This time he answered. He'd ducked into Safeway to get more drinks.

Eventually, the phone records, from Gerald's phone and the Walgreens payphone, would show that those four phone calls took place between 6-6:15 p.m. This became hugely important when MCSO detective Paul Smith tried to put Gerald and me in Cave Creek at this time, by bullying Gerald's phone records and coercing Kenneth Schafer to change his time.

Rather than me driving north to Cave Creek at this time, the trap and trace locations from Gerald's phone actually show us going *south*, pinging at 30th and Greenway Parkway, Drew and Max's apartment, just after 6:30 p.m.

A week later, Max would tell the MCSO that Gerald and I were there, at his apartment at the time we said we were. He told them he got off of work at 5:30 p.m., had come home, and a short time later I had shown up with Gerald. He said we had stayed briefly and left.

Around the time it started getting dark," he said, which, in July is about 7:30 p.m. Max also told them I had a "conflict with someone that day, regarding a girl from the night before," which the MCSO overacted to, thus spotlighting me.

When Gerald and I showed up at Drew and Max's apartment that night, I told them the apartment complex on Central and Bell "would not be getting a check from Freddy anymore." I started to explain why to Max, but he laughed and brushed it off, saying, "don't tell me."

I introduced him to Gerald and told him what Gerald wanted. Max said he was sorry and could not produce.

Max said, "Sorry."

We left.

"At least I got rid of Freddy," I told Gerald in consolation.

However inadvertently, I was thinking maybe Kellen could come home now. Little did I know that on this very day, Kellen was hiding in a house eighty miles away in a small desert town south of Phoenix called Maricopa.

As we finally began traveling north, Gerald's phone pinged twice at Cave Creek and Union Hills at 7 p.m. and 7:18 pm. Tragically, at 7:25 p.m., just seven minutes after the 7:18 ping, a homicidal madman with a penchant for knife violence and arson was pouring gasoline all over Liz Hermann's house, just minutes after brutally killing her and setting her house on fire at 7:30 p.m., and disconnecting the flex line from the dryer in order to accelerate the fire. At that exact time, Freddy and I were a full thirty-minute drive south of Cave Creek.

On our way home we stopped at Zack Shaefer's house at I-17 and Carefree Highway, where Gerald's phone pinged at 7:50 p.m. Zack wasn't home, so we waited, and spoke to his dad, Kenneth Schaefer, for a few minutes. Finally Gerald took me home where we passed my brother and Krystal Boughman in the driveway at nine p.m., exchanging greetings.

Exhausted from the Gerald coco-coca marathon, and glad to finally be reunited with my own bed, I went inside and slept solidly for the next 16 hours.

However, when he dropped me off, Gerald was just getting started. He went to the *Hideaway Bar* after he left my house. He was drunk when he rolled his white Monte Carlo up into the dusty dirt parking lot of the *Hideaway*, stumbled up the wooden steps, through the umbrella-tabled patio and into the bar. He he pulled up a seat and ordered a drink from the same bartender who I'd ordered drinks from the night before, Rebecca Harding. She had witnessed me being introduced to Liz Hermann by Mark Lofgren. As Gerald drank, he began picking up on conversations around him.

"The murder was all that people were talking about that night at the bars," said MCSO detective Kristina Bucaro in a tape-recorded interview. Bucaro was combing the bars that night with other detectives, looking for solid information, and trying to separate it from gossip.

Word had spread into the bar scene quickly because onlookers that had accumulated at the house fire before personnel arrived. Fire personnel, unprepared for the discovery of Liz Hermann's body, had extracted it from the burning house. They laid her on the driveway in plain sight of onlookers, prompting phone calls and panic. Within minutes, Liz's Hermann' friend and fellow bartender, Joy Gorski, was on the scene. So were numerous unwanted individuals. The connections between Hermann, Gorski, the pool of potential interviewers, the actual killer, MCSO personnel, both professionally and socially, and layers of other seedy characters, were all together embodied in the social petri dish that the *Buffalo Chip* brought to life. It was a microcosm of the bigger Cave Creek bar scene and adjoining dysfunction, which went largely unnoticed by the untrained eyes of newer community residents. It is unclear to me which deputy contacted Joy Gorski upon discovery of Liz's body.

The Buffalo Chip

MCSO retired Chief Deputy Larry Wendt founded and owned the *Buffalo Chip Saloon*. He was very close to Sheriff Joe Arpaio. Wendt started the business while accepting his tax-dollars-paid-for salary as "Chief Deputy"- a position created by Arpaio for several of his personal friends, which tabloids complained provided a six-figure salary for Wendt, but no actual work or role in the MCSO.

Apparently bored with law enforcement work, Wendt, whose position indicated that he oversaw the county jails in downtown Phoenix, actually spent most of his time 45 minutes away in Cave Creek. The *Buffalo Chip* provided a good extra income for him and a place for MCSO personnel to cool off when in need of a good watering hole. After Arpaio himself was criminally charged, convicted, then pardoned by President Donald Trump, he could be seen at the *Buffalo Chip* on TV as local media covered his retirement party. They were all drinking and laughing at the bar with Larry Wendt. He was shiny-faced and flushed, with his big-ole broad-rimmed cowboy hat darn near knocking stuff over, having a heckava good time.

Ironically, each year when Sonny Banger's birthday came around, and he and ranking members of his outlaw biker gang, the *Hell's Angels*, needed to determine where best to have a party, with no worry of law enforcement intervention, they flooded the *Buffalo Chip* in droves, as they also did at bike week every year and partied unabated.

As a result, and due to the unbending effects of proxemics, *Buffalo Chip* bartenders became friendly with MCSO personnel and bikers. Hermann's association with the Hells Angels became a point of contention between her and her husband, and the MCSO staff came to feel endeared and protective of colleague Wendt's Buffalo Chip employees, including Liz Hermann and Joy Gorski, who was married to an MCSO deputy.

Aside from all of that, and rather peripherally, individuals like Sam Parker made a business of selling stolen guns in the *Buffalo Chip* parking lot to people like Mark Lofgren. People such as Spencer Schaefer, Zack Schaefer's brother, was busted selling drugs in the *Buffalo Chip* parking lot.

Then, there were people like me, who just liked to socialize, drink beer there, and feed quarters to the juke box, yelling "rack' em" to a buddy as we started another game of pool. Inside, at the dinner tables, there might be some mature couples sitting down to a nice steak dinner, contemplating dancing to the Pat James Band's cover of "friends in low places" by Garth Brooks.

As in most communities, business owners and politics were one and the same, law enforcement landing a little bit on both sides. Fellow bar owners Larry Wendt and Mark Bradshaw of the *Hideaway*, sat on the town council, and employed "security" staff who would move on to become MCSO detectives. It was an elaborate web, as an old west town morphed into a plot from "Sons of Anarchy." Sonny Barger actually served as technique adviser and made cameo appearances in the hit Fx TV series "Sons of Anarchy" while living in Cave Creek, which inspired some of the plotlines.

As Gerald Coco pulled out his barstool and sat down into the melting pot gumbo of the Cave Creek bar scene, ninety minutes after Liz Hermann's house was ignited, he had no idea what he was sinking down into. Detectives were combing the establishments, and within forty-five minutes of Gerald Coco sitting down, the ten o'clock news came on the *Hideaway's* TV screens, leading with a breaking story out of Cave Creek.

Russ Boetcher, a personal friend of Liz Hermann, later told MCSO that he too was at the *Hideaway* that Tuesday night, watching news coverage of Liz's murder. Liz's roommate Allen Bauer said Russ had called him while he was at the Hideaway watching the news coverage. Allen said that Russ was also at the *Hideaway* on Monday night and saw Liz there in person, although Russ told MCSO he had not seen Liz Monday night. He said he'd only called her at nine p.m. and asked if she wanted to come to his house to watch a movie. According to Russ, she said no, and that she was "not in the mood" to go out.

I assumed she turned down his attempt at an apparent "booty call" because she was leaving the *Hideaway* with another man who she'd just met — me. Russ told police he had heard details that Liz came home to find her back door open, while he was at the *Hideaway* bar, whether from Coco or Allen is unknown.

Because she had left the bar with me, and the same bartender, Becca Harding, was on duty, it became quickly and widely expressed that the murdered woman had gone home with Justin Lunsford "last night." I can only imagine what Gerald Coco thought when he heard this.

In his own head, Gerald began connecting the dots, one beer at a time, between taking a few Xanax pills. He was with me after the phone call to Freddy from the Walgreens' payphone, the one that Freddy said Liz was a C.I., and her presence the night before had all but up-ended his whole operation.

It was obvious to Gerald what had happened. He didn't know Liz Hermann, had never met her, had no idea where she lived, what she looked like, but he knew what his gut was telling him. The same Sinaloan drug dealers who he feared might kill his wayward little brother, really were murderers, and they had obviously killed this "Liz" because she was a C.I.

MCSO detectives, including Kristina Bucaro, may have walked right past Gerald Coco at the bar that night. We'll never know because they didn't speak to him. Or did they? And just not record or disclose it? Gerald drank as much as he could until he left the bar at around midnight to drive home. He'd been drinking for twelve hours straight at this point. MCSO deputies would have another chance to speak to Gerald on Cave Creek road, nearing the *Azure Creek* apartments on Tatum Boulevard.

As Gerald struggled to keep his white Monte Carlo between the white lines, and failed, he was stopped for DUI by an unknown MCSO deputy, just as Liz Hermann's house was filled with crime scene investigators. It is unclear why no arrest or incident report was made, but for some reason, the MCSO deputy let the sloppy-drunk Gerald Coco call his dad, Gerald Sr., and go home.

Wednesday July 9, 2008

In the early afternoon of the following day, I woke up in the upstairs guest room at my dad's house, which I had moved into upon my return to "the creek".

When my brother and I were growing up we shared a large downstairs bedroom, extended by an addition we had added onto the northeast end of the house, making our "room" like a small house or apartment in and of itself. The great thing about being raised in a family of homebuilders was that we could add features and rooms onto our own homes at will.

At this point in 2008 my brother and my niece's mom were beginning to construct an impromptu family of their own, occupying the rooms he and I shared growing up. So as a conciliatory prize, and in light of my own failed attempt at an impromptu family, my dad had gifted me the upstairs room for as long as I wanted or needed it. It was perfect. It was not connected to the interior of the main house- you had to go outside, and up or down patio stairs to get from one to the other- offering privacy, yet a bustling family atmosphere was always available. My brother, my dad, the babies, the moms, both young and old, had a full dynamic, fun-loving 26-year-old uncle upstairs who rode a crotch rocket, and loved to cook.

The Lunsford family thrived on closeness, with a positive and easygoing approach to everything. We never argued, there was never a raised voice in a Lunsford house, and we were all proud of each other and ourselves as a family, a tradition we inherited from granny and grandad next door.

When I finally crawled out of bed on Wednesday afternoon I finally activated my new phone. Buying a new phone was the only reason I had even left my house on Monday evening. Once activated, I saw the barrage of text messages and voicemails that had been sent to me in the preceding hours, including one from my mom. She said that she had gotten a phone call from Jill, and that she needed to see me. So, I got dressed and walked the single block to my mom's house. I had also gotten a text from Jill sent at 1:59 p.m., this same day, saying, "please call me." It was strange because we were both spending time with our exes and I knew she was not happy with me at the time.

When I arrived at my mom's she was standing outside waiting for me, with a couple of her friends. She told me that Jill had called her, saying that she had heard that a woman I'd left a bar with on Monday night had been killed on Tuesday night. Everybody was talking about it. They said the woman was killed by blunt-force trauma, maybe a shotgun wound to the neck and that the house had been burned down with two children inside of it.

"Oh my god!" I thought. She handed me a business card for a MCSO detective named Chris Osborn, who had been asking around about me. I immediately called him and told him who I was, where I was, and that I would do "anything I can" to help them. I explained to him how to get to my mom's house and waited for him to get there.

July 9, 2008—First MCSO Interview

Within ten minutes, Detective Osborn showed up with a female detective, Kristina Bucaro. I initiated introductions and handshakes. Detective Osborn asked if I wound mind going with them to the station to talk about what I observed on Monday night.

"Absolutely," I said, getting into an unmarked S.U.V. with them. On the way to the station, about a five-minute ride, I was still waking up, still groggy, trying to wrap my head around what I had just been told.

I asked Detective Osborn "Is it true, that this happened, a shotgun blast and the house was burned down, *and* two kids died in the fire?"

Osborn said no, most of that was untrue, the young woman did die, but there were no kids involved. That was just where some of the competitive gossipers had gone with the rumors they'd found.

Osborn asked me, "Justin, I gotta ask you, you've lived here awhile, right? Is Cave Creek a dangerous place, does this type of thing happen here?"

"No, nothing. I've lived here my whole life. No one has ever been murdered in Cave Creek, nothing like this has ever happened."

I thought of someone I'd known in middle school had died in a car accident, the whole town had felt the weight of the loss, but there really wasn't a reference point for something like this.

We pulled up into the parking lot of the Cave Creek MCSO substation, directly across Cave Creek road from the *Territorial Bar and Grill*, owned by good friends of mine, exited the SUV, walked into the station, down a hallway and into a small room on the right, and sat down at a small interview table, just Osborn and I, across from one another.

Osborn was lumberjack-sized but with a quiet demeanor, not unlike myself. He was very sincere yet also professional. We started with the basics, my name, date of birth, and then he led with this. "Alright, again, I appreciate you're calling me. Um, I just want you to know right off the bat, you know, you're not under arrest, right?"

"Yeah."

"Again, I just want to make that clear. You know, I just want to sit down and pick your brain a little bit"

"Yeah."

"Talk to you um, just kind of wanted a little bit of privacy. That's why we came here."

"Yeah."

I knew I was not in any trouble. I hadn't done anything wrong. I was glad to sit down with Chris Osborn and help. I was just as curious as he was, I wanted to know more about what had just happened that had everyone in my small hometown up in arms, and I wanted to know what had happened to the person I had just met, and why. We had to figure it out.

I walked him through Monday night, methodically, still unpacking it in my own head, as I had just woken up minutes before I had called Osborn. Just a casual, socializing night with alcohol involved, I did not know as I was living it that I would be asked to recount every detail forty-eight hours later. Still, I did well. I told him everything I told Gerald. I was honest, even about the cocaine purchase and use. Self-preservation never crossed my mind, that this was a serious situation. If I had to take a drug-possession charge in order to help Osborn figure out what had happened to this young woman then I was fine with that.

I took him through Mark Lofgren introducing Liz and I, and into a little bit of his background, whatever Osborn wanted to know. A little bit about Sam, though I could not quite remember the girl's name who was with him, Ashely Madison. We went through the phone call to Freddy, the drive down to Freddy's apartment, the purchase, the awkward suspicion the two henchmen displayed regarding Liz, which prompted an exchange between us.

"So whether they were just hinked up 'cuz it was somebody new you know, is that what the big deal was?"

"No, you know, see it's never been a big deal for me to bring somebody in there, especially if I just vouch for 'em and say, this is my cousin or this is whatever."

"Mm-hm."

"You know? So-and-so. It never has. But for some reason there was something different where he got really upset. And they told me that I couldn't come back and that he's moving out. I don't know if he was just exaggerating"

"Uh-huh."

At the time, I *didn't* know if he was just exaggerating, but eventually, Freddy would have some questions to answer, if detectives could ever find him, because his phone number had now come up on the phone records of a murder victim. The detectives never found him.

I walked Osborn all the way through the drive back to Cave Creek, the "out-of-town" roommate, Liz buying beer at Chevron, the one-night-stand, being dropped off at Sam's, locked outside, falling asleep there, calling Gerald, who picked me up from the Circle K, spending the whole day with him. I thought I was done, but then I remembered the strange cars parked in front of her house and possible intruder inside.

"Wait, wait, wait. When we got to her house, I totally forgot about this."

And I told him about the cars and back door being wide open, still remembering things as we talked.

Detective Osborn asked me if Liz had seemed like she was "scared of" her estranged husband, Sandor Polgar, when she mentioned him.

I said, "I don't know, more aggravated than scared probably."

In any murder investigation, when a guilty person is being interviewed, and they get a chance to cast suspicion upon another suspect, like an estranged husband, they jump on it; I did not do that because I was not guilty. And I think detective Osborn recognized that.

"What was your impression of her as far as her personality?"

"Hmm, she seemed fine. She seemed like a normal person. I mean she didn't, she seemed cool. I actually enjoyed hanging out with her and talking to her."

"Mm-hm"

"I really did. And it was just refreshing to meet a girl that, you know, I mean just the two of us enjoyed hanging out and talking to each other."

"Right"

"It was just kind of nice."

Osborn said to me, "you seem well pretty honest with me, pretty straightforward."

I said, "Oh I'm glad to help. My most serious father figure, aside from my dad, was a guy named Jim Gibbs who is a detective for Phoenix PD."

Jim was my best friend's dad in high school. He was a linebacker coach, his son and I both played linebacker, so we all spent a lot of time together and so it was easy for me to view Detective Osborn as a friend.

"So, I'm glad to help in anything that I can, yeah," I reiterated.

I gave Osborn all of the names and phone numbers of people I had seen on Monday and Tuesday.

Then he asked me, "What's the rumor? I mean any idea, you know, anything going around town as far as what happened to her?"

"I don't know. Nothing that I know of. Um, but I didn't really talk to anybody about it besides my ex that told me, and my mom had told me, and then you, and that's it so far."

As we went forward in the interview I was trying to figure out what might have happened to her.

Osborn, later in the interview asked me, "What's your gut feeling that happened to her?" "I don't know. I feel like there's *someone else,* not the estranged husband, or the drug dealers that she was worried about, especially because the door was opened, and she seemed so alarmed when it happened. I don't know. Like maybe there was someone there, or around there.

"Right"

"And, you know, maybe they didn't do anything 'cuz I was there until I left, I don't know. But I get the feeling there's definitely something going on with her in her personal life by the way she was reacting with the door being opened."

"Mm-hm"

There was somebody else. A methamphetamine-smoking schizophrenic with a penchant for knife violence towards women and arson who left his fresh DNA next to Liz's body after stabbing her to death. He would go unidentified for 10 years, because MCSO did not do basic forensic testing.

Then, as a formality, he hit me with, "Justin, I got to ask. Did you hurt her?"

"No I didn't," I answered.

"No?" he replied.

So to be more specific, I said "I didn't do anything wrong to her at all."

"Nothing?"

"Nothing."

"Have you been honest with me?"

"Yeah."

"I have to ask," he said being polite.

With sincerity I assured him, "Yeah I understand. Yeah, I want to help."

Osborn then said, "Well okay. If it comes down to it, you know, and you seem pretty cooperative, you know, uh, would you take a polygraph?"

"Um, I don't see why not," I said.

Then he said, "Okay. All right. Well let me, uh, let me talk to my boss. Probably I can make sure he's got all his questions answered."

Then he left for a few minutes, came back, and we were done. Nothing further was necessary.

Osborn and Bucaro drove me back to my dad's house. I directed them there, explaining that was where I actually lived. I explained to them, as we sat in the SUV in my dad's driveway, that I worked during the day building houses, but would be there at the house with the family every evening if they needed me for anything. I made sure they had the correct phone number to reach me. We shook hands and said goodbye.

I then called my friend Gerald Coco and said, "Dude, you're not gonna believe this."

I told him what I'd learned and that I'd just interviewed, and gotten dropped off by police. I told him I had given them his name and phone number and they would probably be calling him soon since I was with him all day on Tuesday.

"What should I tell them?" he asked, in reference to the fact that we were drinking, and driving, and interacting with drug dealers all day.

"Just tell them the truth, man," I said. "This was serious."

This Was Serious—Gerald Coco

Much of what seemed like normal life carried on after my interview with Deputy Osborn. I made a couple of failed attempts to get my bike back from Sam's condo, but could not get hold of him. I finally did. I drove to his house, but I couldn't ride my bike home, and drive my car home, at the same time. So I got my motorcycle key from him and planned to come back. Of course I asked him if he had heard about what had happened to "Liz," the woman he'd met at the Hideaway, and that I had gone home with on Monday night. He said he had not heard about it. Even though by now it was Thursday.

Thursday and Friday were uneventful. On Saturday, my twenty-two month-old nephew became sick with an unknown illness and was hospitalized. The whole family was at the hospital, gathered 'round his hospital bed, as the doctors tried to figure out what his diagnosis was, to no avail. My brother was worried sick about his baby boy and I spent most of the day at the hospital.

As I waited with my nephew and the rest of the family for some kind of development, I began receiving strange text messages from Gerald Coco. At 6:55 am., he sent me a message that said, "10 to 12. Thanks." Being preoccupied with our situation at the hospital I didn't text him back right away. But about three hours later my curiosity got the better of me and I texted him back, at 9:38 am, and said, "what r u talking about?"

He responded at 11:16 a.m. "You're fucked and so am I, and I didn't have a single part in this."

I had heard from a friend, Robb Ray, who had called me that day, that detectives had shown up at his house asking about me, with copies of my phone records in hand.

"So what," I had said, they're doing their job, following leads, eliminating people it's part of the process."

Being innocent gives you a sense of safety, or security, so I was not worried. I assumed that Gerald Coco, in his usual anxiety-prone way, had been made unnecessarily paranoid by basic police practices. So as a favor to him, to simply calm his nerves, I texted him back at eleven twenty three a.m.

"Call me and talk to me, they're just trying to scare you."

But he didn't call me, or text me, so I let it alone and tended to our family situation.

Then on Saturday night Zack Schaefer, who Gerald and I attempted to visit on Tuesday, called me and said that police had come to his house as well with my phone records and when I tried to minimize it he said that he believed they were viewing me as a *suspect*. I couldn't understand why.

I didn't really even know Liz Hermann. But as a precaution, I called an attorney who I knew, Jeff Mehrens. Jeff had represented me in a DUI that I had gotten when I was 19, and then a criminal damage I had gotten at 21-years-old when my friends and I had left a bar drunk, WWF-wrestling through the parking lot on our way to the car, when my studded belt had scraped up against the fender of a Mercedes. The owner pressed charges.

Jeff was out at dinner but stepped out to take my call anyway. My cousin and I looked up to Jeff, in our twenties because he was the upper-echelon attorney, Ashton Martin in front of his office, the best suits, and a personality that was laid back, cooler than the other side of the pillow, and he had a great secretary.

I said, "Jeff, I *think* I *might* be being investigated for a *homicide*."

Jeff asked, "Do you have anything to worry about?"

"No," I said. "I don't think so."

"Did you talk to police?"

"Of course I did, they needed my help"

"Ah, I told you, never talk to police, you can't trust them."

"Right, but I didn't do anything. I hear you though, I remember you telling me that."

When I had gotten my DUI, I had a car accident and my cousin was injured. I called 911 and got him medical attention, and I felt so bad that my irresponsible actions had gotten him hurt that I waited for police to arrive, told them I was drinking, and asked them to take me to jail. I wanted to be punished. I was raised to believe that a man should own-up to his actions. After the DUI Jeff had emphasized that I would not have been prosecuted for it if I hadn't "told on" myself.

Wrapping up our conversation about the homicide investigation Jeff said, "Well, okay. Just have your family call me if anything weird happens."

"Alright. Thanks, man. Bye."

Monday, July 14, 2008—More Gerald Coco

On Monday morning, July 14th, I woke up early to go to a job with my dad where we were remodeling an elementary school in Phoenix. When I checked my phone I noticed that Gerald Coco had left me a middle-of-the-night text, at 1:17 a.m.

"U set me up u piece of shit. F—k you. I didn't do shit and u r using me. Be a f—king man for ya own responsibilities."

This idiot, I thought to myself as I read it. Now he was getting hostile. Knowing his lifestyle of floating on a raft of Xanax in a pond of alcohol, and the text being left at 1:17 am, I knew that he probably didn't even remember sending it. I wasn't even going to try to figure out what his thought process was leading up to that text, assuming there was a process. I was sure he couldn't even understand his own logic. He was probably passed out. Drunk somewhere in an awkward position and I was on my way to work. That was the difference between me, and most of the people in the scene. I had a job, and a purpose, and I was done with them. The clean break I'd had with Freddy a few days earlier made it easy.

The fact that someone may have just been murdered related to that scene made it necessary. Directly or not, if I never would have known those people, Mark Lofgren would not have told Liz Hermann that I was "the guy." I had entered into an overly recreational lifestyle two years earlier and I was ready to move on, on this early, pre-dawn Monday morning, headed to work with my dad.

Though school was out for the summer, the elementary school we were working on, inside a hallway, had a function taking place in an adjoining multi-purpose room with laughter, noise, and music blaring. A song by "The Killers" came on, called "When You Were Young." I found myself reflecting on when I was young, when my world was more wholesome, and I was glad to get back to that, to be rid of the dysfunction. My attempt at a family of my own did not work the first time but I was ready to get back on the horse and live an adult life again. It made me feel excited, free. I never texted Gerald back because I was tired of catering to his delusions. If he wanted relief or peace of mind he would just have to stop drinking and doing drugs.

Gerald Coco's Interviews

My biggest problem, one I never could have seen coming, was dealing with the consequences of the ever-inebriated Gerald Coco's delusions. However well intended, they were about to wreak havoc on my life. I was about to find all too well what he had gotten himself into that week that led to all of those bizarre text messages.

When I was dropped off at my dad's on Wednesday evening by Osborn and Bucaro and spoke to Gerald Coco briefly, I told him to be honest with police, and he was at first.

On Wednesday evening detectives met him in the parking lot of the Safeway grocery store across from the Azure Creek apartments, where he lived with his mom and dad. His little brother, Kellen, hid from Freddy and the Sinaloans, in a house in Maricopa 80 miles away.

In the parking lot at Safeway, Gerald told detectives everything we did that day, everywhere we went, and everyone we spoke to. He showed them his phone, was transparent with them, and agreed to take a polygraph, which he said, would "come out perfectly." He verified everything that I had told police, which would also be verified by his mom, Gallagher's surveillance video, and other witnesses.

Since they were in the Safeway parking lot, so close to his apartment, and his mom, Cindy, was with us that afternoon at such a crucial time, detectives accompanied Gerald across the street to talk to Cindy, to verify his verification of my statement, which she did.

Cindy said we were at the apartment from "about one p.m. to three p.m.," eating and visiting. She didn't know at the time, but the MCSO detectives did, that was a crucial time, since the truck was burned, by a red-haired man at two p.m. When asked, Cindy said it was a normal day and that everything seemed fine, everyone was normal.

Satisfied and ready to move on with their investigation, detectives concluded their interactions with Gerald and Cindy.

But Gerald went home and thought...stewed...drank...and obsessed. Little brother was in a house 80 miles away, hiding from these Sinaloans, his mom and dad were worried, their household not the same. Gerald knew what he saw on TV at the *Hideaway Bar* the night before, knew what he heard around him, knew Liz left with me, knew she was the reason Freddy moved, and that she was dead a few hours later. He believed he knew what happened. He didn't have direct knowledge or specifics, but the more he drank that night, the more Xanax he swallowed, the more certain he became that detectives really needed his help to get this investigation pointed in the right direction—at the Sinaloans. So finally, with enough liquid courage in him, at midnight, Gerald pulled out his phone and called detective Osborn, saying that he needed to talk to him.

Worst mistake he ever made.

Detectives picked Gerald up at his mom and dad's apt. and drove him downtown to the general investigations division, G.I.D in the industrial part of Phoenix.

His five and one-half hour interview, turned interrogation, took place from midnight to 5:30 a.m. It's as long, painful, and convoluted as anyone could imagine. For advocates of the usage of proper interrogation techniques, it is difficult to read.

Gerald eventually told detectives that the Sinaloans did it. He didn't have any real information; he just knew the Sinaloans were dangerous. The detectives never asked him how he knew that. They never found out about Kellen's problem with the Sinaloans because they never asked. They had their sights set on something else. Gerald then used me as bait.

This interview quickly devolved into an impulsive argument between Gerald and the detectives about who committed the crimes, the drug dealers or me.

The MCSO was were not interested in information from Gerald. Their priority was to make him agree with them. Neither side had any corroborative facts. Each remained adamant about their position. The "debate" that took place was emotional and non-Socratic.

"No he didn't."

"Yes he did."

"No he didn't."

"Yes he did."

Little did Gerald know his life as he knew it was over. Guided by sheer adrenaline now, these detectives were never going to let him walk this back. They tried to get him to incriminate me, and himself for hours, but he wouldn't. They tried to get him to say we went to the crime scene together that day, but he wouldn't. Because we didn't.

They gave him every chance to incriminate me while keeping his own hands clean, by saying things like, "Did Justin ask you, hey drive me over to this area, and get out and leave your sight for a while?"

"Did Justin call someone from your phone and ask them to burn the house?"

Gerald kept insisting that their hunches about me were wrong.

Then, they accused Gerald of the murder.

Eventually they turned off the recorders, took Gerald outside into the dirt parking lot at two or three a.m., pushed him to the ground, spit on him, threatened to charge him with murder, and give him the death penalty if he didn't incriminate me. One can only imagine what Gerald must've been thinking at that point. Predisposed to panic attacks, having gone hours now without his meds, when detectives turn the recorders back on Gerald projects like a timid, hunched-over victim, his faint voice barely audible, cracking with fragility, trying to save his own life now.

He says, "I burnt the house but did not do the murder."

He said I told him this, and that he, Gerald, did not see me commit any crimes. He said I said the dealers murdered her.

Every attempt detectives made to fact-check the details Gerald gave failed. They all proved that Gerald was manufacturing a story, but detectives didn't care—*that was what they wanted him to do*. It took a lot of *good detective work* to get him to do that. It really helped them to move their investigation along.

Knowing that he and I were in Phoenix that evening, when Gerald is told by detectives that the house fire was between 7-8 pm, he replies, "Well then obviously Justin didn't do it."

The interview ends abruptly. That was Monday morning at eleven a.m. July 14, 2008.

As my dad and I headed north on SR51 Monday afternoon, after finishing up at the school, I called Garett. We decided we would get together for a beer at Gallagher's and I could give him the monthly motorcycle payment. After that I had plans to make dinner for the family, who should all be home by six or seven p.m.

I showered, Garett swung by and picked me up, and we drove across the street to Gallagher's. The same sports bar Gerald and I had been at on Tuesday afternoon while deputy Martinez was at Liz Hermann's house. Garett and I sat down to a beer each a plate full of sliders. I passed on the sliders because I didn't want to spoil my dinner.

Chapter 4

Arrest and Interrogation

∙∙

Man, what a crazy situation it was that hung in the air over Cave Creek, we both marveled. We were waiting for the police to make an arrest, just like everyone else, waiting for the monster to be extracted from his dark hiding place, into the light, so we could see his face, learn his name, and get closure.

After about an hour at Gallagher's we left; I had to get home and start dinner. With somewhat selfish motives, I was cooking one of my own favorites—chicken breast, with fettuccini alfredo, a cracking, boiling symphony of garlic and pesto-infused aromas, while my trademark stuffed-mushrooms baked in the oven, awaiting that shiny complexion.

Once it was finished I was starving, and still, nobody was home. I thought maybe I could sneak a quick chicken breast without getting full so I forked one. As I lifted it toward my mouth I heard heavy footfalls in the guest room, directly above me. I stood barefoot on the kitchen tiles, shirtless in gym shorts, and wondered if the ex had arrived and was angry about something, it sure sounded like a lot of stomping around.

As it continued, I walked over to the window above the kitchen sink, looked through the back patio at the stairs leading up to my room, then I looked at the ceilings, then back at the stairs, and I saw one set of black boots, after another, and another, and another, coming down the steps, detective Osborn now fully in view, with Bucaro right behind him.

They still didn't see me, so I said "Hey, I'm in here, are you guys looking for me?"

They walked in the sliding-glass door guns drawn.

Detective Osborn said, "Put your hands behind your back, you are under arrest for murder." I'll never forget the date—July 14, 2008

In disbelief, I could not understand how they had arrived at such a wrong conclusion. I did not know Liz Hermann, and I had no history of violence. I assumed they would realize their mistake soon, and I would be back home in a couple days.

Little did I know, the MCSO, along with its media sidecar, was pushing all of its poker chips in on me as the suspect. They were not in the habit of reneging on an arrest. To understand why, I would have to learn everything I could about the investigation that had taken place behind the scenes that week, from a police point-of-view, although as it turned out, that didn't make much sense either.

The MCSO Investigation

On Tuesday July 8th 2008, at 2:14 pm, MCSO Deputy Kenneth Martinez responded to a vehicle fire at the intersection of Cave Creek and New River road where he found a white Chevy truck engulfed in flames on the northbound shoulder. Once the fire was out, they discovered a a partially burned orange can, with two-thirds of of gasoline still in the bottom. It was on passenger side floorboard.

Jimmie Larson was an eyewitness. He told Deputy Martinez that he got a thorough look at the arsonist, describing him as 6'2," pale skin, light-colored clothing, with "bushy" red hair. Larson stated that the arsonist sped away, by himself, in a "green colored vehicle." Deputy Martinez stated that Larson was "unable to provide anything further" regarding the "green colored vehicle".

Larson said Deputy Martinez seemed totally uninterested in documenting the tire tracks from the arson suspect's vehicle, the shoeprints left by the arsonist, or even taking down his [Larson's] name or phone number.

While running a record check, Deputy Martinez found that the burnt white truck was owned by a 29-year-old woman, Liz Hermann. After approximately two hours at the truck fire scene, Deputy Martinez drove to Ms. Hermann's residence, a mile away at 5536 E. Seven Palms Ln. At 4:15 p.m., Deputy Martinez knocked on the front door several times but got no response. According to Dep. Martinez, he heard no one inside, heard no dog barking, saw no vehicles at the residence, no gas can at the front door. Later in the investigation, a gas can was recovered just outside the front door, three inches from the ignition point of the house fire, just *inside* the front door. He smelled no smoke or gas, did not enter the residence to do a welfare check, and made no further attempt to locate 29-year-old Liz Hermann.

At 7:44 pm, approximately three and one-half hours after deputy Martinez left Ms. Hermann's residence, MCSO Deputy Todd Johnson noticed Rural Metro Fire Dept. personnel rushing southbound on Cave Creek road and followed them. They went to 5536 E. Seven Palms Ln. and found Ms. Hermann's residence "fully engulfed by fire" at 7:49 pm.

Numerous private citizens had accumulated at the scene, including Ms. Hermann's "best friend," Joy Gorski, who was also her coworker at the *Buffalo Chip*, owned by retired MCSO brass. MCSO officers talked to Ms. Gorski regarding the trajectory of their investigation.

There were numerous people at the scene who were never identified, including a "shirtless man" who "broke a window" and left before first responders arrived, and a "group" of adults "with children." The 911 caller was never identified, and the 911 call itself was never disclosed. Fire personnel did a first sweep of the residence and found no one inside. After an undocumented amount of time had passed by, they did a second sweep and discovered a body on a bed in the west end of the house in the master bedroom, untouched by fire.

Upon carrying the body outside they, and bystanders, observed that the nude woman was badly brutalized, stabbed dozens of times, nearly decapitated, and legs nearly severed, indicating a very personal attack, perhaps mental illness. Multiple 1st responders were unprepared for the discovery, fire personnel lay her body on the gravel driveway in plain sight of the bystanders and continue knocking down the fire.

As they do, MCSO detectives arrive and entered the house, gathering and removing as much physical evidence as possible from the master bedroom wherein the body was discovered, and the adjoining master bath, before fire personnel pulled down the ceilings. The detectives recovered two used condoms near Ms. Hermann's body and a bloody palm print cutout from the wall. Dutifully, they bagged and collected fingernail scrapings and clippings from Ms. Hermann's hands, as well as a sex kit. And they recovered a small, orange gas can from the outside edge of the front door, just three feet from the ignition point of the fire. They preserved all of it for forensic testing and sent to the Arizona DPS Crime Lab for analysis.

At the crime scene, MCSO investigators observed no lividity or rigor mortis indicating that the victim had died very recently. Rural Metro Fire Department captain John Kraetz found "wet blood on his pants" after carrying the decedent out of the house, indicating that RMFD had literally arrived before the blood had even dried, putting Ms. Hermann's time of death sometime between 6:30-7:30 pm. MCSO spokesperson Lindsey Smith, after conferring with investigations, gave two statements to KPHO

(CBS) 5, stating that Ms. Hermann died "right before the house fire" in "what was probably a crime of passion."

By nine p.m. on Tuesday night, within two hours of her death, MCSO officers began combing Ms. Hermann's workplace, the *Buffalo Chip Saloon*," and the rest of the small town bar scene in Cave Creek.

Gossip abounded. Private citizens had seen the body. Phone calls and rumors were all over town. MCSO Detective Kristina Bucaro said in a tape-recorded interview with Gerald Coco two days later that the arson and murder was "all that was being talked about in the bars that night."

Gerald Coco was in the *Hideaway Bar* that night.

It was difficult for investigators to draw distinctions between witnesses who had first-hand knowledge and witnesses who *thought* they had first-hand knowledge, and witnesses who were confabulating due to various types of inebriation. Some claimed to have vital information but were thought by by MCSO investigators to be "fishing" for information *from* detectives, perhaps for their own gossiping arsenal, or perhaps a more sinister reason.

Thankfully, hard evidence would become available for fact checking purposes; objective evidence such as surveillance videos, cell phone trap and trace data, and DNA results from the gas can, Ms. Hermann's body, and the used condoms found at the scene.

Unfortunately, it would take days to obtain any view of the surveillance videos, weeks to receive the cell phone records, and years to obtain DNA results. The MCSO and Cave Creek wanted an arrest *now*. Meanwhile, the gossip became more and more compelling, with tales of murder and arson that would make the most intellectual detective suffer from relentless gut hunches. Through patrons, and friends of Ms. Hermann, detectives learned that she had a contentious relationship with her estranged husband, Sandor Polgar, whose Arizona driver's license showed him to be 6'3" with red hair, matching the arsonist perfectly.

Some of Ms. Hermann's friends, expressed their conviction of his guilt, explaining, "they argued about money all the time, he was "verbally abusive, an illegal immigrant who was involved in various scams, and was resentful that she kept the white Chevy truck, that was burned before the house arson." Polgar drove a "green truck also matching the arsonist, and was now living with his new, pregnant girlfriend."

They said Ms. Hermann posted messages on Mr. Polgar's social media page saying things such as "Thanks for a good time last night" because she enjoyed antagonizing Mr. Polgar's pregnant girlfriend, Naomi McQuaid.

Simultaneously, MCSO detectives learned Ms. Hermann had at least one boyfriend named "Nate." She had slept with her roommate Allen, had regular one-night stands with

46

strangers, and had left a bar called "the Hideaway with a guy she'd just been introduced named Justin, on Monday night, twenty-four hours before the arson and murder. For an entire week the investigation dragged on, as Phoenix news stations opened daily with the unsolved murder, arson, and the disturbing situation in Cave Creek.

Some detectives spent Wednesday night interrogating the estranged husband, while other detectives followed-up on my alibi for the day of the crimes, also interviewing Ms. Hermann's roommate Allen Bauer, and trying to locate her "boyfriend" Nate.

Gerald Coco confirmed that he and I were not in Cave Creek when any of this happened, as did Coco's mother Cindy. At least two other witnesses, Andrew Phillips and Max Piper, also confirmed that we were in Phoenix when the arson and murder occurred in Cave Creek.

Detectives interrogated the estranged husband, who claimed to have an alibi, albeit for the wrong part of Tuesday. Mr. Polgar claimed to have strangely been at work from five a.m. to two p.m. fifty miles away. MCSO detectives ruled Mr. Polgar out as a suspect although neither he nor his girlfriend Naomi McQuaid could account for his whereabouts from two p.m. to eight p.m., on Tuesday, the time of the murder and arsons.

Perhaps they ruled him out because simultaneously with Mr. Polgar's interrogation, Gerald Coco re-contacted detectives and said he felt he knew more about what had happened to Ms. Hermann. At the MCSO General Investigations Division, Mr. Coco explained that the "Sinaloan coke dealers" that Ms. Hermann and I had visited *Monday night* must have killed Ms. Hermann on *Tuesday evening* because to his knowledge, they were very dangerous.

This devolved into a simple but profound argument between Mr. Coco and MCSO Detective Paul Smith about who killed Liz Hermann-- the drug dealers or me.

Much of it reads like a living room spat between 5 and 6-year-old siblings, each side adamant, neither side offering any corroborating facts. It wasn't that different from the conversations taking place in the Cave Creek bars or online.

The record confirms that, as Smith's gut hunches were getting into rhythm, as if playing jump rope with Coco's anxiety disorder, he looked at Gerald and pounced.

"Did you kill her, Gerald?"

Despite this, Gerald Coco was never read his Miranda rights. At length, they pressured him to incriminate me, and himself, but he refused. MCSO Detective Paul Smith turned off the recorders and offered to let Gerald go outside into the dirt parking lot of the MCSO General Investigations Department to to smoke a cigarette. According to attorney David Gurney, Smith and several other MCSO detectives followed Gerald out into the parking lot and surrounded him. They began yelling at him, calling him a "fucking murderer" and "a murdering piece of shit," and shoved him to the ground multiple times. When they took Gerald back inside and turned the recorder back on, he stated that I had told him that I lit the fires, but not the murder.

He said I had told him this while we were at *Gallagher's* on Tuesday afternoon. The MCSO detective told him, "that could not have happened."

The detective explained to Gerald that could not have happened because the house had not even been burned. But the *Gallaghers* video shows me and Gerald entering the bar at 3:30 p.m. and leaving at 4:30 p.m. on Tuesday. The MCSO record confirms Deputy Martinez at Ms. Hermann's residence at 4:15 pm. Her house burned at 7:30 pm. Gerald's statement could not have been true. Instead of recognizing coerced false information, MCSO detectives began trying to persuade Gerald to change his timeline, which he never did. They also manufactured details. Coco told detectives that I had retrieved a gas can "from the garage." But a layout of my home and Ms. Hermann's home confirms neither residence even had a garage. This also proves that Gerald and I never went to her house. Had we gone there, he'd have known it didn't have a garage.

Coco also told detectives that I went to a nearby Circle K to purchase the gas. Detectives then pulled the surveillance of said Circle K and confirmed, "Lunsford was never at the Circle K." Yet, to this day, prosecutors and judges affirm my conviction because, their court records contain the MCSO lie that "Lunsford went to the Circle K to purchase a gas can and gas."

Coco was unable to provide any claims that could be corroborated. All attempts by MCSO investigators to verify his inculpatory claims only proved that he was untruthful. The elephant in the room was the proven fact that that we were in Phoenix when the arson and murder occurred in Cave Creek. But the detectives assumed that if they piled enough garbage on top of that elephant, eventually nobody would be able to see it anymore.

Local news reporters sallied forth, as did the gossipers, as panic began to set in on a small town with a savage murderer and arsonist on the loose, leaving MCSO Detective Paul Smith, who lived in that same small town, looking like the guy who couldn't do his job, on his first ever assignment as lead detective in a homicide case. An assignment he'd gotten at the influence of Ret. MCSO Larry Wednt, Liz's boss.

After their strange encounter with Gerald Coco on Thursday night, detectives located the boyfriend "Nate" on Friday of that week and interviewed him at work—a Cave Creek restaurant called *El Encanto*., It was not far from the Buffalo Chip. His full name is Nate Paramanathan Renganathan. In his thick Indonesian accent, he told them he had not seen Ms. Hermann since Monday at noon. His story was contradicted by a *Hideaway* bartender, either Becca or Dawn, stating in her recorded interview that Nate was at the Hideaway when Ms. Hermann left the bar with me on Monday night.

He told them he didn't know she was killed until three days later. He said he was at home watching a movie Monday or Tuesday night.

While unclear, he was ruled out by MCSO Detective Smith, who had already sunk his fangs into Gerald Coco. He conducted the interview with the goal of ruling Nate Renganathan out. Detective Smith and his colleagues re-interviewed Gerald Coco over the weekend, still trying to get him to incriminate me, and needing him to change his timeline. They offered him every opportunity to incriminate me while keeping his own hands clean, offering theory after theory and pressuring him to adopt each one but he never did. He remained adamant that I did not kill Hermann, that we were together all day, and that we never went to any crime scene.

"I don't even know where that house is," he told them, over and over.

Perhaps exhausted by the two-day argument with Gerald Coco, Detective Smith bowed out and MCSO Detective Stephen Fax stepped in. This happened on Monday July 14 at about eleven a.m. At that time, I was working with my dad on the elementary school in Phoenix.

Detective Fax concluded the interrogation and wrote a lengthy, detailed sworn affidavit requesting a Maricopa County Superior Court Judge to issue a subpoena to T-Mobile. It was Gerald Coco's cellular provider. It requesting Gerald Coco's cell phone records for the day in question Specifically, Detective Fax said in his sworn affidavit, he wanted the "locations," in order "to determine Gerald Coco's and Justin Lunsford's whereabouts on Tuesday 7-8-08," to settle this once, and for all.

If Gerald and I were even in the town of Cave Creek when the crimes occurred, the cell phone data would show it. They now had six witnesses who put Gerald and me together from noon until nine p.m. that day in Phoenix. They had numerous surveillance videos, plus, several phone calls from Gerald's phone were made by me at specific times—from 6:00 pm to 7:18 pm. Obviously, for me to be in Cave Creek at that time they needed Gerald's phone records to put me in Cave Creek.

On the other hand, if we were away from the crime scenes it would exonerate us. While Detective Fax was authoring this affidavit, the interview taking place in the other room ends with MCSO Detective Kristina Bucaro stating, "Well, it, the, the, here's the problem the, the fire occurred much later, while you were with him." Gerald told her, ""Well then obviously he didn't do it." They concluded his interrogation then. The phone records would not be ready for over 3 weeks, and Detective Smith was not willing to wait for them. Nor was Detective Bucaro, who had yelled at Coco "he's a monster!" three times in a row during the interview, trying to get Coco to see it their way. They knew what their gut was telling them, they didn't need cell phone records or denials from Coco, much less forensics.

Daniel Patrick Moynihan famously said, "You are entitled to your own opinion, but you are not entitled to your own facts." Thinking back on it now, decades later, perhaps the biggest hurdle I faced with MCSO after me was the shrinking of what Karl Rove termed the "reality-based community." Adviser to President George H. W. Bush, Rove said with a sense of humor that people "in the reality-based community believe that solutions emerge from judicious study of a discernable reality. That's not the way the world works anymore." But however light-hearted he was, he was also serious. Rove was speaking in terms of politics, and how it relates to people at their core, sidesteps and frog jumps out of the field of politics and applies equally to any other arena involving we humans—specifically we imaginative humans in the over-developed post-2000's U.S. of A. Whether a kid on a living room floor who wants to believe that the characters in a video game are real, a young adult dressing up for comi-con, a UFO chaser, sasquatch hunter, or disciple of Harry Potter, modern Americans are haplessly obsessed with centering our lives around frameworks that are not supported by fact. Perhaps this under-appreciation for facts, this desensitization of fantasy worlds dove-tailing into our own, has installed over time a sort of cognitive cruise control that causes lawyers and laypeople alike to run the timeless red lights that were cemented in to the road to truth long ago by those who did not have the luxury of indulging in fantasy—those hamstrung by concepts we cannot be bothered with today—pioneering, homesteading, survival, putting together a nightly family dinner, teaching our kids instead of just buying things for them.

We have always been entitled to our own opinions but at some point the MCSO decided it was also entitled to its own facts—not just children, not just young adults on social media. Detective Paul Smith, a sworn peace officer, after learning from Liz Hermann's estranged husband that she moved to Cave Creek to be "closer to the colors," i.e., The Hell's Angels, and regularly slept with their members, then assured Deputy County Attorney Mike Gingold that nothing associating her with the Hell's Angels had ever come up in his investigation, among many, many other deceptions.

Deputy County Attorney Gingold, after giving excuses about three years of DNA disclosures postponements for a "first batch" and a "second batch" of testing, and learning behind closed doors that it pointed away from me, declared in open court to her honor Judge Barton, that "no forensics" had ever existed in this case because the defendant destroyed it all by means of a fire—despite the DNA from two used condoms identifying a knife-wielding maniac that ten years later would be overlooked by Detective Smith in 2008.

In 2008, Smith knew that I had no motive to hurt Ms. Hermann, no history with her whatsoever—certainly not the history required to cultivate the kind of hatred and ill will necessary for such an attack. He was told by the eyewitness that I looked nothing like the red-haired arsonist, he knew from the cell phone data and witness accounts that I was twenty miles away in Phoenix when it happened, but he couldn't be bothered with all of those pesky facts. He knew what his gut was telling him.

Stephen Colbert, in his first episode of the Colbert report, in a feature called "the word," riffed on a phrase—"truthiness"—in a rant of ironically spot-on sarcasm. He said, "Who's Brittanica to tell me the panama canal was finished in 1914? If I want to say it happened in 1941, that's my right. I don't trust books—they're all fact, no heart...face it, folks, we are a divided nation...divided between those who think with their head and those who *know* with their heart...because that's where the truth comes from, ladies and gentlemen—the gut."

MCSO Detective Paul Smith

Detective Smith grew up in this Instagram society, so why wouldn't he gloss-over the facts and instead go with his gut. That's what we do. The problem, as it relates to a police investigation, and perhaps every other crisis scenario, is that the word "gut" is synonymous with "imagination" which is why it's so deeply romanticized in the fantasy world that our society has become. And for some people it works. Detective Smith can use his imagination to close cases, and when those arrestees stand trial he can swear under oath, as detective Saldate did against Debra Milke, that "his gut" confirmed his suspicions. Somehow, a police officer's gut hunch is admissible as evidence, even in an age of technology and forensic crime labs. Because we love fantasy, imagination trumps science.

But what do we do when this imagined reality intersects with actual reality? Smith's gut hunches netted a lifetime of police salary, peer recognition, and who knows what else for him and his family. It worked for *him*. But his gut hunches couldn't protect 12-year-old Ariana Valenzuela as Nathaniel Noble stood outside the drive-thru window, stalking her like prey, knife in hand, meth in his bloodstream.

As people, we have a real challenge at hand in acknowledging the marriage between gut hunches and self-deception, embedded deep within our often well-intended, yet self-preserving hearts. It is a matter of temptation. We *want* to believe the policeman, we *want* to believe our spouse, we *want* to believe our son and daughter, as we hand them the car keys on a Friday evening. And we *want* to believe we live in a safe world managed by earnest authorities and that everything is going to be okay, and for those whose challenges actually are irreparable in this lifetime, self-deception really is a proper anesthetic, an appropriate medication; denial, just like opioids.

Philosopher Demosthenes said, "The easiest thing of all is to deceive oneself, for we believe whatever we want to believe."

But some situations, such as mine, and the broader systemic injustice it represents, *can* be remedied. It takes a lot of discipline, and profound self-control, to say "no" to the Carmel coated nuggets of self-deception that sprinkles our fantasy world. It takes a lot of resolve to stand up and inconvenience yourself at the risk of losing popularity, or money.

The Arizona investigative body and by extension the judiciary, is dotted with tiny cancerous tumors that will grow if we do not remove them, and the needless pain they cause will continue to spread, as it has for through my whole family, the ones who are still alive, and maybe someday your own. We can choose denial, and avoid going to the doctor, as if avoiding a diagnosis will prevent the fatal consequences, but we all know better.

The only question now, is can we *do* better? Only time will tell.

No one they spoke to could put me in Cave Creek at the time of the murder, much less at the crime scene. They actually put me in Phoenix. There were no forensic results, no fingerprints or DNA yet, no evidence at all that I'd committed any crime. I had no violence in my history, no motive to hurt Ms. Hermann. I didn't even know her, had no history of mental illness, and I did not look anything like the red-haired arsonist the eyewitness described. Yet *incredibly*, Detective Smith arrested me that night anyway.

I can only assume he assumed that the evidence would appear later.

Just eight hours after the last interview with Gerald Coco, dozens of armed police descended on our family home and arrested me exactly where I said I'd be in the evenings, in the kitchen cooking my favorite dinner for my family.

The breaking news story that aired two hours later stated that MCSO detectives had finally caught their murder suspect by skillfully using cell phone records to track him down, to make it sound like I was running all week. My face was offered to the public as the answer to their panic. They could finally rest; the MCSO had closed the case.

They impounded my dad's green and silver dodge truck as evidence. MCSO Detective Kristina Bucaro would tell the media that night that the door panels of the truck "tested positive for human blood," and that with her trained eye she also discovered a "black tee-shirt" from the truck that "tested positive for human blood." Detectives no doubt hoped it belonged to Ms. Hermann.

Eventually the DPS crime lab would clarify that the truck and tee shirt were "negative for blood of any kind," and ultimately, the truck was found to be of no evidentiary value at all and released back to the owner, my dad, after the media coverage had died down. By then, the media had already done its job. Still, Detective Paul Smith would testify under oath in front of a grand jury that the green and silver dodge truck was used in the vehicle fire and for years, appellate prosecutors would refer to this statement to uphold my conviction.

It is unclear to this day, how the "green colored vehicle" eyewitness Jimmie Larson saw that day, regarding which he was "unable to provide any further information" became a green and silver dodge truck.

I'm five foot nine, had buzzed black hair, wore dark-colored clothes and was riding in a white Monte Carlo that day, not a green truck, maintained my actual innocence from the beginning. Strangely, detectives never re-interviewed me and never interviewed the family members I lived with at all, including my dad, who owned the truck they impounded. Perhaps they wanted to leave things just the way they were. At the moment of my arrest I was in disbelief, but not worried. I was sure that law enforcement would go around interviewing people and find out what kind of a person I was and realize they'd made a mistake and let me go.

After the 45-minute ride to the General Investigations Department in Phoenix, they took me into a small room, hand cuffs behind my back, and left me there for a couple of hours. I sat, quietly waited, tried to get comfortable, no Jodi Arias grandstands. Finally, they brought a woman in with a camera and told me to take off all my clothes.

"Are you serious?" I asked.

As I stood there naked in a room full of people, humiliated, they poked and prodded me, pulled out some of my hairs, and took pictures of my whole body. They spoke about me as if I was not in the room, treating me like a science exhibit. I asked to call my attorney.

"Soon" they said.

They kept my clothes, impounded them as *evidence*, even though the murder had taken place a week earlier, and gave me a white paper suit to wear, with paper shoes. They then drove me into the downtown area and walked me into the biggest jail in the state, which was crawling with people of all kinds, all of which were staring at me like I was a terrorist. Even other arrestees could not look away.

"Can I get a phone call?"

"Soon." They said.

That several hour experience made me question a lot of things. I could not believe that in modern America a citizen could be removed from his home at gunpoint, kidnapped basically, dressed up to look like a terrorist, paraded in public, and denied a phone call, without even committing a crime. I thought this wasn't possible.

I had now been asking for my phone call, the one that every law and order television show I'd ever seen made me sure I was entitled to, for hours. I felt like that had to be a constitutional right, an actual right, not just a TV thing. But they still would not give me one. After taking my booking photo, which I gathered would be on the news; they finally gave me access to a phone, by placing me in a cell with one mounted on the wall.

I was so worried about my family. No one had been home when MCSO snatched me. By now it was probably one a.m. and they must be devastated, worried. I picked up the phone and there was no dial tone, it didn't even work. I went to the door, tried to get the officers' attention, but they all ignored me. I really needed a phone. That was when I began to be scared. I realized now that I was in MCSO's custody, and they didn't care about rights or decency.

I overheard an officer walking by my cell saying "what are we going to do with the high-profiler?" and it took me a minute, but then I realized he was talking about me. I was no longer Justin, I was the "high-profiler," I was no longer a person; I was now an object to them, an animal.

I'm glad I did not know then that the over-whelming majority of the people I'd meet over the next twelve years would view me like that, without ever giving me a chance, or listening to me.

Simple life in Cave Creek was over.

July 14, 2008 Booking and Thinking At the Maricopa County Jail

As I went through the booking process the lady behind the glass asked me if I was okay going into general population.

"Yeah, of course," I said.

Then I sat there wondering what "general population" was. When I got to my assigned "pod," it was crazy, conducive with mayhem, just as seen on TV. A fellow inmate told me that a guy had just been beat to death in "our" pod the week before, and that after he was beaten to death, the inmate who did it drug his lifeless bloody body out of the cell, onto the top tier and called out, "who wants to see a dead body?"

Then he threw the "dead guy" over the rail.

"Awesome," I said, disingenuously. I was going to have to ignore and deflect as much of this human-zoo as I could. I needed to sort out my own situation and get back home.

At my initial appearance later that night my attorney, Jeff Mehrens, was waiting in the back room, looking up at me through the glass, with some papers in front of him. As I walked in and sat down he told me that every room in this building was "bugged" and for me not to talk at all, to just let him do the talking.

He read to me a "statement of facts" created by detective Paul Smith, then looked up at me and said something that indicated he believed everything he'd just read.

"Well, at least you didn't flee the country; at least you've got that going for you."

He lectured me. He was genuinely frustrated with me for talking to police, something he'd implored me never to do seven years earlier when I'd gotten the DUI. He explained to me that it didn't matter if you were innocent, it didn't matter that you said nothing incriminating, the police will find a way to twist your words.

Put simply, he said, "People who talk to police go to prison, period."

Bond was set at $600,000.00. My legal visit with Jeff was nice but unproductive. He was in "wait and see" mode. Not only was I told not to talk at all because every room, even legal visit rooms- were bugged by MCSO sheriff Joe Arpaio, but Jeff specifically did not want to discuss the case until a decision was made by County Attorney Andrew Thomas. That would dictate whether or not I was allowed to have Jeff represent me.

Meantime my family worked on getting the bond together so I could go back home soon. Sitting in my cell I tried to figure out what had happened to this woman. The public had been told by Sheriff Arpaio that she simply went home with the "wrong guy" from a bar on Monday night, me, drank, used powder cocaine, had sex, and got murdered, by me.

I knew that was not true. I knew I was the only one trying to figure out, in my own head, what happened to her. I didn't know her. My experience with her was limited to several inebriated hours. I didn't know about her estranged husband, she didn't tell me about her boyfriend "Nate." I didn't know about her roommate, or the one-night-stands, and it would be almost three years before Detective Paul Smith would disclose that she *was* an associate of the Hell's Angels.

I had no idea what she was in to. I did not even clearly remember her name the day after our one-night-stand. I was told per a phone call from the bar that it was the same woman I'd gone home with who'd died, and that her name was "Liz." When I interviewed with detective Osborn, he confirmed that her name was Liz, but he never showed me a picture of her to confirm that we were speaking about the same person. I knew I'd left the bar with *someone* that night, and I just took the police's word for it that it was the same woman, this "Liz."

I had walked them through the night; we'd left the bar, she wanted coke, then she invited me to her home for a one-night-stand and dropped me back off where my motorcycle was the next morning, around dawn. I told them she'd made the Mexican drug-dealers uncomfortable with her many questions while we were in their apartment and we had to leave abruptly.

We stopped to get beer. When we got to her house there were two suspicious sedans out front and she paused, spooked. When we got inside she panicked at finding her back door open- someone had been inside her home, uninvited. Thankfully, she had immediately called her roommate and he later verified all of this with police.

It had to be the drug dealers. Maybe Gerald Coco was right, maybe he knew something I didn't know. What I did know, and I shared this with the MCSO deputies, was that these Sinaloan drug dealers who she'd upset had said they had to "move" the next day because of her.

Given the cars out front, the back door open, I also believed in hindsight that she must've had something going on in her personal life. Maybe the two intersected—drug dealers and her personal life. I really had no way to know.

But the drug dealers seemed like a good place to start. Unfortunately, my attorney, Jeff, was still waiting. The D.A. had 90 days to decide whether or not to seek the death penalty against me, and if he did, Jeff would have to withdraw from the case because he was not capital certified.

He told me, "I don't do death penalty cases; I have enough problems of my own." He had no problem however, accepting the twenty thousand dollar retainer.

So I sat, for weeks, and weeks, while no one investigated my case.

Meantime my family got appraisals done on their properties and we now had the collateral to bond me out. I could go home, fight this situation from there, finally speak about it with my attorney, and maybe even solve the case ourselves.

That same day, one of MCSO's finest detention officers (detective Paul Smith also started his MCSO career there, as a A.D.O. at the jail, overseen by Larry Wendt) approached me and told me that I was getting "page two'ed," meaning new charges. I had no idea what it could be. I didn't live a life of crime; I didn't have any unresolved legal issues. They handcuffed me and we began the journey back to the ground floor, to booking.

Perplexed, I elbowed and sidestepped my way to the phone in the crowded holding cell. I called home, my family did an internet search, and found out that the state had dropped all the charges against me and that I was being re-charged for the same crimes, except, they had added one count of burglary.

I did not understand how I could be charged with burglary after going home with someone for a one-night-stand.

From the beginning I did not understand how I could be charged with murder without a motive, I had just met this person, much less *first-degree* murder, without premeditation. Again, I had just met this person; I did not dislike her. I did not even know her. Now I was somehow being charged with burglary too?

It was explained to me that in Arizona they didn't need a motive in order to charge someone with murder. Additionally, the Arizona legislature, in an effort to give a leg-up to prosecutors, who shoulder the "heavy burden" of proof, had worked the archaic felony murder rule into current state laws, despite most of the United States abandoning it long ago.

And how did they get around the invited entry into the house in order to allege burglary? The Arizona legislature had also decided that even if you were invited into someone's home, and then were alleged to have committed a felony after being invited in, you could also be charged with burglary.

So in my situation, they used the baseless allegation of murder to create the idea of burglary, then used the allegation of burglary in order to invoke the felony murder rule, to enable a first-degree murder charge, in order to give County Attorney Andrew Thomas a discretionary privilege to seek the death penalty, remove my paid attorney, and replace him with a public defender.

I began to find out that there was no lack of evidence that prosecutorial manipulation, coupled with a defense attorney's indifference, could not overcome.

Most citizens in Arizona believed at the time, that in order for the state to seek the death penalty, there must be overwhelming evidence of guilt, but it was exactly the opposite. I would find out that County Attorney Andrew Thomas was carelessly filing a notice of intent to seek the death penalty in a record number of Arizona cases at the time, regardless of evidence, creating what was later called the "capital case crisis" in Maricopa county. It contributed to his being disbarred later for abuse of power. But the damage would remain for decades.

After discussing my new charges with my family, I hung up and remained in a "holding tank" with dozens of other arrestees, most of them in their civilian clothes, me in my black and white jailhouse stripes. Traditionally, the same group of arrestees would remain together, be moved together, through a series of holding tanks, each one bringing them closer to the courtroom, as new groups of arrestees were brought in to fill the ranks. It was called the "horseshoe."

Finally, my group got to the last holding tank, situated next to the courtroom. The detention officers started calling out names, several at a time, to go see the judge. But they never called me.

Eventually all the guys I had been with were gone and new ones brought in; then the cycle would repeat itself. I was being held back for hours.

Then at about one o'clock a.m. my attorney, Jeff, appeared at the door of the tank. He said the state was trying to get me in front of a specific judge during the graveyard shift, and that the MCSO had agreed to hold me back. He said that they knew he was in the middle of another trial and wanted to inconvenience him, by keeping him up all night, and that they intentionally misspelled my name in the computer so that he could not find me. He said that they "do this all the time." Their intent was to get me in front of a judge of their choice, without my attorney, so that I would have to argue for bond by myself.

I couldn't believe the lengths they would go to, in order to violate my right to an attorney while trying to make it look "accidental." It began to sink in; the state was very manipulative. But I was glad Jeff was there. It made me feel safe.

Once in front of Comissioner Christine Mullineauk she read the charges and asked Jeff, and the prosecutor if they had anything to say. Jeff said that he was unsure why I was re-indicted on basically the same charges. He assumed the state had made some mistakes during the first indictment, and asked that the bond stay the same.

The prosecutor agreed, asking that the bond amount remain the same, only that it not be lowered.

I was ecstatic, and relieved. I thought for sure that the state would ask the court to raise or revoke my bond. Instead, it would now stay the same, and since my family had gotten the collateral together, I could now bond out and be home in a couple of days. After two and a half months, this nightmare would be over.

But then, Commissioner Mullineauk shuffled some papers in front of her, looked up at me, and said, "Mr. Lunsford, I have a note here from detectives, MCSO Paul Smith, asking that you be held without bond, so you are now non-bondable."

I couldn't believe it. I didn't know a detective had that much power. I was standing in a room full of licensed attorneys and yet their words were completely ignored in the interests of a Cave Creek cop's wishes.

Jeff was quiet, but furious. He said he had never seen that happen. I now knew I would stay in jail for months, and maybe a year and a half if it became a capital case. It was tantamount to a minimum one-year jail sentence.

Later, County Attorney Andrew Thomas instructed prosecutor Mike Gingold to file their notice of intent to seek the death penalty against me. Jeff withdrew telephonically. I never saw him again. The government was now literally trying to kill me, and I had no attorney, no help.

I began to feel like a paper boat tossed at sea. I realized that they could do whatever they wanted to. My "rights" were fantasy and I had no control over what happened to my life from one day to the next. Everything I thought I knew about the fairness of the society I lived in, from watching those old westerns as a kid and saying the pledge of allegiance every day in school—"and justice for all"—to courtroom TV dramas. For me, all of it disappeared in just ninety days. It wasn't real.

Three Months In the MCSO Fourth Avenue Jail

I had been in jail for three months already for a crime I did not commit but still no one had interviewed a single "witness" in my case. Evidence didn't matter, facts didn't matter, and nobody was even looking into it. There were still no DNA, or fingerprint results, and no one had even tried to locate the red-haired arsonist, or the drug dealers. There was literally no evidence that I committed any crime. No one told me what the state's theory was because they hadn't even disclosed the police reports to my attorney yet, in part, because *I didn't even have* an attorney at this point.

My face was all over the news, I was called a monster, bloggers were demanding my execution, stating there "had to be a ton of DNA" incriminating me, and I could only wonder what the people I knew were starting to think of me, what was happening to my life. And I knew that the longer I sat there the worse it would get.

Eventually Rena Glitsos was appointed as my attorney by the court. She represented me for over a year and a half without interviewing a single witness, or obtaining any evidence for or against me. She drafted and filed legal documents regarding the constitutionality of the death penalty, and many motions to disqualify the MCAO due to the gross wrongdoings that were going on in Maricopa County at the time.

Eventually, MCSO Sheriff Joe Arpaio was convicted of criminal contempt charges-only to be pardoned by President Trump. County Attorney Andrew Thomas was removed from office and disbarred for abuse of power. Among the things they did together were intimidating judges and defense attorneys, especially in capital cases, and making false arrests of politicians, Don Stapley and Mary Rose Wilcox, and manufacturing phony indictments.

Chapter 5

Grand Jury Indictments, Pleas and Defense Lawyers

•••

A s frustrating and head scratching as my first two weeks in custody were, there was hope on the horizon, in the immediate
future. There was a hurdle the state would have to clear, something called a *grand jury
indictment*, and they didn't have the tools to do it—Detective Smith would have to lie
to a grand jury, under oath, in order to convince them to indict me for murder.

On July 21, 2008, the grand jury convened in my case, in front of Commissioner
Passamonte, for what would be a casual conversation about Detective Smith's version
of the situation, between him and Prosecutor Jeannette Gallagher, albeit in a formal
place—a courtroom. They, the twelve members of the grand jury, and Commisoner
Passamonte would be the only people present in the otherwise empty courtroom, which
is the norm in indictment proceedings. No members of the defense could attend; there
would be no one there to question anything that was said.

First, Ms. Gallagher explained the case to the grand jurors, who were then asked
if they had seen media coverage of it, and if they had, would they nonetheless be "able
to render a decision based solely upon the evidence presented during the hearing" and
not be prejudiced by what they had seen on the local news. The jurors remained silent,
no one even responded to the prosecutor, reminiscent of countless classrooms we have
all been in as kids and teenagers. Classrooms where our fellow students, due to the
silence, and we are beginning to wonder if the teacher might have just asked a question.
No one was paying attention.

Undeterred, the prosecutor said, "I take it by your silence each of you will be able to render a decision in this case based solely upon the evidence presented during the investigation."

Detective Paul Smith was then sworn in, hand on the Bible, swearing to tell the truth—the whole truth, nothing but the truth, so on, and yada-yada. He began with the basics, his name, experience, the house fire at 7:44 p.m., female victim, etc. Ms. Gallagher walked him through his testimony, one leading question at a time, enumerating the basic narrative that the entire public had already heard on TV.

As a bridge between that, she cherry-picked segments of the interview I voluntarily did with MCSO Detective Osborn, emphasizing my "admissions"—That I met Liz Hermann, accompanied her to Freddy's Sinaloan coca dispensary, had a one-night-stand with her, and as of about five a.m. Tuesday morning, claimed that I never saw her again.

None of my "admissions" were crimes—except for cocaine possession, which they chose not to charge me with. None of the "admissions" had anything to do with murder, or arson, but the stigmatic word "admissions" is so helpful to law enforcement when trying to create suspicion that it would be used over and over in my case, for years. 'His admissions, his admissions, his admissions...'

Ms. Gallagher, in an effort to get Detective Smith talking about the pets who had perished due to smoke inhalation, reminded him of that topic, to which he mentioned "a cat."

"Okay" she said, "anything else?"

There was the dog. The whole town had read about it, in the small town newspaper, "*The Sonoran News*," which printed, among many articles, an article detailing a dramatic sequence of events wherein the dog, in an effort to protect its owner, had jumped through the air at, supposedly *me*, whereupon they reported that I, like a ninja, had stabbed the dog mid-air. But nobody stabbed the dog. It died of "smoke inhalation" according to the reports, and had no injuries. Detective Smith here, at the grand jury proceedings, did not even remember that there was a dog. When Gallagher asked him "anything else," besides the cat, his dismissive answer was "no."

"What about the bow-wow?" she asked. Oh yeah that, there was that," he said in a longer, more evasive way. Perhaps he was distracted, thinking about how he was going to put together this story, create a nexus between me and murder charges.

He talked about Gerald Coco, telling the grand jury "he admitted that he went and bought gas in the gas can [sic] and put gas in her truck . . . and then burned the house." Nothing about the dirt parking lot beating.

Ms. Gallagher added, by way of a leading question, "Did Gerald tell you that Mr. Lunsford told him to alibi for him for the day?"

"Yes," Smith said, even though various witnesses, surveillance, and phone records proved that I *was with him* all day—20 miles away from the crime scenes. Smith didn't tell the grand jury that part, didn't tell the "whole" truth, or any of it, in that exchange.

In Coco's interviews, Detective Smith tried to get Gerald to say that I asked him to lie for me, over, and over, and over, ad nauseam. *"Please*, just say it," Smith might as well have said. Gerald assured Smith, over and over, that I never asked him to lie, we were together all day, and we never went to any crime scenes.

"I don't even know where that house is," Gerald told him, over and over. Detective Smith couldn't get Gerald to say it for him in an interview, so Smith said it *for* him under oath to the grand jury.

This became a theme in Detective Smith's investigative style. When he couldn't get the dots he had created to connect, he would manufacture something. Smith brought up Max Piper, at Ms. Gallagher's nudging. Gerald and I spoke to Max, in person, at Max's apartment in Phoenix, thirty minutes away from Ms. Hermann's house, *at the exact time it was being burnt.*

Detective Smith and Prosecutor Gallagher dutifully avoided whereabouts or timelines. In Detective Smith's interview with Piper, he and his cohorts were told on page one of the transcript "he [me] didn't tell me anything" and that the only accounts he heard were secondhand (gossip) accounts from his roommate days later. Detective Smith ticked rumors out of Piper, and each time he got Piper speaking about one he would pounce; and try to get Piper to assign it to me, which he never did. Piper told Smith, over and over, that I never told him anything about "a girl who died" and that he got all of his information from his roommate.

Max Piper wouldn't—*couldn't*—incriminate me, so Detective Smith did it for him, saying to Ms. Gallagher and the grand jury, "He told Max he was out in the desert and this girl Mary [Liz] was in her vehicle with a couple of other guys that he didn't know and he wasn't in—Justin was in another vehicle. Some kind of scuffle occurred and the way he described it is she hit the ground, and Max and he [sic] assumed that she was dead. This was the police-favorite, of all the rumors they'd heard from Max. But the MCSO Interview reveals that Max said he got this from his roommate, Andrew Phillips, not me.

Andrew Phillips, however, told Smith et al a *different* story. After three, standoffish, then hostile interviews between Phillips and Detective Smith, Phillips says over and over, that he has no incriminating information about me. In response, Detective Fax threatens to charge Phillips with hindering prosecution.

Phillips responds, "You can't charge me with hindering prosecution, I'm not hindering anything!"

The day after my wrongful arrest a defeated Andrew Phillips told *yet another* story. It was not consistent with what any witness said, it was not even consistent with what he himself said to Piper. It was not supported by any fact and was so outlandish it could've come out of a scene from Pulp Fiction. Indeed, Phillips' story itself was, by definition, *Pulp Fiction*.

No matter. Smith would take whatever he could get. If it didn't make sense he could fix it up—or not, the grand jury wasn't really listening anyway. Detective Smith told the grand jury, ". . . Justin told him that he was over at this girl's house and they were doing coke and he said that two guys came into the house. He said they were undercover narcs, policemen, he didn't know who they were, but they made me [sic] watch them slice her throat and that's pretty much in a nutshell what he said. He didn't get into too much detail after."

My new attorney, Rena Glitsos, challenged my grand jury indictment, due to the false testimony of the only witness sworn in that day, MCSO Detective Paul Smith. But she could not do a thorough job because Detective Smith still had not disclosed the police reports to her.

Continuing the theme of embellishment, Detective Smith told the grand jury that I had "access to a vehicle" that "fits" the description of the truck that eyewitness Jimmie Larson saw at the truck fire, and that it was my dad's truck. He left out the description of the red-haired arsonist altogether.

He then opined that I used Liz's cell phone in the "early morning hours" to call "people that she did not know." Ms. Gallagher asks, "detective, how do you know she didn't know them, she is dead?" and "As far as you know, she didn't know them?"

"Yes," Smith said. "And as far as you know, she wasn't alive to be calling them?"

"Correct.

Detective Smith had no idea whether or not she knew them. And she *was* alive to be calling them. She died Tuesday *evening*. There was abundant evidence of that—wet blood on the fireman's pants, at 8pm), no rigor, no lividity. Nevertheless, Smith told the grand jury that there was no "evidence or estimate of what time she died." Again, dutifully avoiding a timeline or specifics, keeping their narrative as malleable as they could in case they needed to "adjust" or add to it later. Smith also made some admissions of his own to the grand jury. He admitted that Liz was panicked at finding the two suspicious cars outside her home that night, and the backdoor open. He admitted that he had no idea who was in the cars. He admitted that he was never able to locate the Sinaloan drug dealers, and he admitted that their apartment was vacated when he went to the house with MCSO investigators the day after Liz's murder.

He admitted that Liz had an estranged husband—but qualified it by saying he was "at work Tuesday," omitting the actual times. Polgar was at work from five a.m. until two p.m., that day. The truck fire occurred at 2:15pm and 7:30pm, respectively. Polgar had no alibi.

Detective Smith also admitted they did not recover her cell phone, or any alleged murder weapon. And he admitted that I met her on Monday night for the first time. I had no motive whatsoever.

He admitted that none of the pulp fiction came from me. He said the stories he told Gerald, Max, and Andrew, were not repeated when he interrogated me. He had to admit that I cooperated fully and answered all questions, without a hint of the fanciful stories he'd gleaned from the grapevine.

As passive as the grand jurists were in their listening, a couple of them had questions for Detective Smith. The first one, noticing holes in the truck fire scenario, asked Smith, "Did you talk to the father of [sic] the truck?"

A great question. One would assume, if law enforcement alleged that a specific vehicle had been used in a capital-murder-arson-cover-up, they would *certainly* interview the owner of that vehicle. They would want to know who drove it that day, where it was that day, et certa. But they didn't. They avoided that, again staying away from specifics. But one grand juror was on to him. Detective Smith was in a bind…what would he do? Tell the truth, "No we didn't contact him."

I think when Detective Smith found himself in a jam, along with many other bad actor policemen we've seen in cell phone videos doing shameful things, the go-to mantra becomes, '*Just lie.*'

It's so easy. 'Just lie, you're a cop, no one will question you,' they seem to tell themselves. And that's what he did. He told my dad, who was present at our family home for hours after my arrest, as Smith *et al* impounded hundreds of pieces of "evidence" including the truck, "He is not talking to us. We tried."

That wasn't true. The truth was, that my whole family were made to sit outside our house for five to six hours as investigators rifled through our house. My dad waited patiently to talk to them trying to find out what was going on, and where they had taken me. They never spoke to him. The only person they took a statement from was my ex-wife, who, by happenstance was also present. Since she was with or around me basically all week they asked her if she knew anything, or if I had said anything about the incidents.

She said "no."

I assume they approached her because they knew who she was, since her mom, my ex-mother-in-law, who despised me, worked at the MCSO substation.

But they never spoke to my dad, and Detective Smith told another lie to sidestep that question. Perhaps noticing his discomfort, prosecutor Gallagher then interrupted, and took it a step further; telling the grand jury,

"And just to be sure, nobody has to talk to the police. Everybody has the right to say, no, thank you very much. So I am going to ask you to disregard the 'fact' that his father exercised his rights, and ask if there is any member of the grand jury who cannot disregard that in determining probable cause in this case?"

And perhaps she spoke too long, losing the classroom's attention again, because again, no one answered or acknowledged her... or maybe they weren't buying it?

No matter. Gallagher answers for them, again, with, "by your silence I take it you can all disregard that."

One grand juror seemed to notice Smith's omissions of anything relating to a time-line. He asks, "What time was Justin to have lunch with [Gerald's] mom?"

Smith gave a long, evasive answer about me eating lunch, with Gerald, at his mom's, but again, studiously avoided a time line.

Not satisfied, the juror asked again, "What *time* was that?"

He did his best to muddy the waters. "That was in the afternoon or somewhere around two o'clock, three o'clock. The times weren't very specific," he said, lying, again.

Cindy Coco's statement was very specific. In her transcript interview she states, plainly, that I was there from one p.m. until three p.m., which lined up perfectly with the Gallagher's surveillance video, which was also specific, showing Gerald and I arriving at 3:30 p.m. It also showed that I could not have been at Cave Creek and New River road burning Ms. Polgar's truck at 2:15pm. In a reality-based community, this is called an alibi.

At that, the juror then says, "But a witness had testified that he saw a man in his green pickup truck at this Mary's truck that was in some state of fire?"

Detective Smith—"Correct."

Juror—"That was around?"

Detective Smith—"2:15"

Juror—"2:15 and maybe I lost it..." Finally the juror essentially gives up on trying to build a timeline, perhaps in an act of submissiveness to the detective.

After a few more questions highlighting the lack of clarity, and the jury's lack of understanding of Detective Smith's wiggly testimony, a juror states "After listening to this, I have heard it on the news."

The prosecutor asks if the juror can disregard the media stories and base his decision "solely on the testimony of Detective, Smith?"

And he says, "Yes."

But after Smith's choppy, hide-and-go-seek "testimony" everyone might have been less misled by just listening to the local networks.

Satisfied with Smith's non-answers, the grand jury foreman announces, "Case 448 GJ 619, a true bill. My signature appears on the indictment as a true bill."

Two months and one week after the first indictment was crafted—then later thrown out—the grand jury convened, again, in front of a different judge. One might assume that due to the creative testimony of the first indictment, the state might put this second one together in order to produce something more factual in nature, but it was essentially the same testimony, with only two new wrinkles, and two new prosecutors. Ms. Gallagher was out. Maricopa Deputy County Attorneys Ann Alexov and Michael Gingold conducted the second grand jury hearing. Mr. Gingold would be my prosecutor going forward.

The first wrinkle was a slight one, but significant to the trained eye. Perhaps after the first indictment wherein the grand jury began asking about specifics, Detective Smith learned he would have to begin formulating a timeline, however nebulous. He would at least have to look and sound like he knew what he was doing.

Flirting with time of death was something the state would run away from for years. Mr. Gingold asked Detective Smith, "Have you been able to determine if she was dead prior to the fire being started?"

"Yes."

"And what determination did you reach?"

"With the autopsy, there was no inhalation of any kind of smoke."

"Which would indicate she died prior to the fire?"

"That's correct."

In a later reading of the medical examiner's *actual* interview, Dr. Vladimir Schwartz says he did not check for smoke in the lungs, nor does he ever, because it is "a waste of time." He gave no estimation of time of death because, he said, 'The internal organ he would examine in order to determine time of death, the spleen, would in this case, have yielded inconclusive results because it would have been 'dried out' from the fire—even though the body was untouched by fire, and had 'wet blood' on the outside of it, getting blood on a first responder's pants."

There was a second wrinkle. In an effort to create a theme that I was generally dishonest, Detective Smith testified essentially, that the Sinaloan drug dealers did not exist, and that I had made them up." This despite their phone number being on the cell records of a dead girl's phone.

"Were you ever able to contact the drug dealers?" Mr. Gingold asks, knowing the answer.

"We contacted one guy that he had—he gave us a name. We contacted him, and we have no proof that he was a drug dealer. The residence we were able to locate, we went to several times and it was vacated from there

The truth was that in the two months that had lapsed, Phoenix police did stumble across Freddy's underling, Jesus, who had greeted Liz and me at his apartment the night of July 7, 2008. In a phone conversation, an undercover police officer asked Jesus for "two ounces of coke."

Jesus said, "Okay."

The officer asked how long it would take to get it and how much it would cost.

Jesus said, "Five minutes and $800 dollars."

Jesus and his cohort were arrested near the parking lot where Gerald and I were on July 7, 2008. I was on the payphone; he had ducked into Safeway. Jesus and his crony were caught with a bunch of coke, money, and cell phones, and arrested and charged with drug possession, sales, and distribution. Phoenix PD forwarded the reports to Smith, who then testified, under oath—"we have no proof that he was a drug dealer."

I doubt Jesus' prosecutor would agree with that, but mine did.

The Maricopa Medical Examiner established that Liz had cocaine in her system; it was part of this case. The fact that the grand jury asked no further questions about where the cocaine might have spoke to their trepidation about asserting themselves and questioning the detective.

"A true bill," was again their finding.

As in many other cases, sheer coincidence has once again unearthed something compelling. While my brother was taking trips to Florida to see Garett, an old friend from Cave Creek, Ashley, who was a fixture in our home growing up, had moved to Florida to take up bartending in Key West. Ashley moved back to Cave Creek. My brother and she started a life together. She became an amazing mother to my nephew, and continued her bartending trade once she was back in Cave Creek.

Through bartending she met many people, including, fellow bartender Rebecca Ball Harding. Harding was the *Hideaway* bartender that Monday night I met Liz Hermann at the *Hideaway*. She also tended bar the next day—whereupon she said she saw Liz at the *Hideaway* with "Nate," on Tuesday, the day *after* Liz and I left together.

Harding says, to this day, she cannot understand why the MCSO arrested me, and told the public that Liz Hermann was last seen Monday night, July 7, 2008, leaving the Hideaway with me, because she, Harding, saw Liz *the next day* with another guy and told them that. Ashley said, over and over, that she and Harding have had this same head-shaking conversation, too many times to count. She never brought it up to me because she thought I already knew.

I *kind of* did know. But I couldn't prove it. I had seen a tidbit of Harding's claim that she saw Liz Hermann Tuesday July 7 or 8, 2008, perplexingly tucked away at the *end* of a typed summary of yet *another* witness, Russ Boetcher. MCSO said they decided that Harding was mistaken.

Boetcher was the man who apparently called Liz to ask if she'd like to come over to his house and "watch a movie," at about the same time Mark Lofgren was introducing Liz and I on Monday night. Coincidentally, Boetcher was at the *Hideaway* on Tuesday night, simultaneously with Gerald Coco, watching the news coverage of the situation and talking on the phone to Allen Bauer, Liz's roommate.

MCSO detectives, Bucaro and Fax, contacted Russ Botcher early Wednesday. He told them he was at the *Hideaway* talking to Becca Harding on Tuesday night and that as sure as the sky is blue, Harding had seen Liz at the Hideaway *that day*, Tuesday, with "Nate."

Detectives never ask if it was Nate Renganathan or Nate Noble because they did not know Liz actually had two "Nates."

Boetcher became the *reason* Bucaro and Fax seek out bartender Becca Harding, and her *Hideaway* colleague, bartender Dawn Hofer, who was also at the *Hideaway* Monday night.

When they interviewed Hofer, she told them "Nate" watched Liz and I leave together. Then, Hofer called Becca Harding, and asked her to come to the *Hideaway* to speak with them.

She agreed. She went to the *Hideaway* and verified everything Boetcher had told them. She saw Liz and me at the *Hideaway* Monday night, and then saw Liz return with "Nate" on Tuesday.

Boetcher had also told Bucaro to simply view the *Hideaway* surveillance cameras. He seemed to have inside information about it, he told Bucaro, over and over, that "the surveillance was there; it worked, was brand new, and only installed a month ago."

Bucaro and Fax asked Hofer and Harding about the video surveillance. They said of course you can have it; contact our security guy, Rich Stahl, he's in charge of our surveillance.

In light of Harding's recent comments, I dug up her 2008 interview summary, among others. Her summary, typed by detective Fax, says that Harding last saw Liz "Monday night." But according to Harding now, and then in 2008 is not what she said. Boetcher, *and* Liz's estranged husband, who was friends with Harding in 2008, both said in their 2008 interviews, that Harding told them she saw Liz on Tuesday with "Nate." Harding never changed her story.

I listened to Harding's 2008 interview—her words, the actual audio recording, rather than MCSO's "version" of it. I dug through the box of seventy-seven audio CD's, which I had thanks to Joy Riddle and Ashton Coleman. To my amazement, it was not there. So I looked for Dawn Hofer's CD, since they were interviewed together, thinking they might be on the same disc, but hers was missing as well. I checked the itemized list of audio CD's--both were missing. MCSO never disclosed them.

They disclosed audio recordings of Russ Boetcher's interview, even though he had nothing substantive to say. The audio of Ashley Baird, Sam Parker's girlfriend, who also had nothing to say—but did not disclose Sam Parker's audio, even though he was the *reason* Baird was interviewed. They never disclosed an audio recording of the eyewitness, Jimmy Larson. They never disclosed the surveillance from the *Hideaway*, or the 911 call about the house fire, or the 911 call about the truck fire, and now, it was apparent, they also did not disclose the audio recordings of the last two people, per their theory, to see their victim alive in public, with, according to their public narrative, their suspect. What three interviews could be more important than those two witnesses' and the only eyewitness in the entire case? All missing, thanks to the MCSO.

And now we know why. Rich Stahl, the *Hideaway* "security" guy who was in charge of surveillance, allegedly said that there was no surveillance—though it is unclear why they would have a security guy in charge of surveillance if there is no surveillance. Stahl is now an MCSO detective.

MCSO personnel frequent the *Hideaway* bar regularly and mingle with staff, just as they do the *Buffalo Chip*. This includes the husband of Liz Hermann's self-proclaimed best friend, Joy Gorski, a *Buffalo Chip* bartender. Gorski was at the crime scene simultaneously with first responders. Gorski claimed she was Hermann's best friend and that Hermann frequently went to Mexico with her and her husband. They had just returned from their last trip a couple of days before her murder.

It is unclear how the wife of a MCSO deputy, cop, was "best friends" with a young woman who, according to Botcher, binge drank "three times a week," used cocaine, and was, according to Detective Paul Smith associated with the Hell's Angels. One would think that an MCSO police officer would want to keep that influence away from his wife—not take it to Mexico with them. And we can only imagine how the Hell's Angels, who Liz Hermann partied with, and slept with felt about her going to Mexico with MCSO deputies once a month.

In his audio interview, Hermann's estranged husband told Detective Smith that the whole reason she moved to Cave Creek was to be closer to the Hells Angels, who he referred to as "the colors."

Detective Smith told Polgar, "I bet it *pisses* you off, her sleeping with those guys," the Hells Angles.

To which Polgar slams his fist on the table and says "Hell yeah, it pisses me off!"

Polgar said he "hated" the Hell's Angels, that they "force themselves on women" and think they can "do whatever they want." He said he fought with Liz about the H.A. all the time, telling her to get "out of there," the *Buffalo Chip*. But Liz insisted that the H.A. actually "protected" her.

Two things are sure. First, Liz Hermann's world was a complicated one in a very strange town. A town where no doubt Sonny Barger pulled ideas from, as he worked as "technical adviser" on the hit FX series "Sons of Anarchy," bringing the fictional small town of "charming" to life, and appearing for the occasional cameo.

Perhaps Liz's boss, retired MCSO Chief Deputy Larry Wendt, was the inspiration for the likeable yet corrupt "charming" town sheriff known as, "Unser." Unser pushed an investigation or two in a wayward direction in order to avoid embarrassing or exposing the "pillars" of the community. He had a what's-good-for-the-goose-is-good-for-the-gander sort of approach to law "enforcement."

Perhaps *Hideaway* bar owner Mark Bradshaw, who looks exactly like a S.O.A. cast member, as he sits on the Cave Creek town council, was the partial inspiration for a shady charming town council member whose favorite hobby was unethical real estate and getting extorted by the motorcycle gang.

Perhaps Liz Hermann was one of a dozen nameless women shared on the show. We could draw as many imaginative parallels as time would allow. Cave Creek is the real life charming.

The second sure thing is that Detective Smith knew the day I was arrested that I was not the last person seen with Liz Hermann. He and his cohorts got the statements from Becca Harding and Dawn Hofer, and probably the *Hideaway* surveillance video, and then destroyed them all, along with the eyewitness Jimmie Larson's audio, and Sam Parker's.

Sam Parker confessed to involvement in the murder. When Sam Parker's right hand man from 2008, Nathaniel Noble, was implicated by DNA, they covered for him too. They have been letting him run loose through the community high on meth and anti-psychotics, lighting things on fire and chasing young women around with knives and machetes.

It is no small irony that the *Buffalo Chip Saloon* recently fell victim to a "random" arson, burning to the ground—another network news story that I shook my head at from prison. But, whatever. The appellate courts can't be bothered with petty stuff like this. They are too busy looking for clerical errors.

After my arrest I thought there was no way they would be able to indict me, because I was innocent. Detective Smith would have to lie under oath in order to get a grand jury to indict me, and due to my upbringings and understandings of American society I still believed that police officers did not lie; a view shared by most people in 2008. Even if one did, surely a judge like Rosa Mroz would quickly correct it. I was sure they cared about the truth, and the people, even my family, people like my gramma.

But they didn't. Detective Smith lied, Judge Mroz saw nothing wrong with it, and I stayed in jail. When my grandmother died while I was in jail, it broke my heart. She must have spent the last year of her life heartbroken too, wondering why I wasn't coming to visit anymore. Maybe she died of a broken heart. If you spend the last year of your life like that, then die like that, does anything that had happened in the seventy years leading up to it really even matter anymore? Each one of the old memories you could call upon in your mind just becomes a catalyst for sadness, a reminder of what you're never going to have again.

Judge Rosa Mroz

The following week Judge Mroz issued her ruling. She said that the indictment would stand because although the defense had proven that Detective Smith had misled the grand jury, that didn't prove that he "knowingly and intentionally" lied. In other words, he didn't mean to.

To this day that grand jury believes that I am a tall, red-haired guy and the drug dealers never existed—Lunsford made them up. I guess powder cocaine just grows on trees in Cave Creek.

It killed me that my gramma died. But when Jill told me, I was afraid to grieve. I continued my routine. I hung up the phone, went back to my cell, and kept doing pushups, staring at my blurry reflection in the puddle of tears that was accumulating on the floor beneath my face. Up-down, up-down, I had a war to win, however unfair, otherwise I could lose the rest of my family like this too. No judge or detective was going to save us.

First Defense Lawyer—Rena Glitsos

We had another basic status conference. During it, Ms. Glitsos said she still had not read all of the police reports. The prosecutor, Michael Gingold, still didn't know when the DNA testing would be done. Undeterred, our new judge, Janet Judge Barton, just wanted to know if we were going to be ready for trial anyway.

This is what they call railroading.

I couldn't believe that the judge was railroading me into a death penalty trial when my attorney still hadn't even read the reports, which I also could not believe, while allowing Gingold to sit on the DNA results. I had been sitting in jail for a year and a half for a crime I didn't do and no legal professional on either side had done anything.

Judge Janet Barton

My whole family was appalled. Everything was backwards. My attorney seemed to agree, as she offered little pushback. She answered the judge's question about whether we would be ready for trial. "I don't think that is realistic at this point based on my conversations with my mitigation specialist."

Judge Barton said, "All right. Well, the problem that the court is confronted with is we do have our trial date in this case of March 8th, and do not have the authority to continue that trial date."

Ms. Glitsos said, "Well, your honor, I intended to file a motion to continue the trial date, because it is clear that we won't be ready to try the case as scheduled."

I could not believe that the judge did not "have the authority" to continue the trial date. Judge Barton gave my attorney a "heads-up" that her motion to continue would be denied before she even read it.

Ms. Glitsos said, "I'm not trying to threaten you. . . I understand. It's just that, you know, it seems like the way things are right now, there is a lack of recognition about what—and I'm talking institutionally, systemically, a lack of recognition about what is required to litigate capital cases from the defense standpoint. And there is this rush to push cases along, and they are all going to come back on habeas or appeal because counsel isn't prepared. And it's very frustrating as a defense attorney to be out in this position. And I have been doing this for 20 years, not capital litigation for 20 years, but I have been a criminal defense lawyer for 20 years in this system, and I have seen the permutations it's gone through, and this is beyond anything I have seen before and completely ignores what is required for the defendant. I'm sorry. I'm just . . .I'm appalled."

Judge Barton explained that Presiding Judge Donahoe was currently denying motions to continue, stating that she had "seen two denials…within the last ten days."

You see, there was a bigger picture, a bigger problem in Maricopa county at the time. County Attorney Andrew Thomas' wanton practice of seeking the death penalty in a record number of cases for sheer publicity and election purposes had created a colossal mess in county courtrooms, leaving attorneys and judges grasping for straws to patch up a capital system that was bursting at the seams.

Of course it didn't help that judges were inclined to allow phony indictments to stand, such as the one in my own case to ease the congestion on the dockets and lighten caseloads. The office of court appointed counsel, OCAC, the administrative predecessor of the office of public defender services, OPDS, had begun appointing and paying a number of private attorneys to jump into the mess and help clean it up. Attorneys who were interested in helping however, such as Ms. Glitsos, were disturbed at what they saw, once inside the "capital case crisis."

In a November 27, 2019 motion to dismiss the case, or as an alternative allow her to withdraw, Ms. Glitsos pointed out to the court that "Assuming eighteen months as the norm for capital trial proceedings, the systematic overloading by the state of the Maricopa county capital trial system- at a rate of 13-to-15 times greater than our next largest county- has led to delays in appointment of counsel and trial preparation that should be charged against the state."

She cited Vermont v. Brillon, 2009 U.S. Lexis 1780, 5-6 (U.S. Mar. 9, 2009). She pointed out that, "here, in Maricopa county the 'systemic breakdowns' is hardly from mismanagement of the public defender system, but from the state's indiscriminate use of the death penalty, our county attorney, Andrew Thomas, is an extreme outlier among jurisdictions that employ the death penalty, asking for death from 325-375% more often per hundred thousand of population than Pima county."

She went on to say, "When counsel accepted appointment on this case, the average time for a capital case to go to trial was 4 to 6 years… counsel relied on previous assurances from OCAC…that the courts would allow sufficient time to prepare capital cases… now the court has changed the rules."

She pointed out that Judge Donahoe cited an administrative order from the AZ Supreme Court, on October 30th, 2009. She said, "This was incorrect as the Arizona Supreme Court never issued such an order."

One could speculate as to why Judge Donahoe was really doing this. Judge Timothy Ryan later attempted to testify in a matter relating to my case, about death threats he'd received as a result of Andrew Thomas' dislike of him, to which MCSO's finest told him he was on his own, he could walk himself to the parking garage.

The reasons do not change the outcome. The dysfunction within the Arizona judiciary was even more complex than the dysfunction I'd left behind in the Cave Creek bar scene. Justice was perverted. Propriety had gone away, and at this point nobody was even looking into what had really happened to Liz Hermann or the *Buffalo Chip* bartender from Cave Creek, who worked for retired MCSO Chief Deputy, Larry Wednt.

And everybody seemed fine with that. Maybe that's what they wanted.

Ms. Glitsos summed up her position by stating simply that my case would not be ready, and that wasn't my fault, and that I shouldn't be executed over the government's dysfunction, and that "failing all other relief, counsel must withdraw to avoid this ethical breach." She cited the United States supreme court's statement that "It is intolerable that one constitutional right, (my right to a speedy trial) should have to be surrendered in order to assert another (my right to high-quality representation)."

What took place in Judge Barton's courtroom on July 29th 2009, when my lawyer, Rena Glitsos, was candid, will forever be known by the Lunsford family as "Rena's meltdown," but in the most endearing way. It was the first time we had seen a legal professional humanize herself by showing emotion and genuine concern about what was happening. I made sure to call her that day and tell her how much we appreciated her. It made us trust her. She had accepted the OCAC contract because she wanted to help indigent defendants, but upon getting inside the dynamic she found that it was nothing more than a contract to throw away human lives without due process, in order to clean up the mess made by County Attorney Andrew Thomas and preserve the spotless image of everyone in local government, from Judge Donahoe to MCSO Detective Paul Smith, whose actions and inactions now over a year after my wrongful arrest had yet to even be analyzed, much less questioned.

Judge Janet Barton, upon realizing that there was no way around the fact that this stubborn attorney, this Ms. Glitsos, would not participate in herding people like cattle, removed her from my case against my wishes, and appointed someone who would, career Public Defender Rick Miller.

I never learned the exact manner in which Ms. Glitsos was removed from my case. Somewhere in the middle of all the arguing between her and the court, or at the end rather, I was asked by an MCSO detention officer in the jail if I wanted a haircut. This confused me because it was custom for inmates to have the option of getting a haircut each Friday. Only the ones who had a scheduled court date for the upcoming week got haircuts. To my knowledge I did not have one.

But I got a haircut anyway, just in case. I called Ms. Glitsos, and her secretary told me I actually did have one scheduled.

When the detention officers came into the pod at three o'clock in the morning, on the day I was told I had court, to gather the inmates who had court, I was not called. I asked an officer if I had court; I told him I should be on their list. He said I was not.

So I waited for my daily access to the phone, and called Ms. Glitsos' office. Her secretary answered and said "Mr. Lunsford, why aren't you in court?"

I told her they said I didn't have court.

She explained to me that the MCSO deputy, Hoffman, who routinely escorted me to Judge Barton's court, was from the Cave Creek beat. He had told the court, and my attorney, that I "refused" to be transported. I explained to her that I did not refuse; I would never do that. It was important to me, and to all of my family, and friends, that we be at every court appearance, involved in all proceedings.

She then said that it basically didn't matter now, that Judge Barton had removed Ms. Glitsos from my case. Because, Judge Barton said, Rena was "too emotionally unstable to handle a capital case."

I think what Judge Barton meant was "not callous enough to do it unethically."

On July 22, 2010, the secretary said that Rena was no longer my attorney and that as of four p.m. that day I was no longer allowed to call her office. I never spoke to Rena again, and the minute entry, the transcribed report of what was said that day between Judge Barton and Ms. Glitsos was never produced, never included in my file. It was "sealed" by Judge Barton and has never been read by anybody. It was clear to my family and I that Judge Barton did not want anyone present that day, and did not want anyone to read about it either. I now sat in county jail without an attorney, again, for weeks, waiting to hear what the government was going to do next with my life.

Defense Lawyer Rick Miller

On Feb 5, 2010 I met Rick Miller. My new public defender. He had possibly the warmest demeanor of anyone I'd ever met. He was easy to talk to, easy to listen to, and charming. He was in his element quarterbacking serious situations, relaxed yet vigilant. My family and I, after losing Ms. Glitsos, "Rena" to us, who we'd realized had actually gone to high school with my dad at Central High in the early '70s, would eventually come to love and trust Rick Miller entirely. I personally trusted him with my life—fifty per cent for the above-mentioned reasons, and fifty per cent for another reason, which will have its own chapter later. Being "poor" forces defendants into "non-consensual" attorney client relationships. You have to trust your public defender.

In my first meeting with Rick I immediately told him I was innocent and would never consider a plea. I told him we had to spend all of our time on facts and evidence, preparing for trial. I was direct about this because I had lived in the "4th Avenue Jail" for a year and a half around thousands of other defendants. Thirty-six of them were capital murder defendants.

I knew public defenders set their sights on plea agreements, especially in capital cases. They wanted to ease the capital caseload backlog. There simply weren't enough resources in Maricopa County to conduct trials in all capital cases. Capital-certified defense attorneys had by now collectively agreed upon a single, unified goal—to save their client's lives. The safest way to do that was to avoid a death penalty trial altogether, by pleading out.

Additionally, empirical research was now showing that mitigation was impactful, even game changing. Studies and anecdotes revealed that when jurors learned about the difficulties an alleged murderer had gone through before becoming an alleged murderer, they actually became sympathetic, finding him or her more relatable and often sparing their life. So, nationally capital defense attorneys had taken the approach of accumulating mitigating factors, such as childhood abuse, or drug use in the home, and using it to get a favorable plea for their clients.

In Maricopa County, with the capital case crisis as bad as it was, they favored this approach all the more so. Mandated it. Even worse for me, and all innocent defendants, was the fact that almost all court-appointed attorneys had completely abandoned the practice of scrutinizing the state's theory, or challenging detectives' "evidence." This is assuming that they once held that practice.

Of course, most arrestees are guilty any way, at least guilty of *some* of the charges, so what was the point in an attorney's going anywhere outside the police narrative in their own thinking? To many attorneys, especially those who had experienced burn-out over time, interviewing the state's witnesses, requesting subpoenas, and going to the MCSO warehouse to actually view the physical evidence, instead of just taking the detective's word for it, had simply become an extra, unnecessary, waste of time that they did not get paid extra to do, and might undermine the harmony enjoyed between them and police.

No self-respecting lawyer was going to do all that running around for another lying client. Their colossal tendencies, systemic or individual, to fall in love with mitigation, to prioritize plea bargaining, to avoid going outside the police narrative, these were the societal tidal wave that I was trying to push back on in my first five minutes with Rick. It had to be done quick. It had to be done hard. Poor Rick, he probably had no idea what they'd assigned him to, or how hard a sell I was going to be until that first meeting.

Or maybe he did. He received it well, he seemed moved by what I said, and he made me believe one hundred per cent that he was onboard. I felt really good about it afterward. That was the first of two really important things I needed to discuss with Rick on that first day. The second was a question that I had to get his response on, fully measured, which people outside Maricopa county would be perplexed by, but those inside understood perfectly.

"Are you afraid of MCSO?"

Without hesitation he said, "Yes."

Maricopa County Attorney Andrew Thomas

I was surprised and relieved by his candor, but not at all surprised by his position. A lot had happened, and was still happening, leading up to that point. County Attorney Andrew Thomas had been elected on a law and order platform. Quickly, Maricopa county had "more capital cases than Houston, Las Vegas, and Los Angeles combined. The judiciary was crippled by that. Mr. Thomas and Sheriff Arpaio began their scheme to take over the world, starting with Maricopa county.

Arpaio would use Thomas to craft phony indictments against his foes, Thomas would use Arpaio to arrest his enemies, usually judges and defense attorneys who argued or ruled against them.

Judge Timothy Ryan was to testify that granting an evidentiary hearing in a capital case, or a hearing to strike the death penalty, was "political suicide."

This hurt my defense tremendously, especially in the appellate process. The appellate court cannot review a case unless there is a "record," and if those hearings do not take place then there is no record. The appellate court cannot find grounds for relief because there is nothing to read. This is especially true if a trial is denied by way of a coerced plea. Bad actors within the criminal justice system will go out of their way to make sure that their bad actions do not go "on the record."

Chief Presiding Judge Barbara Mundell in May of 2009 told Channel 12 news that she and contractors at her home had seen "unmarked sheriff's cars" parked near her home even though she lives "in a neighborhood patrolled by the Phx police dep't." Any Judge who crossed the County Attorney or the Sheriff would experience the same thing. Relevant to my case alone, five judicial assistants stood to testify that MCSO deputies had made visits *at their home,* after hours, to "interrogate them" about their bosses, the judges. The purpose was intimidation. The sheriff knew that the first thing each county attorney would do was pick up the phone and call their boss.

My attorney wrote, "Consequently, counsel is legitimately concerned that she could become a target of Thomas as a result of filing this motion."

Harassment turned into arrests when Thomas indicted county supervisors Mary Rose Wilcox and Don Stapley. Soon, the FBI was investigating Thomas.

Thomas brought in Yavapai County Attorney Sheila Polk to help sort things out for him. She eventually told him and Arpaio, "She did not believe there was evidence of any crime." She dismissed the charges against Stapley.

Arpaio, indignant, said "[I] can arrest anyone [I] want to" and "nobody can tell [me] to get off [my] own cases

Against Ms. Polk's wishes, Arpaio re-arrested Commissioner Stapley that day, at his office.

After Ms. Polk removed herself from the utter hullabaloo that Maricopa County had become, she became a whistle-blower of sorts, speaking out against the tyranny. She said, "I could not believe that Mr., Thomas or a person of my profession was willing to use the awesome authority of a prosecutor and bring criminal charges in a case where there is not one shred of evidence."

I could. I was experiencing it.

And by now, thanks to Jill purchasing and sending me a subscription to *The Arizona Republic,* I was reading about it every day, learning about the people whose hands my life was in.

In an article titled *"No Higher Form of Corruption,"* the author wrote, "They [Arpaio and Thomas] are capable of intimidating perfectly innocent citizens…there is no higher form of corruption than this."

By this point Arpaio and Thomas had filed a racketeering influenced and corrupt organizations (Rico) action against "a fraction of at least four judges of this court, the Maricopa county board of supervisors and others."

This included my mitigations master, Judge Donahoe. The RICO act was originally designed by the Federal government to help them prosecute Sonny Barger, founder of the Hell's Angels.

After Liz was murdered, rumors about Hell's Angels involvement in her death abounded. So my mother asked Sonny Barger one day, while he was at her house picking up some leather goods, face to face, if they'd had anything to do with it.

He said, "I don't know Joyce, they don't tell me anymore when they do things like this." Due to the advent of RICO, the H.A. adopted the policy of shielding Barger from prosecution with plausible deniability. I found it ironic, that the only other person I knew or knew of, who was "hit" with the RICO Act, was Judge Donahoe, who I sat down with informally at my mitigation meetings. I marveled at the symmetry, but was concerned about the effect on my life.

Just when the men and women of Maricopa County thought they'd seen all the dysfunction a small-market county could stomach, the "Free Stoddard" movement made its place here. On October 19th, 2009, MCSO Deputy Adam Stoddard stole a letter from an attorney's file in open court, while she and the defendant were occupied at the podium. It was an attorney-client privileged communication. Stoddard gave it to another deputy who took it out of the courtroom to copy it. The entire incident was captured on camera. Defense counsel demanded the letter be returned and Judge Flores told her, "Calm down, I allow the deputies a lot of leeway in my courtroom."

At a contempt hearing, Judge Donahoe ordered the deputy to either apologize or do twenty-four hours in jail. Arpaio wouldn't allow him to apologize. Judge Donahoe sent Stoddard to jail. The following day, nineteen deputies inexplicitly called in sick and were "unable" to transport defendants to court. That same morning, someone called in a bomb threat to the entire court building, necessitating an evacuation of all judges and judicial assistants, who by this point had moved staff meetings from judge's chambers to the chamber's bathrooms, due to fear of listening devices. The following day, yet another bomb threat emptied the building again. The MCSO said they would "look into it."

This was the circus environment in which I was seeking and needing justice. So if anyone is to wonder why MCSO Detective Paul Smith would arrest me without any evidence, ignore red flags, lie to the grand jury, expect the judges to insulate him, and expect my public defender to go along with it all, I ask in return, why *wouldn't* he?

Culture, whether in a Fortune 500 company, a sports team, or a sheriff's office, starts at the top and runs down like water. Thanks to Arpaio, by this point the entire MCSO was drenched in arrogance. So I just stared at Rick Miller, he stared back at me, and I thought, "Okay, how are we going to do this?'

In the months preceding Rick's appointment to my case, and during Rena's ongoing entanglement with MCAO, evidence and insight had begun to trickle in from police reports and other sources.

Sam Parker

Sam Parker, the wayward friend I'd visited and gone to the Hideaway with the night that I'd met Liz Hermann was being talked about, and asked about. *Arizonafamily.com*, an online news outlet, had released information in narrative form. The Cave Creek residents who read it clung to every word. Sam Parker's name was mentioned prominently since I was with him the night before the murder and stuck on his porch the next morning

Sam Parker's problem was his desire to be viewed by people as either tough or violent. He had successfully achieved this status through years of violent and aggressive behavior, and intermittent bragging. On the other hand, I was viewed as big and strong, but more cerebral, and a gentleman. So, when people who knew the dynamic, basically all of Cave Creek, they read, Justin Lunsford, Sam Parker—violent incident."

They naturally concluded that Sam Parker did it. What also did not help Sam was the fact that the silver sedans that I described to police (parked in front of Liz's house), and that Liz Hermann described to her roommate, were consistent with Sam's silver Cadillac and his girlfriend's silver Corolla, or Altima. The eyewitness description of the truck arsonist, while looking nothing like me, looked exactly like Sam.

He was also calling members of my family, very emotional, expressing guilt, saying he should be in jail instead of me, and asking if he should get an attorney. He expressed the same thing to me over the jail phone, crying, saying he "knew for a fact that I was innocent," saying MCSO deputies in Cave Creek were "crooked." Then he had my date of birth engraved on his leg. Whatever the case, he was unable to cope with what had transcribed.

That was also the case with Sam's friend, Nathaniel Noble. He was the briefly mentioned Michigan transplant who was working at "Hammerhead Jacks" the night I met Liz. But unfortunately he would go unnoticed for over a decade.

A Cave Creek couple had begun talking about seeing Liz fighting with Sam Parker at Larry Wednt's *Buffalo Chip* bar twice within the week preceding her death. She threw him out of the establishment and embarrassed him in front of other patrons. Adding context and concern to all of this was the fact that Sam's parents being "high level drug dealers" was "common knowledge throughout Cave Creek." He was bragging about getting, "patched in" to a well-known motorcycle gang.

A federal indictment for a multimillion-dollar tax evasion case against Sam's father, James Parker, seemed to support people's belief of their involvement in organized crime. That took it a step further by mentioning thousands of acres of prime real estate in in Belize. It was in conjunction with straw companies and straw owners, including Sam, the purported owner of the $325,000 Rolls Royce that sat in front of James Parker's mansion. The elder Parker, James, would never let his loose-cannon drug-using son, Sam, touch, much less drive. James Parker put a lot of things in Sam's name. Being a straw man was Sam's major role in the Parker family, and he definitely had the brains for it.

In the weeks and months after Rick Miller's appointment, he would suggest to me that if I would give incriminating statements about Sam then the state would view my situation differently.

From the beginning, prosecutor Mike Gingold told my first attorney, with whom he'd been childhood friends, that he did not think I "did it." He just thought I knew more than I'd told police. He thought that I was a witness and thought he could coerce me through confinement. I couldn't understand why Gingold would move forward with the prosecution of a man who he didn't think "did it." I think that after, and as a direct result of MCSO Detective Paul Smith's hasty arrest of me, no attorneys on either side really knew what to do with the case, because there wasn't any real evidence of anything.

Private Investigator Joe Otero

Private investigator Joe Otero asked me a lot of questions about the Parkers. Otero was a former homicide detective with either Chandler or Mesa police. He explained to me that he had grown weary watching MCAO prosecutors twist his own cases in the courtroom. Even though it was for the purposes of convicting the defendants he'd arrested, he said he couldn't stomach it anymore, so he'd come to work for "the other side," helping indigent defendants.

Otero wanted to know from me, how careful should he be approaching these people. He explained that while at the police department he had exchanged gunfire with a member of the Hell's Angels. Both were injured. The Hell's Angel member told him specifically that he would kill him as soon as he could. That was a member of the Mesa chapter of the Hells Angels.

Now getting involved in my case would necessitate him poking around in Cave Creek—the home and haven of the founding member of the Hell's Angels, and Sonny Barger. Otero's main suspect was supposed H.A. associate Sam Parker. Otero wanted me to tell him whether or not he should "take somebody with him" as a precaution.

"Sure, take somebody with you," I told him.

After several trips to Cave Creek and multiple threats from James Parker, Otero disappeared. He didn't die; I just never saw him again. He quit investigating the case. But before he did he left me with this thought. He said that for the first time he was genuinely concerned that police had the wrong person in jail—me. And he said that he believed MCSO personnel in Cave Creek were "on the take." I found that compelling, coming from a former police detective.

April 2010—Preparing For Trial

By April 2010 everyone was really happy with where we were headed. Rick had been on the case long enough to be familiar with the evidence, and my family had really warmed up to him. Rick had taken the time to sit down with them, to talk to them, to listen to them. He had quickly become an important part of our dynamic.

Countless friends of mine were waiting with eagerness to see what would happen next. Some I had known since I was born, like Becca (Steinegger), her cousin Josh (Muetz), and others. Becca said she wanted to go back to law school and finish her degree due to my situation. At the time, she was working at the *Smokehouse Restaurant* (formerly the "*Satisfied Frog*") in "frontier town;" the western-style tourist attraction in the center of Cave Creek. When we were kids Becca and I used to idle through that part of town as part of the Cave Creek parade during the Cave Creek fiesta days, and rodeo weekends every spring. We would be riding with the Cave Creek 4-H club, which my mom had founded and was president. Whether on horseback, or on the hayride float, which all of us had decorated at my grandma's house, we loved riding by and waving at all the people lining the crowded Cave Creek road, and throwing candy to the kids.

Now in 2008-2010, Becca and others heard frustrating rumors about me, which oftentimes was still leading to arguments in Cave Creek establishments. The town divided. I would hear stories about my buddy, Garett, my sister-in-law Ashley, and others, having to assert themselves from time to time. Though two years had passed, the small town certainly had not forgotten about the case. It was daily or weekly that I would hear that someone I'd known sent their support and was defending me, while the other half of town was gathering at the courthouse steps with their nooses. For a small town made up mostly of bars, where not much had ever happened, this was the controversy of a lifetime.

With multiple generations of the large Lunsford family, all living in Cave Creek, and having made countless genuine friends throughout those generations, there was an enormous amount of support for me, a lot more than one would normally find in these situations. In addition, those were people who, from the outside looking in, just felt that the case didn't make any sense, and could not understand why MCSO arrested someone who looked nothing like their red-haired suspect, people still wanted to know who the red haired guy was. There was a lot of criticism of MCSO; older residents were already inclined to dislike. I'm sure Detective Paul Smith had to hear some of it since he still lived in Cave Creek.

A lot of the older Cave Creek families missed the days when there was only one lawman in Cave Creek, the Cave Creek Marshal. It was like Mayberry. Sure, the dirty dozen motorcycle gang was in Cave Creek at that time but they didn't cause any trouble, they were just good ole' boys on bikes, instead of horses, and they actually got along really well with the marshal.

The quiet older "creekers" were not big fans of the menacing black MCSO cars on every corner, the condescending young deputies who drove them, gobbling up their hard-earned tax-dollars, or their loud-mouthed Sheriff with his high-sounding empty speeches. It all ran contrary to the quiet Cave Creek way. The only time those creekers got loud was when Sheriff Arpaio's MCSO float came through on parade day, Arpaio himself sitting atop its perch, waving to the crowd like Caesar, only to be met with resounding boo's all around.

MCSO and Arpaio, it seemed, had forced the small town into a non-consensual relationship, absorbing the old lawmen the same way the Hell's Angels had "absorbed" the dirty dozen some years earlier. Sure Marshal Stein was still around, much the way some members of the dirty dozen were, just so long as he and they both kept quiet and out of sight, yielding to the new establishment.

Becca and friends wrote me every week, passionate about proving the naysayers wrong. Online trolls were anonymously declaring my execution to be inevitable, and the small town newspaper, the *Sonoran News*, was feeding it all, now using bar room gossip as its confidential source.

Jill was ready, Mom and Dad were ready, old friends were ready, the Lynch mob was ready, the whole town was ready for the showdown.

Noah Todd

Some took it even more serious than that, stepping outside of and above the gossip in an effort to change the situation. My lifelong friend, Noah Todd, started his own investigation into Liz Hermann's death and lost his life for it.

Noah and I grew up and went to high school together, as so many of us did. We had countless "good buddies" who'd gone to school together from K-12 and remained close friends into our adult years.

Noah graduated from U of A in 2004 and then went to acting school at UCLA, (the west coast equivalent to Julliard), where he graduated in 2007. Then he came back to "the creek."

The first time I saw him back I didn't even recognize him, he had long hair and a beard for a role he was playing in a film. We picked up right where we left off, now at 25 years old. We were together on most weekends. Noah was interested in what he saw as my ability to "move between worlds" overseeing the building of multimillion dollar private homes for esteemed clients during the week, while casually walking in and out of the midst of cartel-connected Sinaloan coke dealers on the weekends.

In quick order, Noah decided he wanted to do a documentary about this, similar to the "Vice" documentaries. I brought Noah to the Sinaloans, after calling Leo and explaining it to him. Noah met Leo and brought a portfolio of his acting and filming credentials in order to make Leo comfortable and assure him Noah was not a cop. I myself actually wondered if Noah was a cop at times.

In 2008, Noah had just played lead role in a film called "Work Week," about a young man being groomed by the mob, *loved* the "Sopranos." Noah, in real life, did not do drugs of any kind, did not do any crime, didn't even get drunk; just sipped his beers when we went out, but he was *enamored* with documenting the criminal element.

He got a $60K budget for us to begin from his production company, took me to his editor's house for introductions, and told me "we start filming the first of 2009. Whatever you do, don't get arrested or killed in the meantime." He was just kidding. It wasn't that serious. Our friend Chuck arranged for us to do documentary-style interviews at the J.W. Marriot (Desert Ridge), a resort. Chuck was the front desk manager. The problem was, about a month after that, I was framed by MCSO for capital murder.

Noah was in shock, but knew I was innocent. Everyone who knew me knew I was innocent. I was the most easygoing guy in the crowd on any occasion. My family was routinely receiving phone calls from people we hadn't spoken to in years- including even the father of an ex-girlfriend I'd had in high school, Ronny Olmstead, who, after seeing it on the news was literally laughing at MCSO, he said, for arresting the wrong person.

Noah and his mom, Catherine, visited me at the jail frequently. Catherine was the most benevolent lady I had ever met. The three of us spent many golden-sunset evenings on their poolside patio in Troon North, a north Scottsdale golfing community, discussing everything from barflies to quantum physics.

Catherine was a widow now; Noah's dad died with cancer while he was at UCLA. So Noah, her only child, moved back home to keep her company. The two were best friends, Noah included Catherine in everything he did, and she seemed to get a lot of entertainment out of us, carefree and young.

On Monday May 12, 2010, Noah came to visit me at the jail, excited, saying he finally had proof that I was innocent. After my arrest Noah had begun ingratiating himself with the Parkers, spending *a lot* of time with Sam, even though they were polar opposites, and even getting inside the Parker family mansion, on the east side of *Black Mountain*.

Black Mountain was a two-mile long razorback of a mountain running north to south. It was the Cave Creek "loop" I rode my motorcycle around on July 7, 2008. About a thousand feet above the town at its top, it is an island of high-end housing, with mostly mansions on its east side.

Noah viewed the Parkers as the real-life Sopranos, with all the suspicion around Sam Parker. Noah believed he could solve the case, exonerate me, and together we could continue our filming project with its new, elevated plot. I told him to be careful.

I told Noah not to tell me specifically what the "proof" he found was over the jail video visit. I'd have my attorney, Rick, who visited Sam in Oregon, call him.

A couple of days later, Rick told me he could not get ahold of Noah, his phone was going straight to voicemail, and the voice mailbox was full. When I called Jill the next day she answered with "we have a problem," and I could hear a strong tremor in her voice.

"They found Noah."

"Okay," I said.

She said, "they found his body, on his couch in his living room, with a gunshot wound to the head."

My heart dropped. My eyes watered and composure slipped through my fingers. I was silent, but inside I imploded. I felt so helpless and angry. I finally broke. I went to my cell and cried, heaving sobs, cried like a baby for a half hour.

The day Jill delivered the news to me about Noah; she went to Rick's office to discuss it with him. Rick then came straight to the jail to see me and see how I was doing, arranging an impromptu legal visit while Jill waited downstairs. In the months representing me up to this point, Rick had ingratiated himself deeply into our family dynamic. He was so good at conveying warmth, so disarming of course, with the sentimental open-door policy that the Lunsford family has always had. We were eager to welcome him.

There was little Rick could do regarding what had happened to Noah, or what information he was going to share with Rick that week. We would spend significant time and energy trying to get to the bottom of those two things. Jill on the other hand went home scared that night. Everyone did. My niece's mom saw Gerald Coco in the days after the death of Noah, who was a mutual friend of mine, and Gerald's. She asked Gerald if he had heard about Noah. She said Gerald was shaking and crying, saying yes, that he knew he was up next, and he was going home to get his gun. When I called Jill that night she was deeply unsettled and had a friend at the house with her, helping her install lights and motion detectors. Her life had changed, again. It changed our understanding of what was possible, elevating concerns.

Noah was last seen with Sam Parker and his dad, out at dinner. He had called his mom that day; she was on a missionary trip in Egypt. She said that Noah was excited that day, and that he told her during their phone call that he finally had proof that I was innocent.

To this day she is convinced that the Parkers killed her son, her only remaining family member. Since she was out of town at the time, she was not notified of Noah's death right away. Scottsdale PD had shown up, saw a dead guy, a gun on the floor, and assumed suicide. Within an hour they had asked a neighbor to "clean it up," destroying the crime scene. When Catherine finally spoke to investigators, including an unnamed MCSO detective who responded, she told them what Noah had gotten himself into.

But it was too late; the crime scene had been "cleaned up." Our PI in 2010, Joe Otero, asked Scottsdale PD for the reports on Noah's death.

They said, "Sure, we'll get it to you…" but didn't.

Otero kept calling them. They said it was an ongoing investigation; it was sealed. A month later they told him we didn't need the reports because it was a suicide. Case closed.

Otero said, "Oh, good. Since it's closed you can release the documents."

Eventually they said they would release the reports, but only after redacting "all of the content" first. Otero gave up.

In the middle of all of this, Catherine reached out to our camp to tell us it was still being investigated as a homicide, per what the detectives told her.

Nearly a decade later I received Noah's death investigation report. It was thirty-five pages. It came by way of a simple public records request made by a civilian. The detective that authored it made no mention of his involvement in my case, did not even mention his conversations with Catherine, or what she'd told him. There was no mention of Noah's visit at the jail that day.

The detective had put together a three-day narrative; his version of Noah's last seventy-two hours alive. Noah's body was slumped over to the right on his couch, his TV, that I had installed, glowed blue with the dish network logo, a gun on the floor under his legs. On the coffee table in front of him were some "documents," impounded as "evidence" by SPD. Never disclosed--a bag of marijuana, and seven corona bottle caps. On the end table next to the couch was a glass with a lime on the rim, with a small amount of amber liquid on it, and an empty corona bottle next to it.

Some tried to tell me along the way that Noah probably killed himself. He had relationship problems with his girlfriend, Megan Berlinger, whose brothers Mark and Matt were close with Sam Parker. And Noah had now begun using drugs. That's what they tried to feed me. These were the people who were planning on forcing me to sign a plea later.

I told them they were wrong, Noah did not use drugs.

Noah's toxicology revealed that I was right, he didn't do drugs, he had no drugs in his system, not even marijuana, which stays in a person's system for twenty-eight days. So, *whose* marijuana was on the coffee table? Noah's B.A.C. was .07; 1 beer for a 135 lb guy. The Corona bottle on the table was empty. So, who drank the other six beers, to account for the *seven* bottle caps on the coffee table? And why were the other six bottles gone?

They also found, in his upstairs bedroom, that his safe was wide open; its door obstructing the walkway, and it was empty. What's that about? The case for the gun was found under an end table in a separate upstairs bedroom. And finally, why would a non-drug using, happy twenty-eight year old man, with an ascending acting career, who had been trying to prove the innocence of one of his best friends for two years, upon finding such proof, drive around exclaiming it all day, then go home and kill himself?

We never found out what that "proof" was. SPD never disclosed the documents they impounded as evidence from the coffee table, or *why* they impounded them, since this was just a "suicide." We were left with no answers about Noah's death.

At some point in early 2010 Rick Miller flew to Oregon to meet Sam Parker in person. Sam had moved to Oregon after the murder. I didn't learn of this trip until afterwards. To this day there is no recording of, or notes about their conversations on the trip. Rick told me, verbally, that it appeared Sam was doing well for himself, driving a new Lexus, and running an escort service. Then, in almost a sleazy "wink-wink" sort of way, he told me that he made sure to let Sam know that Gerald Coco was going to testify against me, as if doing me a favor, like Sam was going to "take care of it."

It surprised me that he told one witness, my supposed friend what another witness, the State's star witness, was going to say, especially with all the speculation that the former was a possible murderer and organized crime member.

Of course, with all the H.A. and organized crime chatter, I had to go to great lengths to assure legal professionals that I was in no way affiliated with either. Part of me thought that Rick was trolling me to see if I'd bite and try to use him as a middleman to ask Sam to do something specific. And part of me thought Rick would've gone through with it, just to spite the state, over all of their oppressive bullying of the bench and defense attorneys, just to spite them in this case specifically, wherein everyone involved knew their position was weak and suspicious and they probably had the wrong guy in jail.

What's one drug-addict getting "whacked?" Would the world miss Gerald Coco? Rick Miller sure wouldn't. It would lighten his caseload.

Part of me thought he was trying to set me up. Part of me, due to events that would develop later, began to wonder if he hadn't taken a bribe from the Parkers. Part of me wondered if Rick had gotten Noah killed, by giving Sam a "heads up" about him the same way he'd told Sam about Gerald Coco.

DNA

With all of the speculation, rumors, and underdeveloped theories that gleamed of urban myth, I really wanted to dissolve the heavy fog of conjecture with something specific, something objective, such as DNA results.

After 'Rena's meltdown' on July 29, 2009, when Gingold admitted he still hadn't disclosed the DNA results because he himself had yet to receive them from the DPS crime lab technicians, Grant Bellechick and Kelli Radley. This theme developed wherein every time Deputy County Attorney Mike Gingold, the gatekeeper of all evidence, was asked by Judge Barton what the status of the DNA was, Gingold would blame it on DPS.

Perhaps DPS really was just that busy, that overwhelmed with stories of other major cities having backlogs of dozens or hundreds of untested rape kit in the headlines. It was plausible. But with such a serious case as Ms. Hermann's, a high profile capital murder, with a defendant's life on the line, and so much uncertainty in the investigation itself, one would think that DNA testing in this case should and would be prioritized. It should have at least been done within the one year, two weeks and one day that had passed between Ms. Hermann's murder on July 8, 2008f, to our next status conference. What could the DPS technicians have been doing for over a year, I wondered, sitting in my cell, that prevented them from testing physical evidence from a capital murder that investigators deemed so important that they literally ran into a burning building to save.

Unfortunately, the lack of DNA diligence didn't improve. Two months after the July 29 status conference, at the September 14, 2009 status conference, Judge Barton said, "I did receive a joint case management plan from you dated September 9. ... we have our trial date set for March 8, 2010. It looks like there is some holdup regarding the production of the second DNA."

Gingold goes on to say he is still "working on" getting the notes from the analyst, then they began discussing Rena's motion to continue, which was still pending before Judge Donahoe, awaiting his ruling, despite his response time having already run out. It seemed like *nothing* was getting done in this case.

Then, going back to the DNA, Judge Barton asks, "When do you think you can get those analyst notes over?"

Gingold answers, "Judge, the analyst informed me that she would most likely be able to get those to us this week pending no 'emergencies in her office.'"

What "emergencies" could trump capital murder, I wondered.

Judge Barton retorted, "Well if they can get to you this week, is there any reason why you can't get them produced by next Friday?"

"As long as we have them, that shouldn't be a problem. We can get them out in a couple days. It's just a matter of getting them from the analyst."

Why is it so hard to get a simple "yes" from this guy, I wondered. Every answer had a caveat.

Judge Barton said, "What I'm going to do now is put a deadline in place. I'm going to order that they be produced no later than 9:00 am. on 9/25. That's a week from this coming Friday."

My family and I, present in court that day and observing this dialogue in person, were grateful that the court was becoming more firm with Gingold and giving him an actual deadline to disclose all of the DNA results and notes. Finally.

Unfortunately it wouldn't matter. My attorney, going forward, would remain entangled with the constitutionality arguments regarding the capital case crisis, Judge Barton would remain focused on meeting deadlines, railroading, as did all Maricopa County Superior Court judges, in order to prove that there was no crisis. Gingold's lack of production and disclosures would go unaddressed because of the mess, as he sat quietly in the corner, deflecting responsibility when asked, pointing at DPS and Kelli Radley, and blaming it on her, even though she was never in the courtroom to speak for herself.

Rena would get removed, essentially thrown from the railroad car by train conductor Judge Barton, who brought in company man Rick Miller, who filed his N.O.A. in this case on February 5, 2010.

At a status conference in front of Judge Barton on June 25, 2010, the DNA mysteries of this case still had not been solved. This was very discouraging for my family and me because I had now been in jail for *two years* without having a day in court, and my new attorney, Rick, having been on the case for almost 5 months, still had not even seen the first half of DNA testing. We were somehow moving *backwards*.

Judge Barton, "I did receive your joint case management plan and I have had the opportunity to review that…it indicated that some of the [DNA] testing has not yet been completed."

Gingold, "We have been working on the defense's request. It was some DNA stuff. The first half had been done. We're waiting results on the second half."

Judge Barton, "And when do you anticipate the results will be done on the second half?"

Gingold, "I haven't heard anything back from DPS, your honor, I think I received the results about a week ago, maybe ten days at the most, on the first half, and that was immediately disclosed."

Two years into the case and the first half of DNA testing was received, and supposedly disclosed, only *one week prior*. This would have still been *after* the original trial date, which Ms. Glitsos hotly contested was unreasonable.

Gingold, "And it just indicated that further testing, meaning DNA comparison, would actually be done."

He then adds yet another wrinkle by stating, "That's a different analyst. I don't know how long that's going to take."

I was sitting in the courtroom shaking my head at this point. It did not seem like we were getting anywhere. But even if we had been, it was all negated when Rick, bringing us back to zero said, "Okay, I'm just a little embarrassed because I have not seen that first half of testing."

Two years into my arrest, after a wasted year and half of my first attorney being present for apparently no reason, and five months into the new attorney's appointment, and somehow we were starting over again, again.

After Judge Barton applied more pressure to Gingold, to apply more pressure to DPS lab technicians Kelli Radley and Grant Bellechick, to get the DNA results and notes, and finally disclose them all of them to the defense, Gingold plowed the ground for next month's excuse by saying, "The only caveat, your honor, would be if the analyst is on vacation."

Last time it was "in case of an emergency" at the lab, this time a "vacation, As a young adult with at least a little bit of life experience, it really started to seem like they were hiding something.

Prosecution Discovery Reports

Rick began to bring to me the discovery, several reports at a time. In the year after his appointment I had received a report or two from my first attorney, more from Ms. Glitsos, and the rest of the approximately 2,000 pages from Rick. Rick also, eventually, handed me almost 1,000 pages of a blog site that had been created about this case, which was difficult to read. As I read more of the reports I could not believe how misleading and unclear the collective police narrative was. It quickly became clear that this was an "arrest now, investigate later" situation.

The MCSO had arrested me by default. After one week of a hasty, emotionally driven investigation, with public pressure to make an arrest, they apparently thought I was the "best" suspect and assumed that they could accumulate evidence *after* my arrest that would prove it. Between all the forensics that would come back, DNA and prints, cell phone records, confidential informants, recorded jail calls, and who knows what else, surely something would incriminate the Lunsford guy, they thought.

But out of 500 pieces of physical evidence that was preserved for testing, they tested the first 5 or 6 items, and after those either came back "inconclusive" or even *excluded* me, identifying an "unknown suspect" on two items, they put a stop to all further testing. It was all too risky.

They couldn't find anything incriminating or even inconsistent in the recorded jail calls, or outgoing mail, or video visits, and the confidential informant that Gingold had sent but couldn't really produce. It wasn't getting any better for the state. It was actually becoming concerning for them.

Confidential informant Randy Diehl, a known criminal and meth-addict, worked with Gingold in an effort to entrap multiple murder defendants who Gingold was prosecuting. Gingold was also prosecuting Diehl. Diehl would be moved around the fourth avenue jail, housed with Gingold's higher profile defendants, and befriend them, going through their paperwork while they were at visits, court appearances, medical appointments, and haircuts, to accumulate a story for testimony. MCSO ran the jail, and was happy to cooperate with the process.

Diehl, facing a 2-3 year prison sentence for another methamphetamine case, wrote a letter to Gingold saying that I "backed out" that "night" but didn't really admit to any crimes. Though it was non-specific, it appeared that Gingold might use it to cast suspicion, however nebulous. Unfortunately that trick works on some juries. Diehl was released as a result, but re-arrested 3 weeks later when a Phoenix police officer found Diehl enjoying one of his favorite past times, high on meth, masturbating in public.

In reading the discovery, I also learned that the first responders were en route to the house fire at seven forty-four p.m. I was stoked. This baffled me because I had been in

Phoenix driving around with Gerald, visiting people all evening. For almost two years I had assumed that all of this had taken place during the morning- presumably early morning- of July 8 2008, otherwise why would they attach it to *me*...?

The day I learned that the house fire occurred while I was in Phoenix. I called Jill and excitedly told her that I was coming home to her soon for *sure*. Yes, Jill, the one that got away, apparently I was the one that got away too and so we decided that if we ever "got away" again it was going to be together. We got married in 2009.

There were even bigger problems with the state's timeline. Although MCSO spokesperson, Lindsey Smith, told the media that Ms. Hermann "died right before the house fire, 7:30 p.m., in what was probably a crime of passion," detectives had since then arbitrarily moved their timeline of the murder way back, to three to five a.m. in order to cast suspicion upon the guy she'd went home with the night before. *Me*.

However, the medical examiner would not support that theory. He issued "no time of death" and Detective Smith said, under oath, to the grand jury, that there was "no evidence" of time of death. However, he continued to use his own imaginary time of death to claim that phone calls made from Ms. Hermann's phone that day from 9 a.m to noon "proved" that Lunsford was "in possession of her phone," Because, Smith says, "Hermann was already deceased." MCSO investigators interviewed those individuals called by Hermann's phone. Three of five denied talking to me from that phone.

I did not understand this at the time, and my attorneys didn't care, or notice, but there was abundant evidence of Liz Hermann's time of death. It pointed to Ms. Hermann living *a full day after* she and I had parted ways, including no lividity or rigor mortis at 8:30 p.m. Both should be present within a couple of hours. A *Hideaway* bartender telling MCSO investigators that Hermann was at the *Hideaway* with "Nate" on Tuesday July 8, 2008 at noon.

That bartender said, "MCSO could have their surveillance video." But no surveillance video, either for Monday night or Tuesday afternoon was ever disclosed.

Gerald Coco's phone records appeared to be incomplete. The call logs were there, but there were no locations. There were locations on the other sets of cell records. It seemed that MCSO investigators had begun avoiding specifics altogether in order to keep their narrative as malleable as possible. Especially after they began to realize that Gerald and I were in Phoenix all evening, they began to avoid times, locations, and specifics altogether, in order to preserve the subjective suspicion they had created around their suspect.

The DNA results were coming in. At about the 2½-year mark; despite what the kneejerk internet trolls had said. And also unlike what they said, none of it was coming back to me.

I had candidly told investigators that I'd had unprotected intercourse with Ms. Hermann the night we'd met. But my DNA was not found in the sex kit tests. Clearly then, this woman did not pass away at three or four in the morning, right after being with me. She'd lived on a full day, perhaps even showering, before her next visitor arrived. But *who*? The "unknown suspect?" The complete profile, whose DNA was found inside *two* used condoms near Ms. Hermann's murdered body?

I emphasized to Rick that the totality of this DNA information made it clear that I was not the last person with her. *I was not even the last person to have intercourse with her.* We *have to* identify the man in the condoms.

I said, "Ask her friends when you interview them. Ask her coworkers, ask her roommate, ask everybody, "who left the condoms there!" I urged him. "ask them!"

I wondered whose it was. Was it Alan's, the roommate? Was it this "Nate?" Was it her estranged husband? Her friend Russ Boetcher, who was interviewed by police? Was it a Hell's Angel, or a MCSO deputy she served and went home with from work? Sam Parker? James Parker? Ronald McDonald? He fits the eyewitness description.

A partial profile was also recovered from the gas can recovered at the house. Though no complete profile could be created from it, there were enough markers to prove that I did not handle the gas can. I was excluded, it was somebody else's DNA on the gas can.

The state was beginning to have a lot of problems with its evidence. The "arrest now, investigate later" technique was not panning out.

Sandor Polgar

I also started to notice strange coincidences regarding Liz's estranged husband, Sandor Polgar. Besides the information Liz's friends had given about his money issues and conflicts with Liz's Facebook posts as it pertained to his new, pregnant, live-in girl-friend, Naomi McQuaid, his jealousy over Liz keeping the white truck. The white truck was burned by somebody who was 6'3" with red hair driving a green colored vehicle. Polgar, according to his driver's license was 6'3" with red hair. A friend of Liz said he "drives a green colored truck."

There were other connections. One of Liz's friends said that he called her the night of the fire or early the next day, and said Liz "had fallen asleep cooking." No one else had said or heard that theory. Eventually Ryan Koolstra of Southwest Gas would note during his walk through of the crime scene that the left burner knob on the gas stove was in the "fully on" position, before the fire was ignited. How would Sandor have known that?

I also recalled that during my own police interview Detective Osborn showed me a picture of a mean-looking red-haired guy, and asked me if I'd ever seen him before.

93

I wasn't sure, maybe around town. Then he asked me specifically if I'd seen him with Sam Parker. It was obviously Sandor Polgar. Question is, why, on day one of the investigation, did detective Osborn think Sam and Sandor may have colluded in Liz's murder. What was Osborn on to? Did they know each other?

The thing that really stood out to me was his whereabouts. Nothing is more important in *proving* guilt or innocence than whereabouts. It can quickly simplify an over-complicated case. Sandor was supposedly at work from 5 a.m. until 1:58 p.m. on July 8, 2008. The truck fire was at 2:14 p.m., and the house fire at 7:30 p.m. Liz Hermann probably died between 6 and 7 p.m.

Neither Sandor, nor Naomi McQuaid, nor anyone on earth, could account for his whereabouts from 1:58 p.m. until 8 p.m., when Naomi said he showed up at home. This was the exact window of time that mattered.

Detectives say simply in their charging summary that they eliminated Sandor because "he had an alibi" and couldn't have made it to the truck fire scene from his work 20 miles away. They had "eliminated" him because they'd already beat up and coerced Gerald Coco. They had Sandor's boss mail them a photocopy of his time card, *after* my arrest. But there was no way to prove if it was real, or *who* punched it out because there was no camera nearby.

They printed out the GPS coordinates from his work truck to determine his whereabouts from 5 a.m. to 2 p.m. I compared them to the trap plus trace locations from Liz's phone records. Sandor was in the *same exact area* as her phone during those 9 a.m. to 12 p.m. phone calls. What a remarkable coincidence.

Liz Hermann's Death Wounds

But mostly it was the diagrams of her injuries. 50-60 stab wounds. Front *and* back. As if someone was holding her from behind while himself and another did it. Or was it one person acting alone, who hated her enough to roll her lifeless body over and stab many, many times, *after* stabbing the other side, and near decapitation, legs nearly severed, and she was stabbed many times in the *face*. Who would do that? The M.E. said they were likely post-mortem. Who hated her *that* much? Who could possibly? It *had to be* personal, someone who had a history with her, or mental illness.

To this day, I cannot absolve the curiosity of why Detective Osborn thought I could and would put Sam and Sandor together in the context of this murder investigation. Sandor was, "always involved in schemes," according to a friend of Liz. Did Sandor hire Sam? Did Sam have a psychopathic friend who would help him, or was Sam crazy enough? Did the plan go wrong in the middle of the day? Did Sandor have to drive to Cave Creek and get his hands dirty that afternoon?

If he did, Detective Paul Smith had his back.

There were not enough pages in *The Arizona Republic* to hold all of the stories that would be written about this dysfunction as it developed and morphed daily. Other papers began to cover it, other outlets, and soon the embarrassing inability of this small-market county to govern itself became a national story, ultimately turning the Arizona judiciary into a punchline.

The popular sitcom *"Harry's Law"* in 2011-12 took advantage of this in a court-room setting. Leading actress Kathy Bates, whose private law practice the show was centered around, stated in the courtroom, when offended by something the Judge and prosecutor did, "you can't do that here! This is not south Korea, or Iran...or Arizona!"

When I saw that scene I thought, oh my gosh, even Kathy Bates knows!

As we approached our February trial date my attorneys began interviewing some of the individuals involved in this case, including MCSO Detective Smith, Rural Metro Fire Department Captain John Kraetz, Liz's roommate Allen Bauer, neighbor Lynette Guiz Gynn, eyewitness Jimmie Larson, and others.

Chapter 6

Change of Plea—Taking Away Threat of Death Penalty—Sentencing

● ●

With good information coming in from recent interviews, such as Larson stating that I was not the guy he saw burning the truck, and the neighbor Lynette Gynn identifying "Nate" as the guy she saw hiding in the bushes outside the house-fire, Jill and I were getting excited and making plans for when I would get home in a few months, after trial when this was all over.

Avid road trippers, Jill and I began shopping for an RV and planning a weeks-long road trip. I would read through the classified ads in the newspaper and cut out the RV-for-sale ads that were the most appealing, mail them to her along with my letters, and discuss them with her over the phone. Jill, in turn, had begun mapping-out our route on a large map on a wall in our house. We would jaunt over to California; take the Pacific Coast Highway north, at leisure, through Oregon and Washington, then head east, one national park at a time. It would be just the reprieve we needed. We would start our life soon, still in our 20s with a lot of wonderful things ahead of us.

On Monday February 3, 2011, MCSO Deputy Hoffman, who I'd become very familiar with, escorted me to my "final" pretrial conference. Hoffman, or, "the Hoff," as my cellmate and I used to call him, not to be confused with Hasselhoff, worked the Cave Creek beat when I had still lived in Cave Creek. He seemed to know who I was just from that time, including when I was interviewed by MCSO in reference to the DMX animal cruelty investigation, and of course after my arrest, he was familiar with my name. The Hoff and I always engaged in small talk on our long walks through the underground network of tunnels on our way to the court building. On this specific day he asked me, "What's up with your buddy, Sam Parker?"

"What do you mean?" I asked.

"Well," he said, "he always gets into trouble and makes a big mess and then his daddy has him coming out smellin clean as a rose…"

"Yeah, I don't know. Money I guess." I replied.

Maybe he was fishing, but I just took it to mean that Sam was still getting into more trouble.

When we got into the courtroom and I sat down at the defense table with Rick, Hoffman asked me to tell Rick the joke that Hoffman had just told me in the elevator. "Neh" I thought, I didn't want to. I had laughed at the joke when he told it to me, mostly to be polite, as it was a "lawyer" joke and I was now depending on one to save my life. Maybe Hoffman knew what my lawyer was about to do to me. We were all sitting and standing around, chatting casually, waiting for Judge Barton to enter, and Rick looked at me as if waiting for the joke so I said, fine.

"Why do they bury lawyers twelve feet deep?"

"I dunno, why?"

"Because deep down they're really good people."

Being polite, Rick *kind of* chuckled. The hearing that day was a long one. Many oral arguments were heard on the admissibility of different things, jury questionnaire, and jury instructions. As we left the courtroom Rick and Marci walked with me, exiting behind the bench. Usually they walked out the main entryway with the public.

In back hallway, Rick said that we won every argument except the one regarding residual doubt, which wouldn't matter anyway because we weren't going to get to that part.

Arizona Death Penalty Issues

In a death penalty case, there is the guilt/innocence phase, wherein the trial itself is held in order to determine whether the defendant is guilty or not guilty. There is no such thing as a finding of innocence in the court system.

If the defendant is found guilty, they then move to the penalty phase, which is basically a mini-trial regarding mitigation vs. aggravation in order to determine whether the defendant should receive the death penalty or life in prison.

In the 1990's that was a decision to be made by one person, the judge. Later it was changed and is now a decision made by the same jurors who heard the case at the first phase.

At the penalty phase, the jury would hear different things, perhaps even new information due to post-conviction relaxed evidentiary standards. The defendant's family members would testify about their lives together and other personal things. As a result, some jurors had begun to question their guilty verdicts at the guilt/innocence phase. The new information they received at the penalty phase sometimes created doubt. This was called residual doubt. As a result of the residual doubt about whether the defendant was even guilty- although it was too late at this point, they had already found the defendant guilty after a presentation of evidence neatly trimmed by the Judge through admissibility rulings- the Judge would then at the penalty phase, avoid the death penalty and choose life in prison. In order to satiate at least some of the guilty conscious they may have had. It was like a jury-induced, unofficial plea, wherein the jury "settles" the case independent of the rule of law, in their own imaginations.

The courts and the legislature, especially in a state such as Arizona, were unhappy that a panel of laypeople could, or would take the satisfaction of the death penalty away from them, and the victim's family so, arguments over residual doubt gradually became normal in capital cases.

In my case, Judge Barton's adverse ruling regarding residual doubt would mean that if a jury did find me guilty at the guilt/innocence phase, but experienced doubt later, at the penalty phase, they would be instructed by Judge Barton, to ignore their own doubts and sentence me to death anyway.

It blew my mind when I learned about residual doubt, and what the government's position was regarding it. I learned that a lot of judges were inclined to help the state in evidentiary admissibility rulings, making the presentation of the case and situation as favorable to the prosecution as legally allowed (and sometimes *not* legally allowed), in order to "even the playing field," since prosecutors shouldered the burden of proof and had to overcome presumption of innocence, even though almost no one assumes or presumes that the person in handcuffs is innocent, most sincere American adults will admit that most if not all criminal defendants are presumed to be guilty.

At any rate, being the small-town simpleton that I was, I was disappointed to learn that a judge might manipulate the presentation of the evidence, essentially tricking the jury into issuing a guilty verdict, and then instruct them to ignore their consciences afterwards. It just didn't sound right.

When Rick mentioned that we'd lost the residual doubt argument he quickly followed with saying that it didn't matter, because we were not going to get to the penalty phase anyway, we would win at phase one. I would walk out of court and into the arms of my family and off into the future. It was what we had all been waiting for, and it was finally upon us.

He then mentioned that he and Marci wanted to have a meeting with my family members the next day, and when I asked Rick what the meeting's purpose was, Marci interrupted and said that it was for the purpose of coaching them on their conduct and body language during trial, which was to start in exactly one week, the following Monday, because their conduct would reflect upon me the defendant.

"Great," I said, and the meeting was set for the following morning.

When I got back to the jail a couple of hours later I called Jill and the family and told them about the meeting, and they were all very excited to be included in the process. Jill had already bought me several suits, PI Otero had brought them into the jail pod for me to try on, and we were ready to go.

The following morning Rick and Marci came to the jail for a legal visit. Right away, as I was sitting down, Rick said plainly that the jury was going to find me guilty of first-degree murder, and that I would be executed. He said they had just left the meetings with my mom, dad, Jill, and my brother, where they had just dropped the same bomb on them. That was the real purpose of that meeting.

He was unsympathetic, palpably indifferent. His apathy was almost aggressive, passive aggressive, in a seemingly intentional act of hurtfulness, which was an astounding shift from his 100% warm and helpful attitude leading up to this.

It seemed like he enjoyed saying that to me. It was too bizarre as if it were part of his strategy to scare me into signing a plea. I had never seen him like this, it was like I was meeting the real him for the first time. If 90% of communication is nonverbal, then his real message felt something like this.

> "Hello client. I finally get to introduce you to the real me. I used to work for the prosecutor's office, I basically still do. I was never going to help you. I work for the government. I don't care about you, your future, or your mom, dad, and wife, family, whatever; I care about *my* family and job; you're screwed. This is how it works and I don't care."

I don't think he meant to be hurtful; it was just part of his job. I would spend years trying to determine whether Rick really was that treacherous, or whether he actually did care about me and was just trying to save an innocent man from a broken system, an erroneous death sentence.

But I could never emphasize enough the traumatic impact his change in demeanor had on my family and me. It definitely did scare us. He later admitted he was trained to get clients to sign pleas; especially the hard ones, the ones who still had hope and light in their eyes. He was trained to blend into that hope, to help mold it and become a part of it so that he could crush it at the 11th hour, when it was too late for me to recover. He was trained to gain trust and then to emotionally devastate his own clients and their families. He was really good at it.

Unfortunately he was not unique, not some rogue public defender working for the opposition. Due to holistic advocacy, he was simply serving the role of any public defender. In an article titled *"The Mirage of Justice,"* writer Chris Hedges, of *truthdig. com*, explained it like this:

"The public defender…uses the prospect of the harshest sentence possible to frighten the client into making a plea deal. And, as depicted in "making a murderer," prosecutors and defense attorneys often work as a tag team to force the accused to plead guilty. If all of the accused went to trial, the judicial system, which is designed around plea agreements, would collapse. And this is why trial sentences are horrific

"Judge Jed S. Rakoff, in an article in the New York review of books, titled 'Why innocent People Plead Guilty,' explains how the secretive plea system works to thwart justice. *Close to 40 percent* of those eventually exonerated of their crimes originally pleaded guilty."

Coerced, or forced, pleas are the backbone of holistic advocacy, a national movement that the Maricopa County Public Defender signed on to in the mid 1990's. In an article in *Arizona Attorney Magazine*, October 2015, Jim Haas, the Maricopa County Public Defender, described holistic advocacy this way: "The day when it was my client and I against the world are over. We now work as full partners with law enforcement and the prosecutor's office in the interest of what's best for the public." [1]

To me, that means not what's best for the client. It is no small irony that the police, prosecutors, and the 'public' are the complete opposition to each public defender's own client. It is difficult to imagine a defense attorney wholeheartedly defending his or her own client while said attorney is in the middle of a long-term relationship, a 'full partnership,' with the agencies determined to take said client's life away

At sentencing, Rick Miller would say, on the record, that the PD's office sends him and my 2nd chair attorney around the country to seminars in order to train them to get their clients to sign pleas. He said that they set that goal, and do "whatever you have to do to get there." He would also say that he had "seen the whites of the eyes of jurors in Maricopa county who had been screened for capital cases," and he knows "where that goes."

He told Lunsford family friends, privately, that he believed I was innocent, but had "no idea" what to do with this case. This was who Judge Barton preferred represent me, rather than the assertive Rena Glitsos whom she'd removed against our wishes.

---

1 Jim Haas. "50 Years of Service to the Maricopa County Public Defenders' Office Anniversary," 52 AZ Attorney, October 2015, at page 14.

No Possibility of a Not Guilty Verdict

During that crushing legal visit, through which I sat silent, and poker-faced, staring back at Rick, he went on to say that by law, a jury would have to acquit me for lack of evidence, but that in this county, "they just won't."

He began to take a nicer approach, easing back into character. He said he wanted to get me into a room with my family, he said that if we would please go to the settlement conference, he and the prosecutor had already scheduled, behind my back, continuing our trial date, that he could get me into a room with them. I could hug my wife, my mom, my dad, my little brother, for the first time in 3 years. Because of the circumstances at the MCSO jail, I hadn't even seen the sun in 3 years, much less had any human contact.

Rick told me I didn't have to sign anything. Just "play along," *please* allow him to "explore" a 2nd degree plea, and I could go sit at a table with my loved ones, sunlight pouring in.

As I walked out of the visit room I knew I had to fire both of them immediately. I called my family; everyone was reeling, perplexed, scared and angry.

Jill went home from the crushing meeting that morning to find that our Boston terrier had been massacred in the backyard, blood everywhere. Someone, or something, had torn it to shreds. While she was at what she thought was going to be a meeting about trial preparation, getting devastated by Rick and Marci. The dog was killed the same way many thought Liz Hermann's dog was killed. On our back patio walls, blood splatter was 6 feet high. We never found out what happened. But after what happened to Noah Todd, it felt like a message.

We all agreed that Rick and Marci had planned this the whole time and waited till the last minute because Rick knew, from our first visit, that I would never agree to it. I had told him when I met him that I was innocent and would never even consider a plea. We also believed that this was why they did little to no investigation and focused on mitigation. They never intended to go to trial. It also seemed apparent that this was why Judge Barton removed Rena Glitsos and brought in Rick. This was what he was brought in to do.

I drafted up a motion to fire my attorneys. I did not know how to write a legal filing but I did my best. Now all I had to do was figure out how to file it.

I called an attorney who I knew personally, Jill's dad. I explained the situation to him. Sadly, he told me that it would be a waste of time to file it. He explained that he had just tried to withdrawal from a capital case and the Judge denied his request. The courts in Maricopa County were not allowing changes of counsel in capital cases because, due to the "capital case crisis" at the time, courtesy of County Attorney Andrew

Thomas, later disbarred for abuse of power, there were too many capital defendants, and not enough capital-certified defense attorneys. Every time a change of counsel took place a case was forced to essentially start over, in order to give the new attorney time to study the case and get up to speed. Defendants in the United States were supposed to have a constitutional right to a "speedy trial," as are victims. But due to the capital case overload and the postponements that it triggered everyone's constitutional rights to a speedy trial were already being violated. This was why it was a crisis, and Arizona courts did not want the Federal courts to become inclined to intervene. The small-market county of Maricopa had to prove, as all local governments do, that they could govern themselves. If they encountered impediments to that, then those impediments had to be remedied; made to go away. Though the County Attorney had caused the problem, we the capital defendants were viewed as the impediments.

Our cases had to be resolved as quickly as possible, certainly before uncle Sam got involved, right or wrong. With everyone's right to a speedy trial already being violated, starting a capital case over made it egregious. As a formality, a capital case would be "designated complex," setting a trial date, not the standard six months out, but eighteen months out.

For a case such as my own, wherein I had already been held without a bond, or a trial for three years for a crime I wasn't even convicted of, *another* change of counsel would put it closer to five years and thus be comparable to Guantanamo Bay.

Additionally, I knew that there was no way the MCAO would offer a 2nd degree murder plea in a capital case. It would be a quantum leap to, in a grisly murder case, drop the threat of punishment down from the death penalty, past life without the possibility of parole, past life *with* the possibility of parole, all the way down to 2nd degree with an automatic release date. It would be unheard-of to guarantee the release back into the community of a defendant who they claimed butchered another human being, burned their house down, and the torched their vehicle on the side of a busy road in broad daylight on a Tuesday afternoon, for no reason.

Typical, or basic, capital defendants could not even get second-degree pleas. The whole purpose behind County Attorney Thomas' having sought the death penalty in so many cases was to force those defendants to sign pleas for life in prison, keeping them off the streets permanently.

The attorney who I called that day said that if I filed the motion to fire my attorneys it would just alienate my attorneys from me. It would be denied, just like his recent request to withdrawal was denied, and I would be forced to go into trial with attorneys who would be focused only on protecting themselves. I knew he was right. So that day I decided I would go to the settlement conference and steal some much-needed hugs from my family. I would "play along" like Rick had asked me to, allow him to "explore" a second-degree plea, which would obviously be denied, and then we could rally Rick into the courtroom for trial, a team united. I, the reasonable client who went along; they the careful counselors who led.

Settlement Conference Before Judge Sherry Stevens

We went to a different Judge for the settlement conference. The Honorable Sherry Stevens, most known for presiding over the Jodi Arias murder trial. In the conference room I got to hug my family, one at a time, lifting my cuffs and chains up over their heads to get my arms around them. It was sad. We were all scared, disheveled and confused, but all the lawyers in the room were in a chipper mood.

My lawyer spoke for a minute, then the prosecutor, and then to my total surprise, Judge Stevens looked at me and asked if I wanted to say anything to the prosecutor.

I had no idea I was going to be asked to speak, on the record. My attorney never said anything about it, didn't prepare me at all. So, off the cuff, I said this:

"First of all, I didn't do it. Second of all…it's not fair…I'm in a pretty difficult situation…it's terrible what happened to her but I didn't do it…what happened to me was getting kidnapped by MCSO and held hostage being psychologically and emotionally tortured for the past 2 ½ years with you guys pointing a…gun to my head saying, you need to sign because you're going to get executed because that's what happens to people in your situation…"

I went on for a long time, with something between a rant and a lecture, teary-eyed but angry, directing it all at Gingold, who sat directly across from me, four feet away. Jill interjected with the same assertive and defiant demeanor hurling an "I don't understand why you won't help him!" at Rick and Marci.

Pleading No Contest To Avoid A Death Penalty

Judge Stevens interrupted and reminded me of the dangerous situation I was in. Then she asked me if there was "anything else" I wanted to say. It took me a minute to realize what she was fishing for. We were here to discuss a 2nd degree plea, that was what a settlement conference was for. We had gotten in a room together, gotten our hugs, said some things we'd wanted to say, so in order to complete the meeting I offered that I would "consider" a 2nd degree plea, but made the completion of such even less likely by adding two stipulations of my own. First, I would not plead guilty. I maintained my innocence, so it would have to be an Alford plea, allowing me to continue maintaining my innocence. The state could call it a no contest plea if they wanted to, but I would not say that I did this crime. They could forget about it.

Second, it would have to be capped at 16 years, the presumptive, meaning that the overall sentence would have to be 16 years or less, ultimately.

Without hesitation Gingold agreed. I couldn't believe it. They had had the whole thing set up beforehand, without missing a beat. Judge Stevens took over the dialogue and told me how fortunate I was. When it was determined some years earlier that judges would begin participating in settlement conferences it was decided with the stipulation that the Judge would not participate in coercing a plea. But it was obvious to my family and I that was actually Judge Stevens' only real purpose here. It was designed that way, because it was supposed to impact me, and my family, negatively, to hear the message of doom from an unrelated, supposedly unbiased 3rd party, a Judge nonetheless. And it did impact us. Idealistic and naïve, we had hoped that Judge Stevens might actually intervene in our behalf, especially after witnessing me maintaining my innocence in person, so fervently with tears. We hoped she would say, "wait a minute. This case needs to go to trial," and appoint attorneys who were trained to try cases.

Instead, it went like this:

Judge Stevens: "Okay...it's an extremely good offer, you do know that?"

Me: "Yeah, it's very uncommon (trying to be polite), I understand these cases, and these situations, it doesn't make it an easy decision though."

Judge: "I understand that. But you were the one discussing the risk the "figurative gun to my head" and what you have been experiencing, "psychological and emotional torture when gramma and Noah died '.

Judge: "This is an incredibly favorable offer to you.

Judge: "This is an extremely favorable offer."

Judge: "I just want to stress again this is extremely, I'm surprised the state came up with such a favorable offer."

Gingold, however, did not have the authority to settle a capital case so we would have to disperse and reconvene in a couple of days, after he had discussed it with his superiors at the MCAO. Nothing was signed. It was just like Rick had said. I got into a room with my family, hugged them all, and I didn't have to sign anything. And I knew there was no way Gingold's superiors would agree to it. Nor would the victim's family, or the community, who had been demanding my execution for almost three years now.

I did not sleep for the next three days and nights. Right after the settlement conference my 2nd chair atty, Marci Kratter, had pounced on Jill, telling her this is it; if MCAO agrees then it's over, no backing out of it now. Even though that's not what Rick had told me going into it.

Marci also attacked my wife and marriage that day by telling Jill, "Justin's been lying to you, he *did* know Liz..."

I'd never met Liz, ever. I did not even know she existed before the one-night-stand. Marci had heard gossip from someone that I'd taken Liz to their apartment one night and "made out with her" in the bathroom.

I knew the person who'd said that, and I knew what night they were talking about, but the young woman spoken of was actually a "Lacey" that worked at Fry's.

I couldn't believe my own atty would immediately accept gossip as truth, not fact-check, not show the "source" (a known drug-addict) a picture, not ask me for clarification, and just run to my wife on the hardest day of our lives and try to break her.

But in hindsight it actually fit perfectly into Marci's disposition toward me. As my 2nd chair atty, she didn't even bother to come to the jail and introduce herself until one year after she was "assigned" to the case. When I did finally see her it was at a mitigation hearing (Donahoe) that she was obliged to attend. There was no smile from her, no warmth as there was with the others.

It seemed obvious, and it was just my perception, that she had appraised my human worth based solely on what Detective Smith had crafted into his charging summary and thus did not like me. Couldn't stand me. Couldn't even fake it.

Maybe she was experiencing burnout, maybe she was exhausted professionally, tired of catering to the dishonest derelicts that the OCAC contract forced her to interact with. Whatever the case, Jill and I had Marci's gossip to deal with, over the recorded jail phone, additional to the shotgun-wedding plea situation the state had escorted me to.

I still wanted to fire them. They killed us, emotionally. What they did to my fragile mom that day, to Jill, my dad, my little brother, changed their lives forever. My dad would never be the same. A small-town small businessman, hardworking and honest man, he had raised us on Wyatt Earp and John Wayne, to believe in the American justice system, which never made mistakes, blessed by God. We were to not even question authority. Now he questioned the world he lived in, and everything he'd taught his sons about it. He worried that instead of endorsing it to us, he should've been protecting us from it. All of my grandparents, including his mom and dad, would pass away while I was in prison. Jill would have anxiety issues for the rest of her life, especially when an MCSO patrol car pulled in behind her, and dangerous depression, with no husband there to comfort her. My brother at 24 years old would be lost without me, searching for my ghost in the places we used to go, on the snowy slopes we used to snowboard on. And my mom, who liked to drink, would drink, a little bit more, for years, until the cancer came.

The three nights between the two settlement conferences consisted of spells of me laying in my bunk thinking. Trying to fall asleep, shattered by what felt like lightning strikes through my brain and heart, shooting me up out of bed to keep drafting a motion requesting that the court fire my attorneys.

I didn't know what to do. Maybe I was panicking for nothing. The MCAO would probably deny the plea idea, or the victim's family would strongly object, Gingold and Rick would start arguing again, Rick would become genuinely frustrated with the annoying Gingold, which would unite him with me the client again, and we would go to trial and win. I'd be home in a month.

And I'd lay back down in my bunk, believing that. Ready to fall asleep, and then *ZAP!* It would start all over again.

I didn't know what to do.

An "Alford" Plea—A No-Contest Plea—Any Plea to Avoid Death

Because we had promised our lives to each other, and meant it, I gave Jill the final say in what would happen, should the state accept.

Rick, on the "good" side of his good cop-bad cop monologues, had went on and on at length about this not being the end. This was the selling point. Of course I did not want to die an early death by way of an erroneous death sentence, like Jeffrey Landrigan just had, but the real motivator towards possibly going through with this plea was my licensed attorney, bound to me by ethical guidelines and human decency, telling me that my case wasn't over. He said I could sign the plea, which was an Alford plea, relabeled no contest by MCAO, then called a guilty plea by the national media. I could sign the Alford plea, and then, instead of fighting the case in county jail (no human contact; no sunlight; no radio, no t.v.) with the death penalty hanging over my head, I could go to D.O.C. (hours-long contact visits w/ wife and family every week, plenty of outside air) and keep fighting my case with an automatic release date on the horizon, at the age of about 42 years old.

Dangling Post-Conviction Relief to Coerce A Plea Change

Rick Miller advised me to go to the Arizona Department of Corrections and immediately file a "petition for post-conviction-relief" alleging actual innocence and ineffective assistance of counsel. He said if I alleged that he was ineffective, he would not defend himself against such a claim, he would agree with it.

I found it remarkable that my own attorney was advising me to claim that he was ineffective, incompetent, and promising to agree with it when it got back into court.

'What kind of a system is this!' I thought. What a bizarre world. So different than I had thought.

As compelling as all of that was, the selling point *of the selling point,* was what Marci was about to say. She said that I could go to D.O.C. and request DNA testing and that if the DNA inside the two used condoms came back to the boyfriend "Nate," it would exonerate me.

That convinced me that I had *automatic relief* ahead, because I knew the DNA was not mine. I knew it belonged to someone else, probably the boyfriend. By now we had found a witness (Lynett Guinn) who identified his picture as being a suspicious character who was hiding in the bushes outside the house as it burned. We learned that a *Hideaway* bartender had contradicted his earlier statement that he had last seen Liz at noon on 7-7-08. This bartender said that *he watched her and I leave together that night.* So, by now I assumed that he must've been the intruder inside her house that night. He must have driven to her house to spy on us, found it empty, let himself in, got spooked when we showed up, tip-toed out the back, came back the next morning after I had left.

But that was the hook. Marci told me that a DNA match for the condoms to "Nate" would exonerate me.

So, for those 3 days and nights, Jill and I, and the rest of our family, really did have a lot to discuss and think about.

Why would I sign away some appellate rights? "Jailhouse lawyers" will tell you that when you sign a plea agreement you forfeit a wealth of valuable legal advantages and rights. Actual lawyers will tell you the same, and they will also tell you not to listen to jailhouse lawyers, even though the truth is that the one is no more disingenuous than the other. This is my experience.

Forfeiture Of All Appellate Rights

The forfeiture of appellate rights, as a result of signing any kind of plea, is a reality. It is true. But it is a good example of a statement that is technically true but wholly misleading. If you go to trial in Arizona and get your rights trampled upon by lying witnesses, greedy prosecutors, indifferent judges or your own attorney, you do have a right to file a direct appeal. In a death penalty case you have even more rights regarding appeals. That is true. But you also have "the right" to throw a coin into a wishing well. You have "the right" to tell your celly you are innocent for the rest of your life. You even have "the right" to ask the governor for clemency and after he denies you, you still have "the right" to declare your innocence as they execute you. Rights don't dictate results.

Jeffery Landrigan's Execution

A perfect example of this was Jeffrey Landrigan, and it impacted my decision greatly. I read about Jeffrey Landrigan weekly, sometimes daily, as his execution date approached and last minute appeals escalated. He seemed to have three solid grounds for relief, on three different plains. One was mitigation. His trial lawyers hadn't presented any. His appellate lawyers had argued that the sentencing Judge would have spared his life had she known about the mitigating factors. The appellate court disagreed- even though that judge, now retired, came forward and wrote a letter to that court explaining that it would have *completely* changed her determination. They still disagreed.

His second ground was the fact that ADOC had illegally smuggled the execution drug across the Mexican border a month earlier. U.S. prisons had previously obtained it from the U.K., but since the U.K. did not believe in executing humans, they stopped providing the drugs to the U.S., after finding out what U.S. prisons were using it for. Adept at problem solving, ADOC has taken up the practice of drug smuggling. Neither the DEA, nor customs, ever batted an eye.

His third and I thought most compelling ground was the fact that DNA testing had been conducted on the victim's pants and two complete DNA profiles had been identified, belonging to two "unidentified males"- neither profile was Landrigan's. The two unidentified males were *never* identified or contacted, never even interviewed as witnesses.

So the only question now was, what was the governor going to do? He or she had to do something.

Well, at the 11th hour he simplified his whole controversy by ordering ADOC to execute Jeffrey Landrigan and thus, Mr. Landrigan's appeals died with him. No more controversy.

So, did Jeffrey Landrigan preserve impressive-sounding appellate rights by going to trial? Yes, he absolutely did. Does he have a pulse today? No, because those impressive-sounding rights didn't mean anything to the AZ Court of Appeals.

As a not-so-casual observer of the Jeffrey Landrigan saga, I could not believe that the government had just executed a citizen who had just brought forth exculpatory DNA evidence. The death penalty is a serious concept. Every law and order tv show I'd seen made it clear that DNA evidence was the be-all end-all of a case. Witnesses could lie. DNA never lies.

Jeffrey Landrigan's execution was the completion of my own process of realizing that appellate rights in Arizona were basically meaningless, litigious fool's gold. And for anyone motivated to disagree with that statement, motivated to debunk it by giving a sanctimonious speech about the letter of the law, tell it to Landrigan's mother while she was picking out Jeffrey's casket. Even soviet prisoners in Stalin's gulags were allowed, "to write petitions twice a month to officials to proclaim their innocence or decry mistreatment."

Both prisoners of Stalin's gulags, and modern Arizona's number one industry (the prison system), should be careful not to confuse the right to complain with the right to actual results.

Making My Decision

I realized in early 2011 that if I was going to go home I needed to *prove* that I was actually innocent, and if I could do that, I would go home no matter where I was going home from- county jail, death row, or the moon, because the presumption of innocence was every bit as disingenuous as my right to a phone call the night I was arrested, or my right to have an attorney who would defend me at least *half* as viciously as the state was attacking me. It became apparent to me that those "rights" were actually *privileges* to be enjoyed by an extremely low percentage of criminal defendants, such as the wealthy and politically advantaged. As a simple working class man from small town U.S.A., I had no right to those privileges.

My family also realized this. It especially affected my dad, who was the personification of America's perceived identity, hardworking and honest, accepting all humans with a come-as-you-are smile. We spent many 4th of July celebrations roadside in Cave Creek, holding hands with our patriotic heads tilted up at the velvet night sky, watching the bright colors explode and fall all around us. Now my family and I watched as the American mosaic of truth and justice- justice for all and good always wins, exploded and shattered, falling down all around us and burying us alive in its rubble, like a natural disaster. There was no one coming to dig us out, no one we could call, because you can't call 911 when the authorities are the ones hurting you.

To this day I wonder who the two unidentified males in the Landrigan case were, what neighborhood they live in today, if they appreciate the Arizona judiciary, if they've hurt anyone else since then, and from a sociological standpoint, why nobody cares.

Whoever they are living with today, their roommates, or spouses, do *they* know that their semen was found on a dead body? They certainly deserve to know.

On the last phone call the night before the last settlement conference, which was the last of a three-day marathon of phone calls, Jill and I made our final decision together. If the state accepted the plea, we would sign, go through the sentencing, and actually be eager to get me into an Arizona prison quickly so I could file my petition for post-conviction relief, start getting DNA testing done, and start telling people what our lawyers had done to us.

We wanted to make sure that we made the decision the night before, so that there would be no surprises. We had more surprises that week than we could handle. I especially wanted Jill to know that since she was my wife, and vowed to always be my wife, it was her decision too. It was *our* life.

110

Nonetheless, during the middle of the night, through lightning strike-infused thought processes, I changed my mind again. I just couldn't plead out to this.

In the courtroom the next morning I was seated in the jury box, like always, and my family was in the galley.

I mouthed across the courtroom to Jill, "I want to go to trial."

She shook her head "No."

I silently mouthed again "I can't sign this plea; I want to go to trial."

She shook her head "No."

I just stared at her, she kept staring at me, and she shook her head a little bit more.

I exhaled, my shoulders dropped a little bit, and my faithful lawyer was standing right next to me. He had snuck up on me like a leg cramp, looking at me like I was caught doing something wrong.

We all went into the conference room. Not much was said, I was in a trance, the state was ready, I didn't move or speak, my lawyer pushed the papers closer to me and said "Come on, let's get it done." Through wet, blurry eyes, I signed it.

Second-Degree Murder Plea & Mitigation

They walked me out into the courtroom, Judge Stevens headed up toward the bench, adopted good posture, and court was in session. I was asked my name and a few other basic questions that were part of the plea soliloquy, and then, with a straight face, she asked me whether or not anyone had threatened me.

"Besides the state threatening to kill me? And my lawyers threatening to help them? I thought.

"No your honor," I said, playing along. I thought it was incredible that lawyers and judges would view the ritualistic recitation of the plea soliloquy as anything other than tightly scripted theatre. Everyone in the room knew that the coerced plea was a direct result of the state's threat to kill me. It wasn't that complicated. The chance of plea change was the most pretentious adult gathering we had ever been to. It was all fake.

When I got back to the jail later that day and called Jill she told me that she wasn't shaking her head "no," she just couldn't understand me.

Sometimes I wonder how different my life would be today if she'd understood what I was mouthing across the courtroom to her that day. We might be together out there right now, this evening, with two kids of our own running around, 6 and 8 years old.

Or I could be alone on death row right now watching my appeals run out, trying to figure out how to make a noose out of a sheet, how to stop the pain like so many others do, who never thought they would.

But I'm no different than you are. We all have forks in the road that we glance back on every now and again. It's what's ahead that matters.

When I woke up the next day it was the first time in almost 3 years wherein I woke up and the death penalty was not a part of my life anymore. Sometimes you don't realize how much weight you had on your shoulders until it is lifted. That lighter feeling lasted about twenty-four hours.

I knew I had to get right to figuring out how to win in court on sentencing day. I was going to be convicted, at least temporarily, but the sentencing range was enormous. With one count of second-degree murder (10-22 years) and one count of arson of an occupied structure (3 ½ - 12 yrs) my minimum would be 10 years, my maximum possible sentence would be 34 years.

If I was given the minimum I would be released at the age of thirty-six. If I was given the maximum sentence I would be released at the age of *sixty*.

Really, the only thing that mattered now was mitigation. After focusing on mitigation for three years and finding none, like I said they would, my attorneys were still going to try and convince the judge that I should get a lesser sentence because my dad worked too much and him and my mom weren't perfect.

It was ridiculous. I had been housed around young men now for three years who really did have difficult and tragic upbringings. I thought my attorneys argument was offensive to them. And those were the people in front of Judge Barton every day.

I had to find a different way, different mitigation.

I wanted my attorneys to focus on facts and evidence. I wanted a mini-trial. I wanted Judge Barton to know that I did not do the crimes MCSO has arrested me for.

I wanted the whole world to know that.

Amazingly, after three years of this, I still had tremendous support from countless friends and family. I received mail and video visits from people who I'd known for years.

I knew they would be confused as to why I signed the plea. My attorneys had emphasized that I not discuss the case with anyone. Rena Glitsos told me to pretend that someone had a gun to my head when I was on the jail phone, because, she said, that's exactly the situation.

As a result no one really knew what had gone on behind the scenes during the last week. All they knew was that the national news had just said I plead guilty to murder and arson.

Justin's Letter of Actual Innocence to His Family

It was important to me that they knew that I was innocent and that they knew what my attorneys had done to us, so I sat down and began writing a letter to them- "to whom it may concern." was piercing the veil. I began writing everything down.

I never told my attorneys about the letter because I didn't trust them. I spoke directly to all of my friends and family, I was candid. I poured my heart out. When I was finished I had a twenty-six page handwritten letter in front of me.

I did the one thing every defendant is not supposed to do. I talked about my case. And because I was innocent, I wanted the whole world to see it. I wanted everyone to know what happened to us. I called Jill, I told her about the letter, and I told her to make copies of it, give it to anyone who will read it. Have my mom, dad and brother make copies of it. Let's distribute it to as many people as we can. And then I mailed it to her.

But somehow-some way, after having sent thousands of pieces of mail back and forth for three years and every letter and postcard arriving without incident, some-how, this twenty-six page letter disappeared. Imagine that. Without missing a beat, I sat back down and wrote another, this one thirty pages long, and then I figured out a way to smuggle it *out* of the jail without it passing through MCSO's hands. I had been studying the bible thoroughly this whole time, I had serious questions now about the world I lived in and I wanted to know if God was real. Some of Jehovah's Witnesses from Cave Creek had been coming to visit me and to conduct services for the inmates in my pod. Spiritually, I was hungry. I read *a lot,* I thought a lot, and I asked as many hard questions as I could think of. Their answers were impressive and my time with them was therapeutic. As a result I had a very tall stack of watchtower magazines in my cell.

I folded each page of my letter in half. I stuck 1 page inside the back cover of every *other* magazine in the stack, brought the stack to bible study, gave it to the witnesses who'd come in that day, and asked them to give it to Jill. I'm sure they thought it was just surplus.

I made sure not to bring it up over the phone until *after* I knew Jill had the watch-tower magazines in her possession. When I did, she thumbed through the stack, removed each page, put them in order and began copying and distributing, along with my mom and brother.

As a result Judge Barton received seventy-seven letters in my behalf, many pro-claiming my innocence and asking her to fire my attorneys. She said at sentencing it was one of the most impactful forms of mitigation she'd seen. No, Rick said that.

There was an abnormally long period of time between the change of plea and my sentencing. Usually after a plea is signed, sentencing is scheduled for 30-60 days later. Mine was going to be five months later.

During that five months, a lot of interesting things happened.

The Alford Plea Before Judge Barton

After maintaining my innocence so fervently in the settlement conference, the prosecutor, Mike Gingold, had told my attorney, Rick Miller, that I had better not say that "innocent" nonsense in open court, or they would pull the plea and go for the death penalty again, because MCAO "doesn't do Alford pleas."

The problem for Gingold though, was that he and Rick had conspired together to arrange exactly that—an Alford plea.

An Alford plea, as explained to me by Rick, was named after an actual defendant in the south in the 1950's. Mr. Alford a black man had essentially told the court "I am innocent, but I will sign this plea because you white people will kill me if I don't." Rick had explained to me that it was for innocent people who do not trust the system. I found out later that he had lied.

Gingold's dilemma was that he was trying to sneak it past his superiors at MCAO by calling it a no-contest plea. He couldn't have the defendant proclaiming his innocence in open court and causing a controversy. They had to get rid of this case in secret. It was bad enough that the state had forgone allocution by allowing a no contest plea rather than insisting on a guilty plea.

No Allocution

Typically, a guilty plea includes allocution, wherein the defendant gives a full, detailed confession on the record, and explains why he committed the crimes and shows remorse. This benefits the state by making it nearly impossible for the defendant to appeal the conviction—because he's confessed on the record, and offers some closure to the victim's family.

In a no contest plea, no allocution is required, and the Judge is not allowed, legally, to aggravate the sentence based on a lack of remorse.

In a brutal murder like this, one can't help but notice that the interests of the victim's family are completely ignored. The defendant doesn't offer any explanation, doesn't answer the questions they've struggled with—doesn't even admit guilt—and gets an automatic release date probably in his forties. A slap in the face.

But the state wasn't concerned with the victim's family, who were part of the process the whole time. The state was trying to keep its own image clean by quietly doing away with a bad case.

I told Rick I would be polite in court. I did not want to upset the victim's family, but if her honor asked me directly, because it had now been brought up in letters to the court, if her honor asked me directly if I am innocent I will be candid with her. It was immediately apparent that Rick had not even considered this scenario. She might actually ask me, he hadn't thought of that.

Defeated, he said "Fine. If she asks you, you're Alford."

And that was the plan, even though the state had threatened to reinstate the death penalty if I mentioned my innocence in open court. Therefore, even for the next five months, I still didn't know if the plea was going to stand.

Soon thereafter, Rick came in to see me and give me a "heads-up" about something. He'd told me that Detective Smith was angry about the plea, he wanted me to be executed and he was still trying to figure out a way to get it done.

Of course he was.

Rick told me that Smith and Gingold were now paying extra attention to my recorded jail calls in hopes that I would say something incriminating. Gingold told Rick, in private, that I might confess now that I thought the case was over, and if I did, they (the state) would pull the plea and reinstate the death penalty.

I found it *incredible* that Gingold was dumb enough to believe that was a possibility.

They'd listened to 2-4 hours' worth of phone calls that I'd had on the jail phone, every day, for *three years*, for a total of approximately 2-4 thousand hours of calls and had no incriminating or even inconsistent statements, and they were still hoping for it. They wouldn't recognize a dead-end lead if it bit them in the rear.

I called Jill, and we both shook our heads about it. We said Gingold was an idiot, a sentiment shared by most of my family.

Then, within hours, I got a very telling visit from Rick.

Rick was livid, very angry with me. I was startled. I couldn't understand what I had done wrong. He told me that Gingold had just called him, throwing "a fit" because he felt betrayed by Rick because Rick had told me that they were listening to my phone calls again. Gingold said that he had felt mocked by Jill and me. We had hurt his feelings. Rick ranted at me and then left.

I learned a lot in those 5 minutes. The prosecutors in Maricopa county really did expect public defenders to help them convict their own clients.

Gingold expected Rick to help him trick me, so that Smith could have me executed later. Rick was supposed to tacitly help set up his own client and when he didn't, Gingold was *genuinely* offended. Sometimes I still don't know what to make of Rick. He had his moments, this tormented man.

Tracy Warren

After the news of me signing a plea was broadcasted on YV, a woman named Tracy Warren approached my mom in Cave Creek. Tracy was a friend of the victim Liz. Tracy said that she couldn't believe I signed a plea because she knew I did not murder her friend.

Shortly thereafter, I received some additional reports from my attorneys. Apparently Tracy Warren had recently been contacted by MCAO. The state called her because she was a friend of Liz, and they wanted her to be a character witness for Liz at sentencing.

Tracy told them they had the wrong guy in jail. She said she had been afraid to come forward before this. She told them about a conversation she had with a guy named Justin Oddo, but the content of the conversation was not included in the report, nor was it recorded. Needless to say, the state did not call her as a witness.

At the same time, they disclosed to me a composite sketch of the truck arsonist, done by eyewitness Jimmie Larson and a detective Weege. It looked nothing like me. But we already knew that, because he was tall, with light skin and bushy red hair. I'm 5'9, dark skin, and black hair. It would have been an excellent visual for the jury. And by now, Larson had said specifically, after seeing a picture of me, that I was not the guy he saw.

Why wasn't I shown these reports about Tracy Warren, and the composite sketch before the settlement conference? Because I wouldn't have signed.

I urged my attorneys to go interview Tracy Warren in person and to raise a Brady violation issue, but they refused.

My family and I would try to locate Justin Oddo after I got to prison, only to find that he had "fallen off a 300' cliff" and died. It would've been nice to talk to him while he was still alive.

Presentence Report—June 24, 2011

On June 24th, 2011, just six days before the June 30th sentencing was to take place, PSI officer K.A. Barnes- Blumberg issued her own findings in the presentence report she authored. It was yet another testament to the state's loose commitment to fact-finding, and a continued forum on Detective Paul Smith's lack of respect for the record.

In her own description of the situation, Ms. Barnes, when describing the truck fire scene, states, "a witness observed a man fitting the defendant's physical description" setting the fire

Clearly, Detective Smith's misleading sworn testimony in front of the grand jury worked not only on the grand jury, but now on PSI officer Barnes. In fact, I was short, dark-complected, and black-haired. I could not have looked more *unlike* the tall, light complected red-haired man who had burned Ms. Hermann's truck.

The grand jury never knew that. Now Ms. Barnes apparently did not know that, nor would Judge Barton. She would use Ms. Barnes' determinations in her sentencing calculus. For years going forward, every appellate court would use fragmented quotes from Detective Paul Smith's false sworn testimony to uphold the wrongful conviction, despite Judge Rosa Mroz herself characterizing Smith's testimony as "misleading" in 2008. She allowed the indictment to stand anyway. Thankfully, on page three of the presentence report Ms. Barnes included a summary of a recent conversation she'd had with Detective Smith about the case.

MCSO Detective Paul Smith Responds to Pre-Sentence Report

Unfortunately Detective Smith forfeited his opportunity to offer clarity and instead used it as a platform to advertise his ability to read minds. Reminiscent of detective Ernesto Saldate' s tactics in the Debra Milke wrongful conviction, Smith does not talk about facts or what witnesses said, instead he talks about what they *meant to say*, what they didn't say, but wanted to—the content you won't find in the police reports or transcribed interviews.

He said, "The defendant planned to spread the body parts," even though the concept was not even hinted of during the investigation.

He said, "One witness likely saw the aftermath and when he was interviewed, seemed to have the image imbedded in his head." He doesn't mention the name of the witness, but he is speaking about Gerald Coco, who, when asked, assured detectives that they were wrong, he [and me] never went to that house. He didn't even know where the house was, he told them, countless times. Nothing put Coco at the scene. Not his words, not anyone else's words, no evidence, and yet, Smith goes on to say here, "that witness still appears traumatized and was manipulated by the defendant into going back to the house."

During MCSO's original investigation, detectives really needed me to be guilty. They really needed Coco to say that we went to the crime scene together. They had surveillance videos of him and me together all day, just like I said we were in my interview. Multiple witnesses put us together- including us. So, in order to convict *me*, they needed Coco to at least have been a participant, to at least have been *present* at the crime scenes, and when they couldn't get him to admit to it or find *any* evidence of it, they kept it as a staple in their narrative anyway.

Detective Smith also said, "the defendant knew the victim had ties with the Hell's Angels motorcycle gang and realized he was 'screwed' and that people would be out to get him." What I knew? I didn't even know *her.*

That Liz Hermann was connected to the Hell's Angels was something that many suspected but no one could prove—until now. Many suspected that the Hell's Angels were somehow involved in Ms. Hermann's murder for several reasons. First, she worked at the *Buffalo Chip*, a place where they loved to hang out—and she also drank there, when she was not working. Second, people thank of the H.A. as violent, and they have a habit of arson and explosives. Third, Sam Parker was rumored to be a Hell's Angel. Just before Ms. Hermann's murder, three Hell's Angels from the Mesa chapter killed a woman in identical fashion, taking turns stabbing her dozens of times and then nearly decapitating her. In that case one perpetrator became an informant, another was arrested, and the third was still on the loose.

As a result of the head-scratching presentence report, I received a surprise visit from Rick and Marci early the next morning, at about 6:30 am. Still asleep, I had no idea why I was being awoken for a legal visit. I didn't know about the presentence report yet, I didn't even know what a presentence report was. As I stepped into the legal visit booth, the excitement in Rick and Marci's faces beamed straight through the plexi-glass partition right at me, they were happy to see me.

Now I was really confused.

They explained the presentence report to me, how ridiculous Smith's statements about reading Gerald's mind were, and that he was going to file objections to those statements, asking that the Judge remove them from the report since they were not supported by fact. The real point of this visit, the reason they had both dropped every-thing that morning and came straight to the jail, was detective Smith's statement about Liz Hermann's association with the Hell's Angels. They had come to the jail to ask my permission to file a motion to continue sentencing, in order to investigate Smith's claim that Liz Hermann was associated with the Hell's Angels, and to pull the plea and go to trial.

It was a lot to take in at 6:30 am, while still rubbing my eyes trying to wake up, after a five month process of finally getting myself and my family used to the fact that I was going to go to prison. At least for a little while my parents had clung to the auto-matic release date the plea provided—a guarantee that they would actually see their son alive again at home.

Of course pulling the plea would renew the death penalty's presence in our lives. It was the state's biggest weapon against me. They didn't lean on facts or forensic evidence, they relied on the fact that their position in government bestowed them with the ability to force my family into a position of having to plan my funeral, pick out my casket, and mourn the loss of me.

Without hesitation I told them to do it.

In Rick's motion to continue, he said he was "unaware" of any disclosure indicating that the victim had ties to the H.A. M/C gang. The prosecution had not disclosed any information connecting the victim with the gang. But they did. It was in Sandor's interview. It was there all along. Is this a testament to Ricks ineffectiveness?

Defense Motion to Continue Sentencing Hearing

Rick filed a motion to continue the hearing, in light of the Hell's Angels comments from Detective Smith. That prompted a phone call from a frustrated prosecutor (Gingold), to Detective Smith. Gingold asked Smith "what the hell he was doing" and why he'd said those things.

Gingold then called Rick and told Rick that Smith said that the things he told the presentence reporter weren't true, Liz Hermann had "no known association with the Hell's Angels," and in Smith's own words, "I was just bullshitting, I didn't know I was on the record."

One can't help but wonder how a deputy turned detective, turned lead detective, in a high-profile capital murder case, in all of his experience and wisdom, did *not* know his interview with PSI officer Barnes was on the record. What did he think interviews and reports were for? Was this all a game to him, did he not take the process seriously?

Without investigating, prosecutor Gingold took Smith's word for it, that his own statements were false. Gingold then asked Rick to also take his word for it, no investigating should be done. Rick held his ground but it wouldn't matter anyway, because Judge Janet Barton was more than willing to take Smith's word for it. She denied the motion to continue and investigate; sentencing was now two days away. Judge Barton had put forth a lot of effort to "resolve" this case. She wasn't going to have that jeopardized now.

From the top down, the Maricopa county judiciary had put forth a lot of time and energy. They had meetings with professionals on both sides to alleviate the congestion created by County Attorney Andrew Thomas' "Capital Case Crisis"—the situation his term had left us in.

Judge Donahoe had denied all continuances based on a made-up order from the Arizona Supreme Court, rubber-stamping them as quickly as they came in. Judge Mroz had allowed a grand jury indictment against me to stand, although she herself admitted in her ruling that MCSO Detective Paul Smith had misled that grand jury into indicting me. Judge Barton had removed Rena Glitsos against my wishes because she was trying too hard to protect my rights and defend me. Then Judge Barton appointed Rick Miller,. Together they carried out the sign-or-die technique, and the railroading was now almost complete. There was no way Judge Barton was going to nullify all of that railroading by allowing my public defender to actually investigate the murder I was charged with. Detective Smith had given his word anyway.

Eight Bankers Boxes—Court Documents and More

Years later, after several post-conviction court-appointed attorneys had failed us, I finally took possession of my file. I got access to eight banker's boxes full of documents.

In them, I found handwritten notes of Sandor Polgar's interview, Liz's estranged husband. He gave a detailed description of Hermann's association with the Hell's Angels; it was well documented. He said they fought and argued about it many times, it was a point of contention in their marriage because Sandor did not want her to hang out with them. He told a story about Liz Hermann witnessing some H.A. members beating and stomping a man unconscious at the MCSO-owned *Buffalo Chip* bar. That interview was conducted by MCSO Detective Paul Smith, a patron of the *Buffalo Chip*.

Judge Barton also ignored Rick's request to remove Smith's statements from the presentence report. In his "notice of defendant's objection to portions of the presentence report" dated June 28th, 2011, regarding Gerald Coco going to the crime scene, Rick argued that "Detective Smith and other MCSO officers [Detective Kristina Bucaro] interviewed Coco several times...[the officers] pressed the theory on Coco and gave him the opportunity to adopt it. He never did. He consistently disputed that he was at the scene of the crime. Smith opined that Lunsford planned to spread the victim's body parts but found the task too difficult. This information is likely part of the detective's working theory of the case. It never got past theoretical stages. There was no evidence to support it. Much of it is hubris; it does not belong in the presentence report."

In other words, sworn peace officers are not supposed to just fabricate storylines to convict people. The evidence has to be rooted in something other than the detective's imagination.

Judge Barton didn't care. She allowed everything Smith said to stand, in a report that I would be judged upon for years, in her courtroom and once in prison, even though Smith himself had admitted that his own statements were 'just bullshit.' I guess that's good enough.

The only thing Smith said in the PSR that was true or made any sense was, "the violence was passionate, cold, with a lot of hate involved." I think everyone would agree that there was a lot of "hate" involved—which makes you wonder why Detective Smith would arrest somebody who did not even know her.

Consequences—2011

With my plea signing having been on national news programs in February and my June 30th sentencing just two days away, the chatter and gossip was warming back up. Many of Ms. Hermann's friends and family had written letters to Judge Barton and I had to read all of them. They said I was a monster, an animal, and that I should die. One or two of them expressed a desire to have me tortured, and then killed. This was okay with Judge Barton. In court these ideas would be repeated verbally, without rebuke.

This was new to me. I had always gotten along with people so well. I was very social. I loved interacting with people of all kinds. I had never had enemies before, people who wanted to permanently harm me, or kill me.

But I had to wrap my head around it. I had to pay attention and be careful now. I didn't know the victim in this case. I didn't know her mom, dad, brother(s), uncles, cousins, friends. I didn't know who they were; or if one was a Hell's Angel, or an Aryan brotherhood member, or just a "basic" murderer, which there are many of in jail and D.O.C.

Jill told me over the phone that her and our friends, Greg and Tina, were worried because they had seen a threat online, stating that the Aryan brotherhood was going to "slit my throat" when I got to D.O.C.

When I hung up the phone with her I went to the cell of an acquaintance I'd made in the max custody jail, Craig Devine. They called him "Spinner," an active Aryan brotherhood member. He was currently in custody for a high profile capital murder out of Tempe. I didn't know if the threat was real, but I figured the quickest way to find out was just to ask an A.B. member directly.

When I did, his head tilted back in full-on open-mouth laughter. He said the Aryan brotherhood had "way bigger things" to worry about than me. His answer seemed assuring but it was still kind of ambiguous. "wait...so I *am* on their radar, just not that "big" of a thing...?" I kind of wondered. I never asked for clarification because like I had said about Sam Parker's "episode" at the beginning of this book, men in their twenties just don't talk about uncomfortable things, or ask specific questions.

Besides that, it didn't matter what I was told at this point. Between Smith stating that the H.A. was going to get me, the victim's family wanting me tortured (in "good conscience"), or the A.B. slitting my throat, what was not ambiguous was that since my attorney's forced me to sign an Alford plea for Ms. Hermann's murder the whole world wanted to kill me and everyone—even people in uniform—felt it was justified.

No matter what details I was given from here on out I would have to watch out for people, because my relationship with the rest of mankind had now taken a drastic turn for the worse, and I was on my way to a place of violence and murder.

On little to no sleep I stood at the metal door to my cell, at about 3 a.m. (we didn't have access to a clock), listening to the loud clanking and dragging of the steel chains as the robotic officers dragged them into the pod and threw them up onto the stainless steel tables I'd eaten slop on for the last 3 years. It was finally here. My stay at this strange and unyielding place was almost over. After somehow getting used to it, I was about to go somewhere worse.

The Gallows—Walk From Fourth Avenue Jail to Maricopa County Superior Court

But first I had to go through the Gallows, to my shooting-squad sentencing, where they would demolish me in every way not literal, erasing my every good deed from the earth's memory, pronouncing me to be a murderer in front of all. As a young boy I always cared about what people thought of me, and as I got older I would care even more about my reputation, which is beholden by others, so it was going to be really hard for me to sit through this. But I had to; government employees on both sides had made it clear that I would die if I didn't, and neither reputation, nor anything else really matters when you don't have a pulse.

The walk through the underground tunnels was always a very long walk, with a couple of stops at holding cells along the way. With at least hundreds of inmates going to court every day, a large and impressive network of tunnels, 20 feet wide, 12 feet high, was built under the city in order to get the mass exodus of inmates from the 4th Avenue Jail building to the court building each morning without disturbing the public.

The public…I was no longer one of "the public," and the court tunnels reminded me of that every time. I traveled underground now, out of sight, no longer privileged to walk in the sunlight and exchange smiles with other passersby. My very appearance was disturbing and I was aware of that. Jailhouse stripes are unsettling, and the sound of dragging chains with each step wreaks of a horror movie. Smiling at people made them uncomfortable; except for my family, I was always happy to see them in the courtroom. It was the only time we got to see each other in person and even though we couldn't touch, it felt good just to be in the same room as them. It felt familiar, comfortable, in this alien place that my world had now become.

Today was different though. As I began the ascension up to the ground floor, in the final segment of tunnels, I felt like I was walking up to my own sacrificial death.

I was shaking, eyes watering, every fiber in my body telling me not to go up there, to what felt like an 8th floor alter, masquerading as a courtroom, where the powers that be would sacrifice me up in the interest of appeasing the people, as if it was somehow proof that their faith in the establishment, though legitimately questioned at times, would be validated today through some righteous vengeance. It was all theatre.

It is a unique experience to be innocent, dressed up in costume, jailhouse stripes and chains, and sit through a formal court appearance, lawyers in suits, deputy in uniform, Judge in a black robe, sitting upon a perch above it all, carrying on an air of propriety and duty, when you know that it is all-for-not and every educated person on the state's side is wrong because you are actually innocent. As an innocent person I sat and watched them carry on, doing harm to their own citizens and purpose, wondering if I would ever be able to tell how ridiculous they look through the eyes of an innocent defendant, and wondering where the real killer was and what he was thinking. Would he be there in the courtroom?

The Sentencing—June 30, 2011

On the way to sentencing that morning my last stop would be in a tiny, cramped, dark holding cell just behind the courtroom itself, where I would find two other inmates sitting—Braden and Brenton, my friends who I had studied with, worked out with, and helped in general.

My three years at the 4th Avenue Jail was filled with bible studies, exercise, and just trying to be a good big brother to the people around me. Being separated from my actual younger brother, Dwayne, left a void. I was a proud big brother, always including him in everything I did and teaching him everything I was learning, which was mostly good but sometimes mischievous, and he loved it all. While most big brothers were picking on their little brothers and leaving them at home when they went somewhere I was bringing Dwayne on snowboarding trips and to Blink-182 concerts. I had never picked on him or called him a name.

That's what most of the guys I met in jail had been missing, so I gave that to them, and they genuinely loved me for it. It was all they needed. In a world plagued with confusion about how to alleviate societal problems and what to do with individuals who *had* problems, I found the answer to be so simple; it was just love. All humans, even menacing ones, understand love. They all love something and they all needed something, or someone, to love them back.

I embraced Braden and Brenton, having not seen them now for some time since they had both been sent to prison months earlier. Braden was a young white male from Awhatukee, a rising high school baseball star and single dad who was blindsided by bipolar disorder and alcoholism. Brenton was a young black man from Tempe, orphaned as a baby, and still searching for his place in the world.

They were both nervous. They were called to testify at my sentencing and had been transported from their two respective prisons the night before, sleepless due to booking processes. God forbid MCSO let them sleep before they testify.

Then we got a surprise visit from my 2nd chair attorney, Marci, who popped in the holding cell to tell us that the courtroom was going to be *really* crowded. The galleria on the defendant's side of the courtroom was filled with my friends and family, as was the jury box, used as an overflow, and the state's side was filled with friends and family of the victim, as well as a couple of unrelated spectators who would use this opportunity to give their personal opinions at the podium, since this was open to the public.

When Marci went back to the courtroom they both looked at me, wide-eyed, and asked, "are there going to be, like, news cameras and stuff!"

"No" I replied, "no way. Nothing like that."

Then Marci popped back in to tell us that Channel 12 news cameras just showed up.

As I walked into the courtroom I saw the news crew with a large camera on a tripod set up in the middle of the aisle pointing it right at me. I looked to my right and saw the jury box full of my loved ones staring at me. Becca was there, the two of us a long ways from the living room floors we played on as babies or the 4-H club we enjoyed as kids.

Jill and my mom, dad, brother, grandad, cousins, aunts and uncles were in the galleria, behind the defense table, as was my childhood friend, Pat, who'd got off work the night before in San Diego and driven straight to Phoenix on no sleep.

Judge Barton came in, and court was in session. She sat down, went through formalities, and assured everybody that she had read the presentence report and was ready to proceed. With such a crowded, emotionally charged atmosphere she told the crowd "try to keep your emotions in check as we proceed here today."

The prosecutors went first, calling their witnesses. The first, a former friend and coworker of Liz Hermann, asked the court "to make sure that Mr. Lunsford does not do this to anyone else ever. Ever."

The second was her best friend, asking the same thing, as they all did, one even mentioning death and torture for me.

But the risks of allowing private citizens to speak on the record became readily apparent. I knew that when I eventually filed my petition for post-conviction relief and requests for DNA testing the following week, as Rick had advised me to do, every appellate Judge would review "the record" in order to decide whether I should be granted relief and DNA testing.

In the years that would follow my sentencing, the problem for me would become the fact that "the record" in my case would consist of MCSO Detective Paul Smith's sworn testimony in front of the grand jury, which Judge Mroz admitted was at least "misleading," the scripted change of plea soliloquy, the presentence report, and now the sentencing transcript.

One friend of Ms. Hermann's got up and said, on the record, that Lunsford "brutally stabbed her dog," and reassured listeners that she had "read all of the police reports and the autopsy reports."

I did not stab her dog. No one did. An actual review of the police reports would show that the dog had no injuries and probably died of smoke inhalation. But Judge Barton did not correct her, in part, because Judge Barton did not read the actual police reports either.

Liz's brother said that I "pleaded guilty" and "admitted his guilt in taking my sister's life."

A random private citizen who did not know the Hermann's or the Lunsfords got up to say, on the record, "One thing they cannot deny is that he has admitted to the brutal savage murder of Lizzy Hermann."t

There was no confession of any kind in this case. I adamantly maintained my innocence, so it was difficult to sit and watch these poor people who were in anguish, misinform a room full of my friends and family, and Channel 12 news, who would push it out into the public. I could not comprehend the damage that was being done to my life.

For years, even investigators who met with me in prison would do it under the assumption that I had confessed to killing Ms. Hermann. When I assured them that that was not true, they heard me with reluctance, because in the back of their own minds they had it filed away that they had read it somewhere on the record in State v. Lunsford, or saw it on the news, spoken by their favorite local anchor. The stink of a phantom confession would soil my defense going forward, and I would lose lifelong friends over it.

The contradictions in the state's collective theory became apparent in sentencing. Prosecutor Mike Gingold said, "What I want the court to recognize in this particular case is that this was up close and *very very personal*."

It was obvious that this was a very personal attack, which made it so perplexing, that they would arrest someone who did not even know her, who even now 3 years later no evidence incriminated, a guy with no history of violence whatsoever who had nothing but healthy relationships with lifelong friends and family.

Echoing the fact that Hermann and I did not even know each other, Hermann's brother said, "Mr. Lunsford was unknown to me. She was not dating him. She was not friends with him."

He went on to say that no "sane human being" could commit this crime, which also seemed obvious. They should have looked for a perpetrator who was *not* sane, someone diagnosed paranoid schizophrenic with, say...a penchant for knife violence and perhaps a DNA connection to the crime scene; imagine if that existed here. Whose DNA *was* recovered from the scene? Could they say? Would they? No, instead, prosecutor Gingold would say this to the court and to the public audience: "It's no wonder that *no forensic evidence* was found just because what the defendant intended to, [sic] which was to cover up the murder, actually happened...couldn't get any forensics in the house..."

The truth was that the MCSO investigators had collected *over 500 pieces of physical evidence*, including the bloody handprint, sex kit from Ms. Hermann's body, used condoms near her body, and a partial profile from the gas can—none of which came back to me, which was why they stopped all other testing and went with the "he destroyed the evidence" position. In fact all of the other hundreds of pieces of evidence, including hairs and fibers collected from Ms. Hermann's body, and residue collected from under her fingernails, was sitting safely down the street in the MCSO evidence warehouse. Gingold had accidentally said earlier in his speech, "the fire itself didn't actually reach the bedroom where Mary was, Mary was Liz's middle name."

The fire actually didn't destroy any evidence.

Not only did I not destroy the evidence—nobody destroyed the evidence. The state was just too lazy or fearful to test it. But I sat there quietly listening to Gingold lie.

Gingold had spent the last three years telling Judge Barton that he was still waiting on the DNA results from Kelli Raley at DPS, a first batch, and a second batch, and analyst notes, and now he was saying there wasn't any DNA.

When Gingold was done putting on his show, and after the court taking a recess (this was going to be a long day), Rick put Braden, then Brenton, then my dad on the stand. For a Q&A that would be, in his words, "more factual in nature," than what we had seen so far.

They were predictable, establishing that I was a good person.

Then he allowed my cousin Tina, my brother, my mom, and Jill to speak from the podium.

Tina explained at length, that all of my family was waiting for my release and that "there is a huge support system for him to come home to."

My brother explained that I'd taught him "pretty much everything [he knew]," and that I was like a best friend" to him.

My mom said she was "dumbfounded" why we were even there, stating "now, I don't—we don't think he [Justin] belongs here."

Jill spoke by far the longest. She said she was my wife, and because she did that in open court, amateur reporters from the small town newspaper in Cave Creek, the Sonoran news, would use this to write articles that would malign her and make her life even harder, as if a young businesswoman who is now by herself due to a tragedy needs more of a challenge in life.

She emphasized that I was always her best friend, and that she'd never seen violence or aggression of any kind from me, whether we were "sober" or in "full-on party mode," and then she finished up with this:

"I just want you to know he is not a violent person. I don't know to this day what happened. I can't believe that he is responsible for it. I can't and I don't. I wouldn't have started communicating with him again had I even had an inkling that he could possibly be responsible for that crime period. And I just beg that you really look into some of the facts of the case and some of the areas that are still questionable (such as the red-haired arsonist, the unidentified male who left two used condoms near her dead body, etc.) and give him the opportunity to have a life because he will make the best use of it that any human could ever make of it. I'm 31 years old and we want children desperately...I just beg you to take all of that into consideration." Thank you.

My Chance to Speak—Barely—At My Sentencing Hearing

Then I approached the podium and spoke at length, emphasizing how important hope is, telling her honor that she had complete control over our entire lives in that moment and begging her over and over for help.

She never asked me if I was innocent. My family had already said it. Her honor didn't go there, so I left it alone. I didn't want to be insensitive toward Ms. Hermann's family or antagonistic to the court. I would have my lawyer touch on it later, if he would.

When Judge Barton finally spoke she said some peculiar things when speaking of and describing me, the defendant, she said, "He has no prior violence whatsoever in his past." She spoke about a DUI I received when I was 19 years old, and said, "But, again, there is no indication of any violence whatsoever out of this individual."

Regarding future dangerousness she said, "Do I think he poses...a danger to society? I do not. I think some people described Mr. Lunsford as true evil...I have seen true evil in this courtroom, and I don't believe that Mr. Lunsford fits that bill."

The Alford Plea

If anyone in the courtroom that day, after noticing the oxymoronic complexion of this case, was wondering why the unlikely Lunsford was going to prison for it anyway, Public Defender Rick Miller explained, diplomatically, how and why a coerced

Alford plea works in modern America upon a client who maintains his innocence. He said, "I usually have pretty good *silent control* and that's where I am in this case... this is one of those cases that keeps me up at night. Mr. Lunsford has maintained his innocence...he didn't plead guilty. He didn't plead no contest out of any disrespect for the court or the victim's side. He pled no contest *because that's the reality of this system* where the death penalty takes control and drives the train. And where Marci and I are trained and we go all over the country and we learn that if you can ever get a plea—and here it was as second-degree plea—you do it. And you get there with your client. *However you need to do that*, you get there. Because we have seen the whites of the eyes of Maricopa county jurors who have been screened for capital cases and know where that goes."

In Maricopa county, only people who believe in the death penalty may sit on a jury in a capital case. Rick went on to say, "I support my client. You are never going to see him again."

Judge Barton retorted, "I will be long retired before he gets out of prison, Mr. Miller, so I don't have to worry about seeing him again." I cringed when she said that.

Sentence—Twenty-Three Years In Prison

Then, she sentenced me to 23 years in prison, 18 for the one count, 5 for the other, running them consecutive because, she said, "There is a completely separate crime. This is an instance where long after the murder occurred, hours after the murder occurred, he chose to return to the house and burn it down." She said this despite the fact that there was no county M.E. issued time of death, "No estimate or evidence of time of death" according to Detective Paul Smith, grand jury indictment. And, I was in prison that evening.

But after this 3-year rigmarole, what the hell. What was one more lie out of the government's mouth? After the crushing 23-year sentence I went blank, I think I was shaking my head "no" involuntarily, with big, sweeping movements. No hugs were allowed. They grabbed my handcuff chain and pulled me over to a clerk whose desk was positioned directly in front of the defense table and told me to sign here, here, and here...and as they did I felt Marci put her hand on my upper back and swipe back and forth a couple of times telling me something about God having a plan for me, some disingenuous gestures in front of the local news camera, making it look like she had concern for her clients, even the worst of the worst. It was the first time she'd ever been nice to me, or acted nice to me. It was unwanted. But she'd gotten what she wanted, she settled a hard case and avoided a lengthy trial, she was in a good enough mood to fake it.

I don't remember Rick saying anything.

But I felt bad for my grandad, Dick Lunsford, who was sitting directly behind me the whole time and had just heard the Judge hand down a sentence that would mean that he wouldn't see me at home again for the rest of his life. All of this while recovering from a blow to the head, courtesy of the Channel 12 news guy who was late and hastily entered the courtroom swinging his camera equipment around. Accidental sure, but it seemed indicative of the way the Lunsford family was now being treated in light of this controversial case. Of course, the local media would do, and had done, much worse to us with their cameras. They showed up at my dad's house for days after my arrest.

I don't remember the two-hour trip back to the jail that day, through the underground tunnels and cesspool holding tanks. When I got back to the pod I went over to Spinner's cell and spoke to him through the door. He was waiting all day to find out what sentence I'd been given. Everybody was. The *Arizona Republic* had run articles about my case in 2008 and again in 2011 when the change of plea and sentencing occurred. Everybody in the jail had read about it.

I told Spinner, "23." He said that was more than what he thought it would be, rather than the 16 my public defender had told me I'd probably get.

Going into the sentencing I had no idea what it would be. Sometimes I thought Judge Barton would give me the max, 34 ½ years, because it was such a horrendous crime, but at other times I'd think that maybe she would notice the absence of evidence, acknowledge at least the possibility that I was innocent, and just give me the minimum--ten years.

All of us, my immediate family and friends, were hoping in the back of our minds that Judge Barton might intervene in our behalf, stop the whole thing, and essentially say 'Whoa something's wrong here, there's no real evidence against the defendant,' and ask me directly to explain my position and why I had signed a plea. But of course that never happened. They were too close to closing the book on a hard case, and by "hard" I mean extremely unclear.

Arizona Department of Corrections

••

Alhambra Staging Facility—Buckeye Arizona

A few days later I was taken downstairs for the last time, staged in a holding tank, put into the back of a windowless van with a dozen other inmates and driven from the downtown area to a place called Alhambra a few miles away.

Alhambra was basically a staging facility within the Arizona Department of Corrections. It was in Phoenix, where inmates from all county jails in the state were brought for evaluative purposes in order to determine which prison unit they will be sent to. It was a place where inmates were on the edge of their seat. Everyone was concerned about where they were going. People from southern Arizona did not want to go to prisons hundreds of miles away from their families, in northern Arizona, because they knew that it meant they would get less visits, if any. For some it meant that they might lose their girlfriends, or wives, or kids. ADOC did not care. The computer did not care.

I personally wanted to go to any unit in the Florence complex because it was closest to my family, and many of the guys I had studied and worked with and grown close to had been sent there. I pictured myself going to Florence, and prayed about it, so I just felt like I was going there. It would be the best place for me to make the transition into a new community, to climb the ladder back up into a position of being liked and respected, which in and of itself can mean life or death in prison.

During my three years at the maximum custody jail I had gone to great lengths to develop the ability to defend myself and survive any vicious attacks, should that ever occur. I tapped into my knowledge and experience as a gym rat and football captain in order to do enough pushups, pull-ups, squats and lunges to maximize muscle mass.

And I did abs and sprinting exercises in order to maintain agility and athleticism, so that even if I went into the cell with King Kong and he bounced me off of every wall I would still survive. That was my main goal, just to survive. With how wrong this whole case had gone, and how I was wrongfully snatched away from my family by MCSO and kept for years, there was no way on God's green earth I was going to die in the middle of it, away from my family, and let the story end like that. I was coming home, period. I refused to accept anything less.

When I entered the jail at twenty-six I was a little chubby, but by the time I left and headed into prison at twenty-nine I was a very muscular 220 lbs with a full six-pack, eight pack on a good week. I was usually the muscular guy in my living area and now I was ready as I would ever be to enter prison with minimal problems. Even with the chatter about every organized crime group in Arizona, and some private citizens, wanting to murder me when I got there, with the blessing of the authorities, that old chestnut.

The nine days I spent at Alhambra were the longest of my life, up to that point. I went from sensory overload in the overly lit jail leading up to sentencing, to being packed into a dark, humid tank with 25 other inmates and only 15 bunks. Many had to sleep on the floor. We were under fed, constantly hungry, deprived of sunlight, clean air, and showers, and were allowed no phone calls or contact with our families.

I worried about Jill, and my dad, brother, and mom. This would be the first time we'd went without speaking and it made every day difficult. I had to work hard to get a look out a small window, through metal mesh, across an empty field to the back door of some business a couple hundred yards away. I saw the occasional worker step outside and sit in the plastic chair to light up a cigarette in the 115 degree Arizona July heat. It was my first look at anything "public" in 3 years. I used to have a life out there I thought to myself, wondering now what kind of media and news stories Jill and our family were dealing with, without me available for moral support.

While at Alhambra I felt like I was being baptized into a new life, but a bad one, a twilight zone parallel of the human experience. I had crossed a threshold, I would be gone for at least years now, and my reality had changed. No more planning an RV road trip with Jill, no more looking forward to being with her. There would be no comfort where I was going, just hot, Arizona dust, old concrete, razor wire, hostile strangers and untrustworthy authorities. If I was going to survive where I was going it was up to me and me alone. A person cannot expect to fully depend on other people to fix or save his or her own life. It doesn't matter if it is a medical situation with a doctor or a legal situation with a lawyer; we are all responsible for our own well-being at the end of the day. We have to do our own thinking, our own research, our own deciding and our own acting. That is especially true for a prisoner. A prisoner cannot call anyone for help in *any* situation; a prisoner has to stand on his own two feet.

My goal wasn't just to survive; it was to triumph to beat a goliath that had taken my life. When all of the primordial prison machismo was gone—or not—I had to be a thinker, a researcher, a writer, an investigator, and it was going to be hard to be an intellect and a behemoth at the same time, but I didn't have a choice. I was realizing this in that hot, sweaty cell, in what society had deemed a human trash heap.

Yuma State Prison

On the ninth morning they filed us all into the chow hall, handing each of us a basic "go-bag" as we entered—a plastic trash bag with toothpaste and soap inside—they told us to have a seat. Sitting down I noticed a row of 50-gallon plastic trashcans along the south wall. Each one had a paper label taped onto it with an ADOC prison complex name written on each one: Florence, Tucson, Yuma, Kingman, Winslow, etc. The state of Arizona was full of prisons. Prison is the only real industry that Arizona has. The state has no natural resources. It is a desert. No more citrus, no more copper, never had seafood, so, they've taken up the practice of harvesting human beings.

The Arizona legislature, and aggressive police and prosecutors keep those prisons full, right or wrong. I stared at the Florence trash can. How symbolic. We were all headed to our respective trashcans. We were being thrown away.

I was anxious when they started calling out names and trashcans, hoping they would call me each time they came back around to "Florence." Round and round they went. It seemed like it was taking forever for them to call me, and then it happened—Yuma.

Almost Killed in Yuma State Prison

I cannot explain what happened in my gut the second I heard Yuma, but every alarm in my body started going off. Something was wrong. It was like a panic attack, and it never stopped. For 2 ½ years going forward from that moment it would never stop, but it would keep me hyper vigilant, and that would actually save my life three weeks later, barely.

Sitting on the prison bus with my trash sack I felt a heavy sense of foreboding. Dread. The drive from northeast Phoenix to Yuma would take hours, and it would take me right past downtown Phoenix, where I had been housed in 4TH Avenue jail and brought to the court building for the last three years. The prison bus actually had windows, so I could see that familiar Phoenix landscape that I'd grown up with. Thunderbird and Camelback mountain to the north, the high desert mountains of Cave Creek, where my whole world was, thirty miles behind them, and the Phoenix city scape to my immediate south, which was on my left, with south mountain setting the back drop.

As I looked at the downtown buildings, among which I had been an earnest and naïve young college student at Phoenix college ten years earlier, I felt gloomy. I felt betrayed. I saw the hospital where I was born. I couldn't understand how the community could do this to me. It broke my heart. But that didn't matter, there was no time for whining or moping like a "sissy-la-la." I had to get to the bottom of this sense of foreboding thing, I had to figure out why every alarm in my body was going off.

I was always in touch with knowing why I was feeling however I was feeling on any given day. I was very healthy, kept track of how much I slept, what I ate, I prayed, meditated, and I tried to come up with an objective reason for this panic; there just wasn't one. I was a very spiritual person, but not wishy-washy, and not superstitious. I don't think God gives us signs or makes Jesus' face pop-up in a pancake on the stove, I don't believe in looking for a divine message in the dreams we have at night. But my goodness, I could not figure out what was going on with me at this time, so I just decided to pay close attention to everything around me going forward. As if I hadn't already.

After about an hour, we pulled off into the hot, dry Buckeye prison complex, where they would divide us up, put us on vans, and send us in different directions. Buckeye was a hub of sorts. They kept us in chain-link cages outside for hours, in the Arizona heat, over 110 degrees on any given day in July.

As they put us vans I was the only one from Alhambra going to Yuma. The other two prisoners getting on the Yuma van with me were being transported for disciplinary reasons from a medium custody (level 3) yard in Winslow, Arizona. We were headed to Dakota, a level 4 yard, where all the bad boys go—criminals who are so dangerous that regular criminals are in danger around them.

Dakota—A Level 4 Yard

Dakota was a controlled movement yard. That meant that it was not an "open" yard where the inmates could roam around within the prison walls with relative freedom. Going to and from chow and "recreation," we were arranged in a double-file line and marched from point A to point B. It was one level below a level 5, special management unit (SMU), which is isolation. A 4 yard is the most violent yard. Inmates have daily access to each other and do not have the "protection" that isolation allows. Not only do inmates have access or availability to one another, as in the *choice* to interact, but also inmates are *forced* to stand and march shoulder to shoulder with each other, making it the worst place I could have possibly been sent.

Due to ADOC guidelines, if I'd have been given a sentence of less than 20 years I would have gone to a 3 yard, much safer. If Judge Barton had not opined that the arson and the murder that I was charged with were committed "many hours" apart—even though the investigation hadn't established a fire start time or a time of death, her timeline was imaginary. She used that baseless idea to run the two sentences together, five and eighteen years, making it a twenty-three year sentence, instead of eighteen. I was headed to the 4 yard courtesy of Judge Barton.

We arrived at the Yuma complex in late afternoon, somewhere in the desert south of Yuma itself. Yuma is real desert. It is all sand dunes, it looks like Iraq, or the middle east, It doesn't have anything green or alive, save for the humans, who somehow manage to survive anywhere, just like cockroaches. Why they built a city and prison out there is beyond comprehension.

As we pulled into the complex on the lovely asphalt road that headed south toward the Mexican border I tried to think positive. A mile in, we started to pass the level 3 yards in the Yuma complex, Cheyenne and Cibola. I studied the chain link fences, the razor wire atop each one and the lifeless grey buildings within them. This place was death. It just looked like death, not a blade of grass, or a hint of anything to smile about anywhere.

As we kept going we approached the end of the asphalt road it came to a dead end at Dakota, the 4-yard. Dakota was the end of the line, the end of all civilization, if you call it that, nothing but rolling sand dunes beyond it, as far as the eye can see.

We drove past the 4 yard and looped around it to the back entrances, and stopped at the sally port waiting for the first gate to open. When it did we pulled up. It closed behind us, and the guard stepped out of the booth, checked us out, and opened the second gate.

We drove through it onto the back lot, all asphalt, and pulled up to the warehouse to await our state-issued blankets and "mattresses." A prison mattress is 28" wide, 6'long, 2-3" thick.

The yard was divided into two sides, east and west, which were completely sep-arated by a network of fences, each of which had a large guard tower in the middle. It was basically a 20' high brick building, 30' x 40', wherein two armed guards walked around the roof whenever inmates were outside.

The two other inmates were sent to the east yard, to building 5 and 6, and I was the only one sent to the west yard, building 8. As they opened the gate for me to walk off of the back lot and onto the yard it was like a ghost town. There was not a single other person out there, no guards, no inmates. I had no idea where to go. I studied the buildings looking for clues, while trying not to look new. The buildings were replete with narrow vertical windows, 5" wide, 36" tall, one for each cell, so it was impossible to know who was watching.

Each building was divided into 4 wings; A, B, C, and D. There was a metal detector in front of each H-shaped building, but no fence to force you to walk through the metal detector. Later I would see that guards and inmates just walked around it.

I found 8-B and approached the metal door on the exterior of the 20' tall grey building, after walking around the metal detector, since my mattress wouldn't fit through it.

There was nobody anywhere. I pushed a button on a metal speaker next to the door, but nobody answered. Now I felt like I was going to get into trouble. I wasn't used to this. In the MCSO jail they wouldn't even let me walk down an indoor hallway without an escort, now I was just standing around outside. It made me feel like I was doing something wrong.

After a moment or two I heard a loud metal "clank" inside the door itself the door jam, and with that sound the door popped open, just a crack. Hands and arms full, I stuck out a couple of fingers and pulled the heavy metal door open. With that, a hallway opened up before me, and prison opened its mouth to me, all concrete, with an elbow bend about halfway down. I didn't see any people, no guards, and no inmates, not a sound; just dead silence. As I started walking into the hallway I could hear the sound of the plastic cover on my mat dragging on the smooth acid-stain concrete floor. As quiet as it was, it echoed off of the concrete walls on each side of me. After I made the quick elbow turn in the hallway the dayroom of the pod opened up to me, big, spacious, with a high ceiling, almost twenty feet above the floor, which was recessed with steps going down to it. On the left I could see the control room, windows all around it, but since those windows were covered with vertical iron rods for the guards' safety it was difficult to see through. I could see some movement inside of it, probably an officer, and it looked like there was another pod—presumably 8-A—on the other side of the control room. Whoever was in the control room made no attempt to walk over to the window or speak to me. So I started scanning the room, all of the cell doors, looking for the number that was on the scratch paper in my hand, 8-B-21.

Ah. It was an upstairs cell. I would have to take the ascending stairs on my right, up to the 2nd tier walkway, around to the corner opposite door I just walked through.

The pod was dead silent, but I could see eyes in the occasional narrow cell door windows looking at me, sizing me up. I've never felt anything like the tension and intensity inside that building. It was overwhelming. It was palpable, more than a cloud or feeling; it was like an external, physical object pushing in on you. If you could imagine a cube of water in outer space, unaffected by gravity and holding its form, and you had to walk through that cube, that is what it felt like to walk through the heavy tension in the air. Unfortunately I could not walk *through* this cube of intensity; I would have to live *inside of it* for years, desperate, while sharing space with other drowning men.

As I approached cell door 21, which would be my new home, I wondered what kind of a celly I would get. It being a level 4 yard, he would be either someone who'd received a long sentence for a serious crime, or someone who'd worked his way up to the 4 yard through disciplinary and violent incidents. I wasn't afraid of any one person. I knew I was big enough, strong enough, and agile enough to handle myself with basically anyone. I might not always win, but I would be hard to kill, 1 on 1. I hate how theatrical that sounds but that was my situation.

Even basic prisoners, their number one priority entering prison had to be—don't die. With my situation as polarizing and unclear as it was I had to be extra careful, and it was not the toe-to-toe fistfight that I had to worry about, it was the sneak attacks. In prison or jail, if there is a "green light" on you, and the would-be attackers are not sure they can overpower you, they will adjust their approach, tactically. Just like in the old west, when dry-gulching and bushwhacking was a sure way to take out the target—the lonely rider who had no idea he was entering a trap. Now it's a cowardly attacker in prison who might sneak up behind a target and put a piece of metal in his neck. That would be easy to do on a 4-yard since we are forced to march in line. Obviously a cellmate can get you while you're sleeping. Eventually, you have to go to sleep.

When I get to door 21 and looked inside I was happy to see absolutely nothing. No person, no stuff, I would be living by myself for now. Perfect. Once inside I looked out the window, facing south to Mexico. I knew I could see into Mexico but it was impossible to tell where the border was because there was no wall or fence through the sand dunes. Ya simply can't build anything permanent on sand. The Mexican authorities were notorious for harassing and extorting American ATV-riders who had gone to Yuma to ride and unknowingly drifted across the border at some point. Nobody really knew where the border was on the dunes, there were no signs.

My dad and my brother and I used to go to Yuma with our ATV's and ride on the dunes south of there, the ones I was staring at now, through my prison cell window. It was sad, but I was wistful, I expected to win my legal case eventually, so it was encouraging to see that the world was still out there, it still existed. It was still waiting for me.

On the way to Yuma from the Buckeye prison I had thought a lot about the last trip that Jill and I had taken together. We'd went to San Diego to watch the Red Bull air races over San Diego bay. An amazing display of acrobatic WWII Bi-planes hopped-up on 2-stroke gasoline, flipping and turning through the inflatable obstacle course on the water. It was like butterflies playing in a field. Jill and I had driven on the same highway, the direct route from Phoenix to San Diego, which takes you through the southwest Phoenix farming town of Buckeye, right past the Buckeye prison complex south of there, through all of the desolate air force training grounds, through Gila Bend, and eventually through Yuma.

In the van from Buckeye to Yuma the guards had the local radio on, power 98.3, it was the first time I'd been outside and really heard music in three years. Coincidentally, a Kanye West song came on, "*The Good Life*," which used to come on when Jill and I were together. It had just come out back then. We probably heard it on the way to San Diego that morning, three years earlier.

It hit me hard. Man I wished I could go back and be in the cab of the truck with her on the way to San Diego again, on this same stretch of road. Now I was on a prison van with the singular goal of trying not to get killed in Yuma, with a 23-year prison sentence hanging over my head, the brutal murder of a stranger erroneously placed on my record. What a mess.

Where did it go wrong? How much of it was my fault? Obviously not the murder. But why was I out at a sleazy biker bar on a Monday night? Why at 26-years-old was I not at home with a wife and kids, like my own dad had been at 26? I regretted my carelessness.

I thought about my choices. Grandad had always said, "make good choices," that was his slogan to all of us grandbabies. And I had tried to. I got a place with an ex at 23 years old, planning an adult life and future. I worked hard for it. But when I caught her cheating it was like I was looking at someone I didn't even know, like looking at her for the first time ever. At the same time my dad had promised me part ownership in his company, which kept getting postponed, and postponed, and postponed…all the while all my buddies were at our favorite sports bars watching Phoenix Suns playoff games, enjoying those huge mugs of draft beer at Cocomo Joe's, playing pool afterwards, mingling, just having fun and it didn't seem to affect their lives in a negative manner at all. I felt like all the hard work I had put into my job and the ex was for nothing, it didn't bring me happiness or any positive developments so I said "forget it" for a while and prioritized having fun after that.

I met Jill, through Isaac, who had introduced me to the Sinaloans, so she already knew them as well, and we partied like Mark Wahlberg and Julianne Moore in "*Boogie Nights*" every weekend. Irresponsible sure, but what a bonding experience. But back then I was too nonchalant to commit to forever, and I wasn't sure we could grow a marriage out of that landscape anyway. So, she walked out and back to her ex to make a point.

I had a one-night stand with a stranger, who'd be murdered by an unknown perpetrator the next day, under the jurisdiction of a Sheriff's office that cared more about its own image than the truth. Now, I was just trying to survive until some kind of help came.

I loved Jill. When I received that first letter from her in that cell in Yuma I smelled it and held it to my chest. It smelled like sweet comfort, everything a woman means to her man, her husband. We were both sorry for our youthful indiscretions, both forgiving. We'd take it back if we could. We looked forward to being back together, hopefully soon. For now, I had to get situated at Dakota and begin my legal filings.

Within the first day or two in 8B21 at Dakota yard I had spoken to a couple of my neighbors through the vent, they told me we were on lockdown due to "quarterly searches." They were Native Americans, "Ta-dow" and "Curly" and they gave me an envelope and paper to write Jill.

A guy named John Stinson, aka "catfish," came to my door while he was out for a shower and asked me who I was. His face lit up, wide-eyed with a smile when I told him I was from Cave Creek. It turned out he was also from Cave Creek. We knew a bunch of the same people but did not know each other because he was four years older. We went to the one high school in Cave Creek--*Cactus Shadows*, at different times. Also, Catfish was in the harder drug scene back then so we did not cross paths due to the fact that I had been a fairly straightedge jock.

The only one of my close friends that he knew well enough to ask specific questions about was Garett Bischoff. I'd bought the motorcycle from him. He was the guy I was with at Gallagher's an hour before my arrest. Everyone knew Garett. His dad, Eric Bischoff, had launched professional wrestling, side by side with Vince McMahon. They had later began creating and producing reality TVv shows such as "*Home At Last*" with Billy Ray & Miley Cyrus, and "*The Devil's Ride*," a show about a biker gang, which men in prison loved to watch and analyze. Eric was constantly on T.V. on "*Smack Down*" in the middle of the ring with his nice suit and perfect silver hair slicked back, bellowing out his declares through the microphone. Being good friends with Billy Ray Cyrus and Hulk Hogan, we would see him on "*Hogan Knows Best*" showing up at Hulk's Florida home, or on "*Home at Last*" dropping in on the Cyrus's.

After achieving success Eric had bought a home on Black Mountain, the "*Island*" of top market homes elevated above Cave Creek. It was on the southwest end of the mountain, opposite the Parker mansion on the east side. Eric was traditional, so instead of pulling his son right into showbiz he made him get a "real job," which is why Garett was serving me beer and calamari sticks at *Hammerhead's* in 2008, across from the

Buffalo Chip. Garett and his dad would watch my situation closely to the end, proving to be some of the most genuine people I knew.

On that second day in lockdown at Dakota, Catfish offered me a bag of instant coffee and asked me if I was thirsty. "Absolutely," I said. I hadn't had a cup of coffee in three years. I had *never* had instant coffee, so I didn't know much to put in the tiny Styrofoam cup. Just to be safe, I put in a lot. I filled it about a third of the way up, enough for a half a gallon it turns out, and drank it. It cleaned the heck out of my cell for the next three hours, enjoying every minute of it. With my neighbors having their ghetto blaster on loud enough to seep through the vents, I might've done a jig or two between cleaning sections of floor.

It was madness, pure madness, and I knew I was in my element as long as that door stayed closed.

It would take some time to get visits and phone calls set up, about a month and a half, which was difficult to bear because I wanted to see my family, or at least talk to them, but at least we could write letters in the meantime.

It would take about two weeks to get my first commissary—food, shoes, and a T.V. In the meantime, I learned the routine, marching to chow each day, morning and noon, the guards delivering sandwich sacks at night. I was given a job working on the maintenance crew. It was the best job on the yard, offering a reason to be outside and moving around the unit all day, working with tools like I used to when building houses. It was a privileged job, one usually decided by seniority, but per D.O.C. policy an inmate had to have a clean disciplinary record for the preceding six months, no staff assaults, and back lot clearance. Out of the 800 inmates at Dakota, I was the only one eligible, since I had just gotten there and hadn't a chance yet to acquire any infractions.

Working maintenance, it was my job to push the cart from one task to the next, and to learn from the others. I would build a 3 million dollar custom home from the ground up but I really had no idea how to navigate a 40-year-old prison-plumbing chase. I got up on the roof a couple of times, working on swamp coolers, and enjoyed the view. Dunes to the south, desert mountains to the north, a bit of black top here and there, nothing beautiful. It looked like a good place to film the next terminator movie, but just being able to see far in all directions, regardless of what I was seeing, felt liberating. There was a freeing feeling in it. I began to notice that there was value and empowerment in the smallest things, so I began to look for more of it in order to gain strength and hope.

Each building received access to the recreation (REC) yard once every two days. The rec yard was about a one acre fenced in area, with razor wire, in the middle of the west yard. The east yard had its own. There was a full basketball court in the middle, with 3 8'x8' ramadas and some random pull-up bars and pushup stations next to it. And it had a dune-sand "track" to run on surrounding it all. Sand was everywhere.

When we went to rec the guards would escort us across the black top, to the rec-yard gate, unlock it, pat us down, looking for weapons as we entered, and then locked the gate behind us. The guards would not enter the rec yard at all. They observed us through the fence while the armed guards on the tower watched from above with live rounds. If anything happened to you on the yard you were pretty much toast. It was up to you to survive.

I was happy to be reunited with a set of pull-up bars and some push-up blocks. Working out and running had become an integral part of my life; I had continued doing it for years now just as much for my mental health as my physical health.

I loved running on the track, even though it was sand, because it was the first time in years I could run big laps. At 4th Avenue jail, the indoor rec room was so small I had to measure its perimeter by counting the 16" blocks at the bottom of each wall, then doing the math to realize that I had to run 104 tiny little laps to get my two miles in before my sprints and workout every day. I did that for three years.

At Dakota, I got to run in a straight line farther than 30 feet. "Yay" most people would say sarcastically, but again, it's the little things. I enjoyed playing basketball. I wanted to see if that 3-point shot I'd always had was still there. It was, and so were the dribbling skills. I also got a nice looking shiner from a new acquaintance named "Demon" playing a game of prison-ball, which is just basketball with no rules. It was all in good fun.

About two weeks later I got a surprise call from a guard who told me to pack my stuff up. I had to move to building 7. It was weird and unexpected. Catfish was surprised, curious, maybe a little concerned. There was no reason that I should be getting moved, I was almost comfortable in my studio apartment covered cell.

As I moved in to 7A-01 I met my new cellmate. His name was "Canada," although he was actually Russian. He was 6'1", 240 lbs, baldhead, black beard, and had just come down from SMU. He was in SMU for stabbing another inmate, for the second time around, was in prison for murder, was never getting out, and was fine with that.

If somebody really wanted me dead, and commissioned another inmate to do it, this could definitely be the guy, I thought, as I smiled and shook his hand, saying, "It's nice to meet you."

He was nice, polite. He was glad to be out of SMU. He offered me a bagel and some music, Shania Twain, since I hadn't heard any in so long. We talked about Spinner. They had known each other from prison when Spinner was locked up the first time.

A guy named John was also in 7A. John had warmed up to me in the chow hall the week before. He said he'd gone to high school in Cave Creek for one year and offered to help me get acquainted with some of the fellas on the yard.

On July 26th 2011, I headed out to afternoon rec with the rest of building seven. About 200 of us. It was hot, and I was already sunburned from going outside two days earlier, blisters and all. But rec was not optional. The population within ADOC was segregated radically. If you were white, and you did not go to rec, you would be beaten when the guys came back in. This was a rule within the other four races as well—blacks, Chicano's, pisas, and chiefs gravitated—because each race wanted to make sure they had as many soldiers as possible out there in case a riot "popped-off."

I remember this day specifically for two reasons. First, it was the first time that I really felt like peace of mind was possible in this horrible place. After working out head-to-toe and running, I was slowly walking laps waiting for our four hours of being locked inside the rec yard to be over so that I could go inside, shower, eat, and finish my letters to Garett and Jill. As I walked, I remember looking out towards the west and seeing that southwest sunset putting its golden touch on the horizon. For the first time, I began feeling like some real healing would take place here, much needed after what my family and I had been through.

When the guards opened the gate we filed out, and as a crowd, began wandering across the asphalt towards the "H" in front of the building, I was walking with "John."

Earlier when I had been jogging laps, as I passed the cluster of phones each time I noticed that the "fellas," the heads, were getting all worked up about something. One guy would be on the phone, then he'd put it down, walk over to the group, say something, and they would throw their arms up in the air and walk around in tight circles. I heard one guy, a "Torpedo," who I was sharing a workout station with earlier, all worked up, asking the head "Do you want me to go get it, do you want me to go get it right now?" The head was telling him to chill out, "not out here," he said. I knew he was talking about a shank and I thought to myself as I kept jogging by, "eeeww, they're gonna get somebody today."

I had no idea it was me.

As I entered through the crowded bottleneck created by the metal detector, it was hard to sift through all the orange t-shirt bodies, but I did. I shook some hands and started to go in.

John stopped me and asked if I'd made sure to shake everybody's hands. Then he told me the Torpedo had to hurry up. The Torpedo hurried inside and disappeared down the hallway. He was going inside to get "it."

Being polite I shook some hands in the crowded "H." John stood by the door with his back against the wall watching me. Something wasn't right. I felt like they were trying to control where I was, so I broke their spell and headed toward the door. John stepped into the door and hallway in front of me, as if he was simply headed back to his cell, walking in front of me with his back to me. When we got to the elbow in the dark hallway he turned in a flash and delivered a blow to the left side of my face and head that almost put me down. At the same time someone who was walking behind me got me in the back of the head. I was in the worst possible place. We were too far from the building for the clueless outside guards to see us, and the guard inside the building, in the control room, couldn't see us because of the elbow in the hallway. That's why they attacked me right there; they wanted to do it somewhere that it couldn't be stopped by the guards. I knew the Torpedo would be back with his piece any second.

I'd been in a few tussles growing up in Cave Creek. I won most of them, only really lost one, and had a right hook that would almost certainly end any fight once it was used. But I knew I had to get out of this hallway if I didn't want to die on its floor, so I out all of my effort into that.

Once I'd jumped out into the daylight I turned around to read them. They stood in the shadow inside the door, wide-eyed like hyenas. I knew I had to leave; the threat was real. Every threat I'd heard before sentencing might as well have been real.

As I walked past the outside guards I didn't even slow down. "I gotta go," I said over my shoulder. I needed to put as much distance between the sea of orange shirts inside the "H" and me as I could. I didn't want to be near an orange shirt and if one came near, I would be swinging. I didn't trust anybody now. No one in that whole yard. But I had no idea who was involved.

Then two guards handcuffed me and said, "What happened? Did something happen?"

They were clueless. They walked me to the back lot near medical and pulled up my shirt, checking me for stab wounds.

"Why? Was I supposed to get stabbed," I asked. I didn't trust the guards either. They told me that sometimes an inmate gets stabbed and doesn't realize it right away.

DDD—Dakota Detention Unit—"The Hole"

They then escorted me to DDU, Dakota Detention Unit, which is "the hole" for Dakota unit. It is identical to the other buildings, but the inmates inside never go to rec and get no visits. It is also where the SSU office is. SSU is the special security unit. SSU is to ADOC what the gang task force is to a police department. Their peers usually admire them. Among inmates they have the reputation of being the most hypocritical and corrupt staff within ADOC, providing prison heads with drugs and cell phones in exchange for a promise that those heads will not authorize any staff assaults or murders. Like every other human relationship on the planet, the one between the heads and SSU relies heavily on mutual beneficence.

The two guards put me in a coat closet sized standing-only holding cell and told me to wait for SSU. A little while later an SSU officer came in and put me in leg irons, then put a chain around my waist and attached my handcuffs to the chain. It had to be after 7 p.m. at this point. Rec was from 2-6 p.m. I could feel the left side of my face swell up, it felt heavy, I could barely see out of my left eye and my jaw hurt. I received no medical attention, but to be fair, I didn't ask for any.

After a while an SSU sergeant came to the door, opened it, and escorted me down a hallway to his office where another SSU officer was waiting. He sat me down in a chair directly in front of a desk; he sat down behind the desk, and began the interrogation.

I don't understand why they were interrogating me. They treated me as if I had done something wrong. They asked me who attacked me, and why they attacked me.

"I don't know, I don't know," I kept telling them.

And then, to my shock and awe, they started interrogating me about the murder in Cave Creek. They asked why I "killed" the person over and over. When I told them I didn't have anything to do with it, they got angry.

"Yes you did! Yes you did!" They kept saying.

"No I didn't!!!"

I started getting angry. They were accusing me of something I didn't do and they were abusing their authority. It made me so angry; it was so unfair. Just when I started to feel like the police had set this whole thing up, the SSU officer told me that if I didn't tell them everything they wanted to hear about the murder in Cave Creek they were going to send me right back onto the yard where I'd just gotten attacked. I sat there in my handcuffs and chains with a badly swollen face thinking, how can they abuse their power like this? I met them shout for shout in the yelling match.

Eventually, they took me back to the tiny standing-only cell and left me there to "think," as a last chance before they sent me back onto the yard. I was in trouble. I stood in that cell trying to figure out what to do, how to improve my situation, but I had nothing. I had no choices. I wished I could call my dad and he could somehow intervene, but my family did not even know what was happening, or where I was. I started to wonder how I was going to make it out of Yuma alive.

For about six hours the SSU officers kept interrogating me, trying to get me to confess to murder, and threatening to send me back to the wolves. Over and over. They took me back and forth from the office to the standing cell and back.

I assumed it was almost identical to what Gerald Coco went through during his 5 ½-hour middle-of-the night interrogation with Detective Paul Smith and his goons.

"No I didn't!"

"Yes you did."

"No I didn't."

"Yes you did."

No evidence, no reasoning, just a cop looking for a soundbite. I began to wonder if Detective Smith was behind this interrogation in Yuma. Why were two ADOC officers in Yuma concerned with what had happened in Cave Creek? Why?

I believed they would send me back to the yard if I did not confess. They had already shown me that they were willing to be corrupt. But there was no way I was going to confess to that horrible crime that I had nothing to do with. I stood my ground, went toe-to-toe with them and threatened them with a lawsuit, telling them that my family knew everything that was happening and would sue them if they put me back on the yard. I was totally bluffing, but it was all I could do.

As I stood in that cell I realized that somehow, my situation had gotten even worse than it was on sentencing day. I knew somebody wanted me dead. It appeared that someone in uniform was helping them. I now trusted ADOC staff even less than I trusted the inmates. I was suspicious of everyone. I had to be. Now I wondered if Liz Hermann had relatives who worked for ADOC.

And Detective Paul Smith. I already knew he was dishonest and didn't bat an eye at lying under oath to the grand jury and assaulting Gerald Coco to get him to change his story, I knew I was innocent, so how far would Smith go? If my case was reopened by someone outside Smith's circle, what would they find? How far would he go to prevent it? Was there something going on between the H.A. and MCSO at the *Buffalo Chip*?

As I stood in that tiny room facing the door trying to think through these things I saw the SSU sergeant appear. He didn't say anything nice, but he had this look on his face like he was finally done attacking me. Seizing the brief opportunity to perhaps connect with him as a human being, I looked him in the eyes and said, "Hey man, I *really* am innocent, I *really* didn't have anything to do with what happened to that person in Cave Creek, I'm a good dude. I would never do anything like that. I wouldn't even yell at or a hit a woman. And as far as prison goes I don't mess around with dope or politics. I don't assault people. I cause no problems for you guys. All I do is work out and bible study and try to help people. I don't know what's going on right now man, but you gotta believe me, you've got to help me"

He didn't really say anything, but a short-time later a couple of chunky white prison guards showed up, opened the door, and motioned for me to come out. "Step out," they said. t was the first time since I'd gotten to Yuma that I'd encountered an officer who spoke fluent English. Most of them were Hispanic. Some of them didn't speak any English.

As I stepped out into the hallway with them in the middle of the night, I asked them where we were going. They didn't say anything, didn't even look at me. As we walked down the hall, in the opposite direction of the SSU office, I got a look into the pod, "the hole," where I had actually been earlier that day with the maintenance cart snaking a drain. I could see eyes through the slits in the doors and windows looking at me. The guys in the hole knew something was going on, they had heard all the yelling and each one of them wanted to know exactly who I was, and what the situation was. Gossip is at a premium in prison, especially if it has to do with violence.

I was hoping that the two guards would not put me in this pod. I needed to get away from that yard as quickly as possible. It's one thing to be assaulted by someone you know, for a reason that you know, but when complete strangers try to take you out, and you don't know who ordered it, or why, or even who all was involved in the assault itself, it's a whole different animal. It's like living in Jurassic Park.

The two guards walked me out onto the asphalt back lot, in the hot dark one o'clock a.m. air. A white prison van was sitting there. They put me in the back seat, got in the front, started it up, and drove around to the other side of the back lot, directly in front of the building where I'd just been attacked. We sat there with the engine idling.

My nerves were at full volume. Why were we just sitting here, I impatiently thought. Where are we going—*are* we going anywhere? They had driven past the sally port, the only exit. What were these guards up to? What had SSU told them to do? And whoever had set up the attack, what was their role going forward? All I knew was I was handcuffed and shackled in the back of a van like a sitting duck somewhere in the desert outside of Yuma and no one I knew had any idea what was happening. I didn't have a friend within 200 miles.

The guards had their radios on. I listened to their radio traffic, unit wide. I heard an officer say they had spotted an "unidentified truck" on the perimeter.

'*What* is going on?' I thought. It was one a.m. There wasn't a good explanation for someone to be way out in the middle of the desert, right up next to a prison. I couldn't help but feel like it had something to do with me. What if the H.A. did think I did the murder? I knew they had a chapter in Yuma. It would be so easy for them to compromise DOC staff down here. Or what if *they* did it and wanted to prevent my appeal?

The van started to pull forward and we headed to the sally port. As we pulled up to it I saw headlights about 200 yards down the fence line to my left. Just sitting there.

The first gate opened, we pulled up, and it closed. The second gate opened, we stopped, and the guards got out, opened my door, and told me to step out.

"Nope," I said. I had been through a sally port before. I knew it was not necessary for the inmate to get out of the vehicle.

"Come on, we need you to step out for a minute."

In front of me was nothing but desert and darkness, all the way to Mexico.

"Not a chance." I said.

In my mind, I honestly thought it was a possibility that they would shoot me and say that I tried to escape. The headlights to the left were still sitting there, just waiting.

"For what," I wondered.

The guards at the open van door gave up and asked me to give them my ID, so I did. They showed it to the guard inside the booth, got back in the van, and we pulled out and went right. I craned my head up to look at the headlights in the rearview, which were following us now. I laid over to my right so that my silhouette could not be seen, having remembered an account wherein an Ontario Hell's Angel, mom Bouche't had somebody killed in transport, even killing a female prison guard in the process, shooting up the whole van.

Cheyenne Detention Unit—CDU

After about a hundred yards we went right at the elbow road and headed north, towards Cheyenne unit about a mile away. Cheyenne yard was on our left, but Cheyenne Detention Unit (CDU) was on our right, and that's where we pulled in. An officer stepped out of the door of the CDU (the hole), as we pulled up. I got out. They opened the back of the van and I saw a net bag full of my few belongings, including the clear plastic 13" flat screen TV I'd received the day before, and my one white banker box, containing my police reports and discovery. That box was my life; I couldn't file my petition for post-conviction relief without it.

The CDU guard took custody of me. He was a tall, athletic built white guy in his 30s and he treated me really well. My nerves were still overwhelmed, I told him over and over "DO NOT put anyone in the cell with me, and DO NOT put me in a cell with another inmate." He could see my swollen face, he could feel my intensity, and he gave me his word that he would keep me separate from others.

When he walked me upstairs and put me in a cell, I was glad to be in my own room with the metal door closed behind me. It was two a.m. I paced back and forth, around the room, trying to wrap my head around my circumstances. I didn't know who ordered the attack, why, or how they felt about the fact that I got away.

And I didn't really get away. I was still locked in prison, stuck in an 8x10 cell, in "the hole" with 50 other inmates who I did not know. And under a 23-year prison sentence that I was just beginning. Additional to whatever the attack at Dakota was about, I also now had a new host of problems due to the fact that I had left the yard. Anytime an inmate "checks in" or "P.C.'s up" he has a green light on him by every other inmate in the entire general population of the state's prison system. So whatever enemies I had 24 hours earlier, I now had about 40,000 more. I had no idea how I was going to survive in prison for the next 23 years, so I put all of my focus into trying to survive through that week.

I still had that overwhelming feeling of foreboding; every alarm in my body was still going off. All week long I stayed ready. There was an inmate who came to the pod every day, from the yard, Cheyenne, to work as porter. He was young and looked ambitious, in a prison way. He mopped the floors and made his rounds. He came to my door more times than I could count asking me questions, mostly small talk about why I was in the hole.

"A fight at Dakota," I told him.

It seemed obvious that he was keeping tabs on me for someone else. I didn't trust him, and I was constantly on alert for my door to get popped open.

In county jails, and prisons, cell doors are easy to manipulate and some of them don't even lock. State funds are always running short, and when there is no money for state parks and public libraries, prisons are definitely on their own. As a result, prison security suffers. ADOC director Chuck Ryan eventually lost his job over this specific problem—cell doors not locking in 2019 when ABC reporters broke a story using videos of these assaults in the Buckeye prison. Staff assaults occurred, and several inmates were killed this way. No one was safe in an Arizona prison.

For my first three days at CDU they made me pack up my belongings and move to a different cell every night. They moved me constantly. On the fourth night they made me pack up and get back in the van. They didn't say a word to me about where I was going, they wouldn't tell me anything. They pulled out of CDU and to my shock turned left, heading south. The only two things south on that road were Dakota and sand dunes. They were bringing me back to Dakota. They pulled in through the sally port, onto the back lot, and over to DDU, and asked me to get out. Then they walked me inside, I didn't say a word the whole time. They took me down the hall, towards SSU's office, but put me in the standing cell and locked the door and left.

I had no idea what was going on. I prayed. I had been praying since Alhambra. I had always asked Jehovah just to get me back to my family, just to not let me die out there away from them. And, believing that one must act in harmony with his or her prayers if he or she wants them to come true, I stood there in my cuffs and chains and mentally prepared for a fight to the death, hopefully not mine.

After about an hour they came back to the door, took me out, back to the van, and drove me back to CDU, putting me in a different cell. They pulled this maneuver twice during my nine days at CDU. During the "down time" at CDU, when I was just sitting in the cell, I was waiting for a violent fight to the death. Every clank of metal, every time a door popped open, I was ready. I knew that an inmate in my situation would typically make a weapon, but I did not want to violate my beliefs, my identity, so I tried to rely on my faith. When I couldn't find my faith I just waited, refusing to compromise, until I found it again.

In the morning I woke up early, to watch the sunrise over the black-char desert mountains some miles to the northeast. I looked at those mountains and I thought about my family hundreds of miles beyond them. I thought about King David, who ran for his life for months from King Saul, hiding in caves. King David had his own government trying to kill him, like me, and I was sitting in a cave, "the hole," just like he had been 3,000 yrs earlier. I hoped God would save me the way he saved David, but I realized now that from the moment I got onto the van to Yuma my odds weren't very good. I probably shouldn't have even made it out of that hallway at Dakota unit. But I was glad I did.

Every morning, after the sunrise, I looked forward to coffee and 30 minutes of CMT videos. They played Taylor Swift's "Mean" every morning. I loved it. So many people out there, "why they gottta be so mean," she sang. And then Jason Aldean's *"Dirt Road Anthem,"* reminding me of Garett and the desert bonfire parties we'd had growing up in Cave Creek, in the federal lands next to Tatum Ranch, by Jill's parents' house.

I drew a lot of strength from the sunrise, coffee, and music, and used it to write my Jill and family, encouraging them, telling them I was fine. I thanked God for the little things. Every day I was grateful just to wake up.

Prison Guard Sgt. Ruiz—Yuma State Prison—CDU

On the 9th day a Sgt. Ruiz took me into his office and sat me down, in shackles. He looked at his computer, looked at me, shrugged his shoulders and hands and said, "I can't figure this out man, what's going on with you? You're not a doper, you haven't been here long enough to get into debt, why is this happening to you?"

I said, "I got tangled up in a murder investigation in 2008, I had nothing to do with it. But from what the lead detective said in the presentence report, some pretty dangerous people might be involved. All I'm trying to do is prove my innocence…"

He said, "What people"

I said, "I can't tell you, I don't know anything and have enough problems right now."

He said, "Where did it happen?"

"Cave Creek."

"Oh, Hell's Angels."

And I just went silent. I didn't understand how a prison guard in Yuma immediately associated Cave Creek with the H.A. I had lived in Cave Creek my whole life and never seen them out and about, wearing their colors. I had heard plenty of stories, but was that what Cave Creek was known for? He went on to tell me that a Hell's Angel was running the yard down there and had probably ordered the attack on me. He said that he could send me to a protective custody yard but that it would take 60-90 days because of the waiting list. And, he said, it probably wouldn't be that safe for me there in this type of a situation anyway. He said that it was important that I get out of Yuma complex ASAP. If would sign a waiver to go to a sex offender unit as a hideout, it would be the safest place. He could have me on a van that night.

"Where are those yards?" I asked him.

"They're all in Florence," he said, "Eyman complex."

"Done." I said, "Where do I sign?"

He also had told me he had a friend in Yuma who was a police detective and was investigating the Hell's Angels, and asked me if I wanted to speak to him.

"No" I said.

I was on a van at 1:00 a.m. heading out of Yuma with no intention of ever driving through there again, in or out of prison. If Jill and I ever went to San Diego again we would drive around it. In the meantime, I had to try and figure out how to meet my deadlines on my legal filings. At my sentencing Judge Barton had told me that I had 90 days to file my notice of intent to file a petition for post-conviction relief (PCR). Now I had wasted over a month running for my life, and I still didn't have the proper paperwork. Jill would have to mail it to me, but she didn't have my address because I still did not *have* an address. She had looked me up while I was in CDU but the ADOC website showed no location under my name. For about two weeks, neither she or the family even knew what yard or complex I was in. When they called central office they said that they could not find me either.

She did get the 58-page letter from the though, explaining what had happened. Meanwhile, she and the family could do nothing but wait by the phone. ADOC would not allow any access to me. Heaven forbid I get them on the phone and ask them to send a lawyer down to Yuma.

Florence State Prison—Eyman Complex

Heading north out of Yuma they put me on a van with one other inmate, a Chicano guy who was getting released. He asked me where I was going; I told him they were just moving me to another yard for fighting. If he'd have known that I was going to Eyman he would have been expected by his pears to try to head butt me, or stab me with a golf pencil. Who knows if the guards would just let us fight or shoot us both?

I could not let any inmate know that I "checked in" and was going to Eyman, the sex offender complex. To General Population inmates, all S.O.'s are scum, the worst of the worst. Baby killers and bicycle seat sniffers. All sex offenders must die, was the mantra in GP, I had heard it many times. There were countless "youngsters" in each race chomping at the bit, eager to stab someone so they could get a political prison tattoo, earn their stripes. If you ever found yourself trying to explain yourself to one of them, or the heads, it was, way too late. They weren't looking for a reason to exonerate you. They were looking for a reason to stab you.

Some of them even studied books on human anatomy in order to learn how to aim for vital organs. So it didn't matter that I was a "good dude," a "solid dude," who had never been accused of a sex offense, almost nothing that was true about me had any value where I was. I was now a "hideout" on his way to sex offender island and I had no idea what it was going to be like. I imagined the worst of the worst, predators and creeps. I was sure now that I would not see my little niece and nephew, there was no way I could have them come in to visit around those people. I wouldn't even be able to have pictures of Jill posted on my wall.

The van stopped in Buckeye in the early morning hours, and they put me in a chain link cage with a bunch of other inmates. I was hoping they hadn't overheard the guards talking about where I was going. I was on edge the whole time.

Hours later they finally pulled me out, with a few other inmates, and walked me to a van by myself, where several guards stood, next to an inmate with a metal rake. They said to each other, "this one's a sex offender," pointing at me, and I watched the inmate with the rake act like he didn't hear it. Good, I thought.

We hit the road and headed east. We had about a 90-minute drive ahead of us to Florence. We sped down the black top high way, through the desert wasteland, with the Estrella mountains and south mountain range on our left, downtown Phoenix hidden on the other side of it. I'd seen the north side of these bare desert mountains a million times, downtown Phoenix in the foreground, but I'd never seen the backside. I had a lot to think about as we shot out through the desert, but at least I was finally going to Florence.

This was the only other time I'd ever seen the small Arizona prison town of Florence. The first time I was on my way to a mission with my cousin John, a youth minister. We went down to a small southeast Arizona town and put on a theatre for the kids at their local church, with "pastor Bob" and his wife, retirees whose dream was to build a church and minster to people. We had such a great time that week. A company called "Kid's Quest" had provided us with scripts and costumes; all we had to do was act.

When I was riding shotgun in John's church motorhome, as we drove past the Florence prison, I remember looking at it and thinking, "Man, how awful, I'm glad I'll never have to live there."

Just the same way the Yuma prison complex was the end of all civilization to the far south, so too was the Florence prison complex out here 90 miles east of Phoenix.

As we pulled up to Eyman Unit I knew it was the end of the line, both figuratively and literally. There was nothing but desert beyond it. And if things didn't go well here, there was nowhere else to go. You can't "check in" from checking in, unless you want to go do the rest of your 23-year sentence in a one-man isolation cell at SMU, eventually cutting yourself and clucking around your cell like a chicken.

They took me out of the van at Eyman unit and deposited me into SSU's hands. While in their office, SSU Sgt. Negrone looked me up and down and asked me, "Lunsford, are you gonna be alright on this yard?" I wondered what he was talking about. 'You tell me' I thought. I wondered if there was some type of initiation. Him and SSU officer Banghart gave me a cell assignment and told me to get to it. 4B111.

As I stepped onto the yard I noticed a large rec enclosure, similar to Dakota. This too was a 4-yard, controlled movement. Inmates were out at rec. As I walked by the rec pen a bunch of big, tattooed white guys came up to the fence, "hey wood, who are you? Where are you coming from?" they started asking me. 'Wow' I thought, 'this is exactly like where I just came from.'

"Dakota." I said, and that was not an answer they were anticipating. Dakota was a GP yard. It was extremely rare to get somebody coming straight from a GP yard to Eyman. Usually they were getting troublemakers from the lower level S.O. yards, now for all they knew; maybe *I* was here to get somebody.

I went into building 4 and found 4B111 empty. I would have my own cell again. Good. I could get a good night's rest. I went to bed early, and woke up early. Then I found the heads, all the tattooed, tough-looking guys and introduced myself to the main one, Cody Williams. May he rest in peace.

We went to breakfast, came back, Cody gave me a bunch of muscle and fitness magazines to read, and an old grandpa-like character, Warren Summercin gave me paper and envelopes to write to Jill and the family.

Things got moving along well while I was at Eyman. I was still uneasy around people, I was aware of the fact that at least some people wanted to kill me. I had PTSD from everything that had happened. I stayed on my workouts, staying muscular and ripped, and I slept with a long sleeved shirt wrapped around my neck just in case anyone tried to make a good on that online threat, the one saying the Aryan brotherhood was going to slit my throat. Every night for the next 2 ½ years I slept with my neck covered up. I also got a celly named Jesse Houser who would end up being a good friend for years. I found out that there were a lot of other people in the Eyman complex who, like me, were not S.O.'s.

When my friends and family finally figured out where I was, the mail started rolling in. It made people jealous. Jesse asked me if I had a fan club or something.

Jill and the family filled out their visit applications. It would take 6 weeks, the process was started over since I had been moved to a different unit, but I was just happy to be making progress.

Chapter 8

Appeals and Innocence

••

Post-Conviction Relief & More

Jill mailed me a lot of information on post-conviction relief and other avenues. I filled out the proper forms and wrote an eleven page, detailed letter to the Arizona Justice Project on Dec. 11th explaining my situation and asking for help, while waiting for a court-appointed PCR lawyer.

Before I knew it, my family was approved for visits and phone calls and for the first time in over 3 years we got to be together, to hug, and sit and eat together. Granny and Grandad came down to visit with my dad and Jill. We had pictures taken of all of us and talked about how to get me back home.

With some time in my cell at relative peace I got to start thinking about my case and working on it more. The *Arizona Justice Project* wrote me back, on Dec. 19th, Lindsey Herf and Katie Puzaukas, and sent me an application to fill out, which I did.

Most of the case was still a mystery to me. After initially assuming the Sinaloans did it, by now I'd realized that almost anyone could've done it. And with the attack on me at Dakota, and the way SSU interrogated me afterwards, I had to think seriously about the fact that Liz Hermann's whole world in 2008 was taking place at Larry Wendt's *Buffalo Chip* bar, the nexus between MCSO and the H.A…who knew *what* she was into, what she knew, who she slept with, what she witnessed. I really had no idea.

I continued to review the discovery, trying to make sense of it. I couldn't. It didn't make sense. I looked for clues within it, but there wasn't any. And the more I read over Gerald Coco's interview transcript the more confused I became. I couldn't understand why he said so many different bizarre things. All I could tell was that there was a break in dialogue during his second interview that completely changed the nature of what was being said. Still I had no idea what had happened during the break.

There were no DNA results, except for the "unidentified male" in the condoms, who was obviously with her after me. But nobody knew who he was. There were no prints, no idea who the redheaded truck arsonist was. No time of death, no cause and origin arson investigation, no fire start time, and I did not even know Liz Hermann. I had no idea what was going on in her personal life, and that was a problem. I had no idea what to tell any lawyers or investigators who would come to visit me. They all expected me to have the answers. From day one in 2008 it was like that, every legal professional put it on me to solve the case, to tell them what happened. MCSO Detective Paul Smith had not done his job, and now, that was my problem. Everyone expected me to do it for him.

Fair or not, that was the way it was, I had to get to it. Thankfully, I could get some help from my father-in-law.

David Delozier—Criminal Defense Lawyer —2016

During 2016 Jill's dad, David Delozier, had become more involved. David had been a criminal defense attorney in the greater Phoenix area for 30 years. He was a private attorney, and had some experience with capital litigation.

Living in Cave Creek, he knew of the situation in July of 2008, watching it play out on the news along with everyone else. Compounding that was the fact that his daughter knew the two young men who were spoken of as having been at *The Hideaway* bar on the night of July 7th 2008, Justin Lunsford and Sam Parker, and she knew the Sinaloans.

Originally, Jill said, She "defended [me] to the hilt" when her dad had jumped to conclusions based on my arrest. In September of 2008, Jill and her dad went to the MCSO GID to speak with Detective Smith. David offered an unflattering portrayal of me, emphasizing that Jill then had a DUI pending. Jill on the other hand emphasized to Smith, over and over, that between Sam and I, he was violent and I was the "peace-maker." She told Smith that Sam had done steroids, that she had seen a kilogram of heroin at Sam's condo, and that Sam looked like the description of the truck arsonist whereas I did not. She told Smith plainly; numerous times that he had arrested the wrong individual for the murder of Liz Hermann.

Smith produced a one-paragraph summary of his interview with Jill that read, "She had no information pertaining to this case." He didn't mention her statements about Sam Parker, or the kilogram of heroin. When David Delozier asked Smith at the end of the interview, "Do you want us to do anything for you guys," Smith gave a dismissive "no."

I found it bizarre that Detective Smith, a Cave Creek resident himself, upon finding that a local criminal was sitting upon an $80,000 brick of heroin, in his own backyard, didn't ask Jill to take a picture or sample of it, or at least refer her to a colleague in narcotics.

David's involvement became a lot more specific about a year later, in 2009, when a man knocked on Sam's front door, and upon Sam opening it, shot Sam once in center mass, and as Sam shut the door, falling back, emptied the rest of the clip through the front door. A mutual friend of Sam and I, Joey McGill, was inside the house when Sam was killed. He ran to rescue Sam from the barrage of bullets. He was hit in the neck and paralyzed. Later he died of complications from the murder of Sam Parker.

The shooter, Dwayne Rucker, needed an attorney so he hired David Delozier. Rucker told Delozier that Sam Parker was bragging about killing Liz Hermann. When Delozier's investigator Lee Damner, began interviewing Parker's associates, several of them said the same thing.

I had no idea that my attorney's suspicions regarding Sam Parker in 2009 were based on something that specific. My attorneys had kept that from me. Jill would only tell me about it after I was in D.O.C., when we would finally have contact visits and long conversations.

The day after Rucker hired Delozier, on Aug 11th, 2009, Delozier called an urgent meeting with my then court-appointed attorney Rena Glitsos. He wanted to participate in my defense. In a letter from Ms. Glitsos to Delozier, dated August 12th, 2009, she says, "I have serious concerns about allowing you to work with the defense on this case." She goes on to mention the fact that in November of 2008, Gerald Coco, the guy I was with all day on the day in question, had stumbled into his Delozier's office feeling that he himself needed a lawyer. The reason being, after my arrest, Detective Smith was finding big problems with the timeline in this case. The "arrest now investigate later" strategy was not panning out, so he really needed Gerald Coco to change his timeline again. Detective Smith's problem was that four months after my high profile arrest, he still could not put me in Cave Creek when the crimes had occurred. He had Coco telling him we were in Phoenix all evening, and Maxwell Piper, who lived in Phoenix, 30 minutes away from the crime scene, putting Gerald and I together, at his [Piper's] apartment. Until "it started getting dark," according to Piper, which in early July is close to 8 pm. The fire was started just after Ms. Hermann's death, at 7:30 pm. This was a problem for the MCSO.

So Coco, having gotten a call from Detective Smith in November of 2008 to do another "interview," wanted to bring a lawyer with him this time, in order to avoid a repeat of the dirt-parking lot tussle and threats that had occurred in his second July interview. Delozier accompanied Coco to that interview. The 20-minute interview consists of Smith pressuring Coco to change his timeline and Coco essentially saying, "I don't know what to tell you man, we weren't there..."

In August of 2009, Ms. Glitsos saw this as a problem that prevented Delozier from being able to help, ethically. She said, "I have additional concerns that you may have a personal interest in this case because of the relationship between Justin and your daughter."

It could be that Ms. Glitsos, tied up in her battles with the court and MCAO regarding issues of constitutionality, was not ready to get into the facts of the case, or any investigation into the murder itself. In the 18 months that she represented me, she did not interview any witnesses.

She ended her letter to Delozier by stating, "I regret that the meeting ended on an unpleasant note, but please be assured that my reasons for not wanting you to become involved in the defense have nothing to do with that… I trust that you will not be making any legal visits to Justin in jail and that you will refrain from any further action on Justin's behalf."

Judge Barton removed her from my case 4 months later.

So, I had an attorney who had come upon exculpatory information and wanted to help me, in 2009, but my court appointed attorney stonewalled him. At the time, she told me not to talk to Delozier because he would try to sabotage my defense in order to keep Jill and I apart. Not knowing the details at the time, I did not know any better. I did not have a copy of her letter to him, or his response, that he just wanted to help "an innocent man." All I knew was that he had represented Coco and thus may have been the reason why Coco had said those bizarre things; maybe he had coached Coco, in order to keep Coco out of harm's way, and to keep Jill and I apart. I really had no way to know.

Years later I would know better.

Delozier's final involvement in my pretrial situation was to accompany Jill to the settlement conference in front of Judge Sherry Stevens in February of 2011. Mike Gingold was furious at Rick Miller that day. He didn't know my wife's dad was an attorney. He wouldn't have let him attend if he did. Now sitting at Eyman in December of 2011, on the other side of all the mayhem and confusion, Jill and I decided to get David involved.

Arizona Justice Project at the Sandra Day O'Connor College of Law at ASU

Right away Delozier made a phone call to the Arizona Justice Project (AZJP) at ASU. He spoke to Lindsey Herf and explained the situation to her; the AZJP had just gotten my letter and application. David had read the 11-page, detailed letter I had sent them, and said that it was written extremely well.

The AZJP had policies. They focused on cases with a high likelihood of DNA potential. They were only able to help people who had exhausted all of their appellate options and had no lawyer. I was just beginning my post-conviction proceedings, but after speaking to David Delozier, Lindsey fast-tracked my case and began reviewing it, circumventing AZJP policy.

She assigned a smart and sincere young law student to the case; David Gurney.

While I was waiting for my first legal meeting with Lindsey Herf and David Gurney, Jill and I were becoming hopeful and excited, and I was starting to get used to the environment and people at Eyman. I was told I should be at Eyman for approximately two years, before my classification would change.

Then in January of 2012, just 4 months after I got to Eyman, an officer told me to "roll-up." I was being moved to another yard. He wouldn't tell me which one. I didn't sleep much that night. I lied awake and thought my way through a lot of different scenarios. There were the obvious dangers, the threats I had received and what had happened in Yuma. There were basic challenges that every prisoner faced. I would have to be introduced to and become familiar with hundreds of new inmates, who I had never met. And I would have to maintain my focus and mental sharpness regarding my case, so I would be ready for my meetings with David and Lindsey. (David Delozier will hereafter be referred to as Delozier)

Cook Unit at Eyman Prison

When I arrived at Cook unit, a level 3 yard, I could not believe what I saw. It was huge, open, 1,500 inmates walking around everywhere. It was like a city. There was no real separation between the two sides of the yard, north and south, like there was at Dakota. It was a wide-open 10 acres of yard with grey, one-story buildings surrounding it. There were basketball courts, softball, soccer, horseshoes, bocce ball, a small and large track for running and countless workout stations. It looked like a public park in the suburbs, sans grass.

My first thought was, "Wow, some people out there in the free world would probably be angry if they knew that this prison was just a really big playground." But there were people everywhere. I had been in controlled movement for four years so I was not used to having that many people walking around me. This was a completely different dynamic, large and elaborate. I would learn that every yard was like this, as if it had its own complex organism. It was like an elaborate network of electricity. You had to work your way into its current, and blend, without getting shocked. Every open 3 yard was like a motion picture, full of color, movement and noise, but it never ended, never stopped moving. It would be a big adjustment, coming from a stagnant 4-yard.

Fortunately, within 5 minutes I saw a friend, Keawe (key-ah'-vee) Cox, who I had studied with and worked out with at Eyman. He was like a little brother to me, and he had gotten rolled-up a week earlier.

"What's up big bro!" he said, in his excited, Philipino charisma.

He walked with me to my new building pointing out people and names along the way. There were a lot of guys who attended our bible study services and were happy to meet me, which made me happy. I loved our faith-based activities and doing positive things with people.

Jill and I, and our family, would sit, talk, and eat with Keawe and his mom and sister at food visits, reminiscent of a backyard BBQ atmosphere. They would be our good friends for years.

Court-Appointed PCR Attorneys

"People who work for the government…work for the government." Me. In January of 2012 the court appointed an attorney for me, Eleanor Terpstra, from the public defender's office. I couldn't wait to talk to her. My family and I were eager to tell our story to a new attorney, and Jill and her dad were eager to show her the Parker confessions. After speaking to Delozier, Ms. Terpstra was very excited about the case. She scheduled a phone call with me soon thereafter, and we had a good conversation. She had a lot of work to do, we had to get my court appearances transcribed and mailed to us. Meantime I waited.

After about a month, I wrote Ms. Terpstra a letter, inquiring of an update. I waited several months to receive a letter back from her, which I did receive on June 1st of 2012. It seemed like we had wasted a half of a year.

And we had. In her letter, she apologized for not getting back to me sooner, and said she had been re-assigned to a different division within the PD's office and would no longer be representing me. She then referred me to her former supervisor. Ultimately, the public defender's office filed a motion to withdraw from my case because, they said, they had been either formerly representing or currently representing at least seven of the witnesses in my case, in their own respective legal situations.

I had no way of finding out which of the seven witnesses they were, or what their charges were, or when those charges came about. Whatever the details were, the public defender's office had a conflict of interest so again, I was left waiting, with no lawyer. I had now been in prison for a year.

Almost two months later the court appointed the Office of the Legal Advocate to represent me, assigning "attorney" Colin Stearns on July 20th, 2012. I wrote him a detailed and heartfelt letter five pages long. I told him about an e-mail I had received a copy of, which private investigator Lee Damner had sent to Delozier in 2009 enumerating that friends of Sam Parker had said that he had confessed to the murder. I told him about the coercion that my primary alibi witness, Gerald Coco, had been subjected to during his 5 ½-hour interrogation.

I told him "I need to know immediately if your office will employ Damner to follow up on these and other leads. He is qualified for OPDS funding and has rapport with Ms. Racz and others in this small town. I need him to secure statements and a DNA match to the used condoms located amid blood spatter..."

Most notably, in a letter I wrote to Colin Stearns dated Oct 3rd, 2012. I stated, "another suspect, who Sam Parker had admitted knowing, was the victim's boyfriend, "Nate." A DNA match needs to be obtained from him; chances are his DNA is in the condoms..."

A fascinating coincidence, in this letter, the "Nate" I was speaking of was Paramanathan Renganathan, the young man from Bali, Indonesia. In a 2010 interview with my attorneys, Sam Parker, when asked about "Nate," admitted to knowing him and connected him to two other suspects in this case, Andrew Phillips and Max Piper.

The name "Nate" appeared in this investigation numerous times, but police investigators and defense investigators alike always just assumed it was Renganathan, never asking for a last name or following up. This became extremely important seven years later, when we found out there were actually two "Nates." As I wrote this letter to Colin Stearns in 2012, I emphasized the DNA in the condoms because it proved that I was not the last person with Ms. Hermann. It had to be her killer. My DNA was not found in her, despite that I admittedly engaged in unprotected intercourse with her on Monday night 7-7-08.

I mentioned "Nate" in conjunction with the condoms because my pretrial, 2nd chair attorney, Marci Kratter, had told me specifically in her plea advice a DNA match from the condoms to the boyfriend "Nate" would exonerate me.

In the same letter to Colin Stearns, I emphasized the need to interview *The Hideaway* bartender Rebecca Ball Harding, regarding statements she had made about seeing the victim at *The Hideaway* with another man, "Nate," on 7-7-08, *and* 7-8-08, the day of the arsons and the murder. This too becomes extremely important later, as it proved that I was *not* the last person seen with Liz Hermann.

I also emphasized the need to interview Tracy Warren, the victim's friend, who had told MCAO that they had the wrong guy in jail just before my sentencing, also mentioning her ex-boyfriend Justin Oddo, who she had purportedly gotten her information from. Tracy Warren had said she was afraid to come forward for fear of her life, but that Justin Oddo had told her exactly what had happened to Ms. Hermann.

Justin Oddo was fighting a sex assault case out of Scottsdale in 2009, and then died in 2012, after "falling" off a large cliff. No one ever interviewed him.

ereereeerereereeeeeereeeeeeeeeeeeeeeeeeeeereeeeeeeeeeeeeeee

In January of 2013 I received a letter back from Colin Stearns, dated Jan 2nd, 2013, stating, "I have been unable to find any claims for relief raised on your behalf." It was crushing. He offered a profoundly bizarre, and inaccurate, line of reasoning for his position: "Based on my review of your trial file, Mr. Miller has in possession of the "pay dirt memo" regarding Sam Parker. Mr. Miller interviewed Sam Parker and her [sic] girlfriend, Ashely. Based on Mr. Parker's statements and those of his girlfriend, Mr. Parker has an alibi for the night in question." "The night in question?" With no estimation of a time of death in a murder case, Mr. Stearns had somehow decided it happened at "night," despite the fact that the truck was burned at 2 o'clock in the afternoon and the house at 7:30 p.m.—and that Mr. Parker had an "alibi" based on his "statements and those of his girlfriend," which read as follows: "Regarding Monday night, when asked how long they stayed at *The Hideaway* bar after Ms. Hermann and I left, Sam Parker's girlfriend, Ashley Madison Baird said, 'Sam and I finished up the drinks that we had and walked home.'" She estimated in another interview that they stayed at the bar for "30 minutes," which would be 10 p.m.

In his own interview with detective Paul Smith (not recorded) on 7-22-08, eight days *after* my arrest, Parker gave a different story, stating that he "Styed at *The Hideaway* until nearly closing with his girlfriend." Bars close at 2 a.m. so, were they the silver cars outside of Ms. Hermann's house?

Regarding Tuesday, the day all of the crimes actually occurred, when asked what they did that day, Ashley Madison Baird's response was, "I have no idea."

Since when is "I have no idea" a good alibi?

Parker himself was never asked what he did Tuesday.

Neither one of them was ever asked what they did Tuesday night. So how Colin Stearns decided Parker had an alibi "for the night in question" was a mystery to me—until the previously mentioned smart, genuine law student David Gurney at the AZJP made it known to me later—Stearns never even read my file.

Colin Stearns never so much as commented on Tracy Warren, Justin Oddo, DNA testing, used condoms, "Nate," or my alibi, Gerald Coco, which was an actual alibi.

Presuming Innocence.

Presuming, as defined by the American Heritage Dictionary, means to have or show "excessive and arrogant self-confidence." Every American citizen—and non-citizen—has a constitutional right to the presumption of innocence. Presumption, in the same dictionary, is also defined as "1. Behavior or attitude that is boldly *arrogant* or *offensive*, effrontery."

David Gurney—Lawyer

David Gurney, four years into my nightmare, was the first legal professional from whom I received the presumption of innocence. I could tangibly see it on his face the moment our eyes connected as I entered Cook Unit visitation the morning of our first meeting. How *arrogant* of him, presuming innocence. How *offensive*, to the law and order culture. How *brazen*, to just assume, that someone who has been investigated by our trusted authorities, arrested, charged by a thoughtful prosecutor and indicted by a grand jury of his peers, under the watchful eye of a superior court judge, is actually innocent. What thinking person would boldly assume that an arrestee is innocent?

A genuine one, with respect for the constitution, who is not hamstrung by impulse.

In the interest of transparency I will make my own confession here, and this will be the only confession properly made—save for the years of youthful, fun-loving indiscretion that I willfully participated in before my arrest. I myself have, or *had*, never presumed a single arrestee to be innocent. I come from an authority-trusting background. We believed in "the long arm of the law," we always believed that justice was served, as shown on the local news, and any detractors were yahoos and conspiracy theorists. I grew up in a small southwest town where as a child, in the backseat of the car, in the early 1990's, during the first U.S. Iraqi war, I was reading patriotic bumper stickers on the pickup trucks around me that said, "Kill 'em all, let God sort 'em out." We never questioned authority, to do so would be offensive and un-American. If they said that an individual was a bad guy, he was a bad guy. Like every other American still breathing, I presumed guilt.

But after I was falsely arrested, I suffered greatly for the presumption of guilt, and so did my family.

A respected author said that actual innocence is like a unicorn. I think that means that we know how to describe it but none of us really believes that it exists, because it cannot be found. If actual innocence is a unicorn, then the presumption of innocence is its sister creature, the Pegasus. Despite what the law says, and what the constitution says, and what the evidence in a particular case might "say," as long as the law, the constitution, and evidence are all interpreted by human beings then the unspoken and undefined tenets of social sciences will trump the law every time.

For lack of time to research, people will go with their "gut," and the cynical species we are, we will always presume guilt—unless we're mindful.

David Gurney's genuineness was palpable. There is a difference between genuineness and politeness, and you can see it if you look for it.

The smile is the same but the difference is in the eyes, which somehow manage to appeal soft yet bright at the same time. Most legal professionals looked at me like I was a subject, which they would politely evaluate—except Marci—but David Gurney looked at me like I was a buddy from high school who he grew up with, like he cared about me. His sincerity opened up to the way for outstanding meetings and discussions. Early on, David and AZJP staff attorney Lindsey Herf met with me, had meetings with Jill and her dad, interviewed my attorneys, and went to the ground and interviewed the witnesses in my case, including Gerald Coco.

Simultaneously, and in between correspondences with Colin Stearns, Jill paid investigator Lee Damner $1500 to begin working on my case, specifically to find Krista Racz, the primary subject he mentioned in his 2009 e-mail regarding the Parker confessions.

David Gurney's Report

David Gurney wrote a preliminary report about this case based on his own review of the record, and him and Ms. Herf's meetings with myself. It reads in part:

> "Justin claims that he is innocence [sic] of the crimes to which he pled "no contest". He states that there is no physical evidence linking him to the crime. This appears to be true. He further states that DNA found inside two used condoms in Mary's bedroom does not match his DNA—this is also true, according to the record. that DNA was ran through CODIS, which produced no match. He also claims that the DNA from the gas can does not match his DNA…according to Justin, neither DNA sample was tested against Mary's estranged husband or her boyfriend at the time." Mary was Liz's middle name. Sometime later, after conducting witness interviews with Ms. Herf, David added summaries to his report.

> Regarding Dwayne Rucker, the individual who shot Sam Parker and Joey McGill, David's report reads, "according to David [Delozier] and Lee, this client alleges that Sam had confessed to murdering [Ms. Hermann] earlier in the evening."

After mentioning speculation that Sam Parker was "allegedly a patch holder with the Hell's Angels" the report goes on to say, "David and Lee also suggested that…Ms Hermann was working undercover to provide information on the Hell's Angels for the Sheriff's department at the time of her murder.

Although this claim might initially sound fanciful, it becomes less absurd when one considers that *The Hideaway* and *The Buffalo Chip* are known hangouts for Hell's Angels members as I myself witnessed when I lived in Cave Creek."

The report then mentions the "murder that took place in Mesa" wherein the female "victim was killed in a similar manner," specifically, "two Hell's Angels" took turns stabbing the woman dozens of times, nearly decapitating her for "talking too much"

After reading and hearing these things I couldn't help but recall a conversation that a guy named Ed Foley had with my dad the first year or two after the murder Ed said that a motorcycle mechanic who lived in the desert hills section of the Cave Creek area, which is the same section where Sonny Barger lived, told him that two Hell's Angels whose motorcycles he was working on told him, the mechanic, that they had killed Liz Hermann.

I also recalled a phone call that Sam Parker had with my brother, around the time I went to prison, wherein Sam told him that he now had "people who would kill for him."

Most concerning, was this excerpt from a report authored by an investigator who wished to be unnamed:

"We initially ruled out the Hell's Angels connection as far as I could tell at the time, but recent events have made me re-think that position. I had the opportunity (perhaps foolishly) to speak with some Arizona Hell's Angels recently, using a ruse. They indicated to me that the Hell's Angels and Sam Parker had colluded in the murder of Liz…"

Maybe they were just bragging, just toying with him. Maybe the mechanic was also just blowing hot air. Maybe Sam was exaggerating ina small town case where so many rumors had been inspired, who could tell what was real and what was not? But I also recalled countless police detectives declaring on television that they do not believe in coincidences. With such an unclear case, so little investigation done in the beginning, and the apparent boycotting of forensics, how could we ever make sense of this?

We would have to get right to drafting those motions requesting DNA testing like my 2nd chair, Marci Kratter, had suggested. Meantime, all of this Hell's Angels chatter did not help me to become more comfortable in prison. I had no idea who was who, who knew who, or what was what. All I knew was that I was not where I was supposed to be and I had to get home.

About two years after I met David and Lindsey, David issued an addendum to his report, mentioning that he had now spoken to Allen Bauer, Ms. Hermann's roommate, Gerald Coco, my primary alibi, Catherine Todd, Noah Todd's mother, and Tracy Warren, the friend of Ms. Hermann who told MCAO that I did not kill her friend.

Regarding Allen Bauer, the addendum reads, "Allen Bauer confirmed that Liz did in fact call him on the night of the murder when Justin was with her because there were two strange cars parked in front of her house. Her house is in a rural area."

In his original police interview with MCSO Detective Kristina Bucaro, Allen had said the same thing. When asked by Bucaro in his second interview if he knew of anyone whose cars matched the descriptions of the cars Liz had described to him, he said "yeah, Sammy Parker and his girlfriend." He called Sam a "scumbag" several times and repeatedly said that I was "a stand up guy." He also said Sam was "violent towards women."

Also, in his *first* interview with Bucaro, when asked who was with Ms. Hermann when she had made the phone call to him on that night Detective Bucaro writes in her summary, she said, "Allen told me that the person may have been Nate. A friend of Liz's, because they hang out frequently." Allen described Nate as a "white male."

I always thought it was weird that Allen described "Nate" as being a white male. I thought Nate was Indonesian.

Could there be two "Nates"?

David Gurney's addendum paragraph regarding Gerald Coco reads as follows. "Gerald Coco was hard to track down, but the Justice Projects PI was able to get an address for his brother. Lindsay and I showed up there unannounced, and he was spooked to say the least because he initially thought we were cops. Once we made him comfortable, he was adamant that Justin was innocent, and he confirmed the alibi he provided for Justin during the next day when Liz's car and home burned."

Regarding Noah Todd's mother, Catherine, David's report reads "Noah Todd's mother was a particularly difficult conversation. She is absolutely convinced that Sam, and possibly his father, killed her son Noah when he began investigating the case."

For what it's worth, I agree with her. Despite how improbable and dramatic it might initially sound, I believe the evidence indicates that it is a real possibility. I also spoke to a number of Noah's friends who all stated that he was an incredibly happy person and would never commit suicide.

The report goes on to say, "Tracy Warren was very reluctant to talk to me because she feared for her life. When I finally convinced her to speak with me—just a few months ago—she was brief, but indicated that she knew for a fact that Sam was the killer."

To say the least, David Gurney's report gave me a lot to think about.

Visitation

During the latter half of 2012, and most or all of 2013, I was fortunate to be one of the few inmates who was able to spend a lot of time in the large indoor/outdoor visitation area. Its capacity was 150 people, which was only 10% of the population of 1500, and it almost never reached capacity, so, it only required a little bit of math to deduce that most prisoners there—and all across the United States—do not have support from anyone other than their own fellow prisoners.

Most inmates come from low income, fragmented homes, if they come from a home at all. Many were "raised" in the broken and disturbing foster care system, orphaned by someone or something long enough ago for no one to care. With no one to stand up for them socially, and having inevitably made the exact bad decisions that we fear any child will make without the proper guidance—and many of the same bad decisions we still made anyway—these full-grown orphans have found themselves in the cross hairs of a predatory justice system, seen as easy prey by full-grown ivy-league educated suburban kids now called prosecutors, and the judges who raised them.

Once in prison these orphans of our society were seen even more so as easy prey, with the "prosecutions" of constitutional rights removed, left somewhere outside the brick and razor wire.

With disadvantages systemically, socio-economically, and practically, most of the men I lived with—some actually very good men—were marooned in prison, deprived of purpose and family.

For those reasons and many, many more, I cherished our family time at visitation. It was a family environment, food, drinks, cards and board games, walks outdoors, no cell phones.

Cook unit had a special arrangement that allowed visits on Fridays as well as the statewide weekend visits, which was great for Jill since she taught hunter-jumper riding lessons on the weekends. We spent quality time together every week, eight hours per visit. I was also able to see my mom, dad, stepmom, brother, niece and nephew, granny and granddad, and countless other friends, cousins, aunts and uncles. I was grateful that my niece and nephew, who were 3 months old and 22 months old when I was taken, were still lap-sized and zealous for toddler games. It was a breath of fresh air, a life-giving contrast, to the prison environment I lived in throughout the week.

On May 3rd, 2013, Jill's dad helped me by filing a pro-per motion for additional funds for investigator and other experts.

Investigator Lee Damner's Declaration

The investigator was Lee Damner, and in a declaration he authored, which was attached to the motion, he referred to his 2009 e-mail in the Rucker case (Rucker shot Sam Parker and Joey McGill) and explained to the court that he had discovered third party confessions to Liz Hermann's murder, and that it was his understanding that the information had been "passed along" to my public defender in 2009 "who then did nothing with it."

The e-mail stated, in part, "as I e-mailed you earlier, I contacted and interviewed Krista Racz her cell is --- --- ----. She is terrified and does not want her name mentioned to anyone. She is an ex-friend of Sam Parker. She has known him for 10 years.

She told me she was certain Sam killed Liz. He had implied that to her directly several times as well as other friends..."

He goes on to list several other "friends" of Parker to whom he confessed, according to Krista Racz, who continued to emphasize how dangerous Parker was, and that it was "common knowledge throughout Cave Creek that his parents were "high level drug dealers."

I remembered Krista. she had hung out with my group of friends during my senior year of high school. She had just moved to our small town from another state and had taken kindly to our school and social activities, with her easygoing charisma, developing crushes on my close friends Sam Gibbs and Dave Cohee. And most of the guys liked her back, as she was fairly attractive and unlike some of them, actually owned her own car, which was usually occupied with several of them who did not, as we caravanned from one desert bonfire party, or house party, to the next, each weekend. It was all innocent teenage fun well within the warm embrace of our small town.

Unfortunately, eight years later she was deeply embedded in Sam Parker's drug routine, and as a result, had become entangled in a murder investigation and scared for her life.

Bizarrely, the Damner e-mail went on to say of Krista:

"Her boyfriend is MCSO detective Dominic Ruello. He has much experience with Sam and can help us out. He has witnessed Sam's violence toward her and others." I found it incredible that while she was doing drugs at Sam's residence, for days at a time on some occasions, that her "boyfriend" was an MCSO *detective!* What was going on in Cave Creek, I wondered. Also, for Ruello to have "witnessed" Sam's violence "toward her, and others," they would have had to be somewhere together, all three of them—Detective Ruello, Parker, and Krista. Where did that happen? At a public place? Someone's house? And why wasn't there an arrest record of it?

Curiously, the e-mail ends, in part, with this. "Krista was very cooperative until a few weeks ago. She recently explained that she has not contacted us because several people who know Sam have contacted her and want to meet with her...asking about the shooting involving Rucker."

In Damner's declaration, attached to my motion for funds, he emphasized that he was perfect for this case because he had rapport with Krista Racz and others in the small town of Cave Creek. My family and I agreed, and were eager to get him involved, get him digging, and hopefully get some answers to the questions created by his 2009 e-mail, additional to the ones we'd lived with for years.

Just after we filed the motion asking for funds to appoint investigator Lee Damner, the attorney general's office cut funding from the Arizona Justice Project down to one third of what it was before that time.

As a result, the AZJP had to cut its staff and caseload down to one third, and this led to some changes. During my last meeting with Lindsey Herf and David Gurney in 2013, Lindsey explained that due to these changes at the AZJP, she was going to Washington D.C. for another job, and that David had drafted a motion for my case requesting the court to authorize DNA testing on a number of items. Also, since we had circumvented AZJP policy, my case would go "off in the wind," while the DNA request was pending. Additionally, Lee Damner, who had now gotten appointed by the court, could find the potential witnesses that the AZJP could not find, such as Krista Racz.

As the three of us sat at the table in visitation, where my family and I had just been sitting a couple of days earlier, I listened to Lindsey explaining these things, methodically, politely, but I couldn't help but notice that David was completely quiet and seemed to be angry. Seething inside, if I had to guess—which I did. I thought he was angry with me, and I couldn't understand why. I tried not to be distracted by it as I listened to Lindsey.

When Lindsey finished explaining everything to me, David began tensely explaining the DNA motion he had authored, which I was grateful for. I couldn't believe it had taken over two years, since my sentencing, to get the pursuit of DNA testing started, but after one year running for my life and the 6-8 months of inactivity with Eleanor Terpstra, and the wasted time of the Colin Stearns debacle, I was just happy to have something in my hand. We could finally get the testing that my public defenders had advised we should get.

After going over the request for DNA testing David told me a couple of things about the interviews he had done and what people had told him. He said that Gerald Coco and Kellen Coco sent strong and sincere support to me, and that Gerald said I was innocent, and that MCSO Detective Paul Smith had turned off the recording during Gerald's second interview, invited him outside for a cigarette break, 2 a.m, dirt parking lot, industrial part of Phoenix, then proceeded, with several other detectives, to surround him, begin yelling at him, calling him a "f—ing murderer" and a "murdering piece of shit," and threatening to give him the death penalty if he did not incriminate me, while shoving him to the ground and spitting on him.

I was shocked. I'd known that something suspicious and significant had happened during that break in dialogue just from reading the transcript, but I had no idea that Detective Smith and his goons would do something that brazen, (without even reading

Gerald his rights.) Obviously MCSO detectives felt that they could do whatever they wished, legal or not.

David also told me that Colin Stearns was "a joke." He said this with disdain. He said that when he and Lindsey interviewed Colin Stearns it was obvious that he did not even bother to read the file. He did not even know the difference between Gerald Coco and Sam Parker. His appointment to my case had been a waste of time and opportunity, and as a layperson it seemed that he had been appointed just to make it *look* like I had PCR attorney, who reviewed the file, and despite his earnest efforts, was "unable to find any colorable issues," said his format letter notice of completion. A review of the electronic index of record, of my case, makes it look like my sixth amendment right to have counsel at this stage was satisfied.

Now I knew why his letter to me about Parker having an alibi the "night of the murder" made no sense. Stearns did not read the file. He was basically a fraud. I became concerned for future defendants who would be represented by Stearns, and their trusting families.

On his way home that day David Gurney called Jill and indicated to her that he was frustrated that the AZJP was basically abandoning us, and that he would never leave us, he would never stop fighting for us and for my release. While he had investigated my case, the AZJP staff and law students would meet at the end of each week to discuss their cases with each other. David had always said that at each meeting, the other attendees wanted to hear what he had found first, what was going on with the Lunsford case. It was the most exciting one. It frustrated him greatly, being impacted by the case, finding strong indications of my innocence, and then having it stripped out from under both of us, and Jill, for purely bureaucratic reasons. He took that with him moving forward into his career.

Eight Bankers Boxes of Court Filings From 2008 to 2014

The one positive thing that came out of Colin Stearns' complete abdication of the role he was paid OPDS funding to serve in my case, was that when he was done making it look like he represented me, he was forced to release my entire file—eight banker boxes—to me.

I was eager to receive them, I could not wait to go through every page—approximately 4,000 pages per box, close to 30,000 pages total. I found that most of the file was made up of duplicates, and much of what was duplicated had to do with the "Capital Case Crisis" in Maricopa county from 2008-2011, Ms. Glitsos' filings regarding that crisis, and countless newspaper and magazine article attachments that went along with it.

Then there were countless copies of Dr. Paul Miller's 65-page report, establishing simply that I was a normal guy with a normal upbringing. Adjacent to that was an enormous amount of personal information, countless copies of pages from my high school yearbooks, there was even a local newspaper article and photo of myself, and several classmates from a 1988-second grade square dancing contest. And from 1987, a picture of myself at 5 years old—though it is hard to tell—dressed up in a Halloween costume.

What all of this had to do with solving—and proving—a 2008 homicide and arson was obvious—nothing. At first I found it surprising that a huge legal file would actually be filled with such a large amount of irrelevant information, but the more I looked back on what my attorneys and mitigation specialist were doing from 2008-2011 the more I began to realize that it was a perfect reflection of their activities.

That is not to say that the entire file was unhelpful however. In line with our theme of pursuing DNA evidence I stumbled upon a report documenting the existence and preservation of fingernail scrapings, and clippings, from both hands of the victim, which had been properly bagged by crime scene investigators. Somehow, detective Smith must have forgotten to include these in the discovery, which was disclosed to the defense while in pretrial posture.

I wondered why I was just learning about this evidence now five years after my arrest and two years after my conviction. It was due to a general lack of clarity regarding who knew what. It was impossible for me to know whether or not my attorneys had overlooked these documents, or if they knew about the nail scrapings and clippings and just did not tell me about them. At this point, it didn't matter anyway. We were about to put them at the top of the list of items we wished to have tested.

Due to the fact that Judge Barton had used the presence of "defensive wounds" in her Chronis ruling in order to support a finding of gratuitous violence and keep the death penalty in play in this case, the question of *whose DNA was under Ms Hermann's fingernails* when she died was one which we agreed all sincere factfinders would want to know. What could be more important in an up close, brutal, hand-to-hand murder, that involved defensive wounds, than whose DNA was left under the victims' fingernails while she was defending herself?

The most surprising thing however, that I saw in the file, was a picture of Liz Hermann attached at the bottom of her brother's letter to the judge, which stated that the picture had been taken the day before her passing. I was baffled. She did not even look familiar. The woman I'd went home with, I thought, had longer hair and a rounder face than the one in the picture I was looking at.

I could understand why I might not be able to give a detailed description of a person I'd only interacted with once, for a few inebriated hours, at nighttime, five years prior, but why didn't she at least look familiar? There should have at least been a sense of familiarity. I felt certain that I was looking at someone I'd never seen before.

Certainly, I'd gone home from the bar that night with Liz Hermann, right, I reasoned to myself. At the time I filed it away in my mind as a given that I'd went home with her, it just seemed like a solid fact. But it would pop up in my mind in the days and weeks to come, so, in order to put it to rest, I looked in my own memory for proof that she was the same one I'd went home with. With a lot of surveillance videos in this case, was there a video of us together? No. The only video of her, at Chevron at Carefree Highway and Cave Creek road at around midnight, Monday night, July 7th 2008, showed her by herself, buying beer.

What about physical evidence? Come to think of it there was none connecting me to her—no fibers, hairs or trace evidence on her person. Even though I'd had a one-night stand with someone, without contraceptives, there was no biological trace of my presence in the obvious places. None. There were no prints or DNA connecting me to this person's vehicle. Nothing connecting me to her phone, which was a centerpiece of the case, and amazingly, not a single print, hair, fiber, no touch DNA, not one thing out of 500 connected me to Ms. Hermann's house, bedroom, vehicle, phone or person. Nothing.

There was actually no evidence that I went home with her. I knew I'd gone home with *someone*. Why had I come to believe it was her? I started retracing my steps from the day I'd interviewed with police. I'd woken up, gotten a phone call, and someone said they had gotten a call from someone else, who said that there was a tragedy and that the woman that had perished in the situation was the same woman I had went home with two nights ago. And I just accepted it as truth. I didn't think to question it at the time. They had heard it at the bar. Detectives wanted to speak with me, after getting most of their own information from bars.

So I'd contacted detectives and told them it was my understanding they wanted to speak with me concerning a woman I'd left a bar with two nights prior. They said yes, and picked me up. I'd said I wasn't sure what her name was. They said "Liz." I said okay and we interviewed. They never showed me a picture of her to establish that we were talking about the same person. So, the only indication that I was with a woman named "Liz" was myself agreeing to it verbally after detectives told me that I'd gone home with a "Liz." This is why my first attorney Jeff Mehrens, was so opposed to any client ever speaking to the police.

In my own mind, going forward, I used the contents of my own interview to support the idea that I had gone home with Liz Hermann. In a bizarre way, it would've been even more difficult to cope with this situation if I'd have found out I lost my life over that small misunderstanding, which came out of my own mouth. In my interview, I seemed to have described a house similar to the one she lived in. Good enough. But could one of her friends have brought me back to her house? The hypotheticals were many, in a case with no forensic effort. There *was* a longer-hair brunette with us that night—Ashley Madison—could I have gotten them mixed up?

Years later, in 2019, PI Lee Damner would tell me that *The Hideaway* bartender he'd just interviewed said unequivocally that I did not leave the bar that night with Liz Hermann, that she'd left with a different man, and the bartender, for years, could not understand why police had arrested me.

The Hideaway video could have cleared this up years earlier, had it not disappeared.

Damner told me that *The Hideaway* "security" guy was in charge of surveillance at the establishment. He was given a job at MCSO and later became a detective. Jilting, for Damner, who also asked for surveillance from *The Hideaway* in regards to another homicide investigation, to no avail.

To this day it would not surprise me if a previously unnamed woman with long brown hair came forward and said that she was actually who I'd went home with. It would actually make sense. Amazingly, there are so many huge gaps in this case that there is actually room for such a development.

It was time to get some DNA testing done.

The Defense's Request for Post-Conviction DNA Testing

Armed with the petition for post-conviction DNA testing that David Gurney had authored, I now felt empowered. I shared it with Delozier, and Jill, and our family of course, and we then collaborated with attorney Evan Haglund (Disbarred in 1991) who Delozier had an ongoing work relationship with. Evan Haglund was perfect for our situation because of his time clerking for the Arizona Supreme Court. Delozier regularly employed Haglund's help in drafting post-conviction filings.

Additional to his experience in appellate scenarios, I knew that Evan also had experience representing at least one innocent client, unlike my public defender, who said he had never represented an innocent client and had "no idea" what to do with my case. Evan would know exactly what to do with it.

George Peterson and the MCSO

Interestingly, the innocent client that Evan had represented was also investigated and arrested by MCSO. The man's name was George Peterson, who had served as a U.S. Marine during the Vietnam war. A peace-loving man and property owner. He had enjoyed camping at the Verde river for solitude where he was mistaken for a transient by MCSO, who used their gut hunches to justify railroading Mr. Peterson for the murder of a woman, Alice Marie Cameron.

After Mr. Peterson was exonerated, it was found that the real murderer, Alex Garcia, before killing Cameron at the Verde river mesquite flats campground on October 18th 1991, killed nine Buddhist monks at a Buddhist temple in west Phoenix. All nine monks, and Cameron, were killed by Garcia for no apparent reason, with a gunshot wound to the head, execution style.

If you are wondering how Garcia managed to get away with the first nine murders in order to kill poor Ms. Alice Marie Cameron two months later, the short answer is that he benefitted from MCSO's incompetence, just like the real killer in my case. MCSO helped him, albeit unwittingly. In the case of the nine monks being murdered, MCSO avoided forensics and instead focused on coercing statements out of four other suspects—all of whom were wrongly arrested and later exonerated. The case is laid out in detailed and methodical fashion in *"Innocence Until Interrogated"* by Gary L. Stuart.

On September 27th 2013 we filed our 5-page petition with the court asking for seven pieces of evidence to be tested, and, for any future DNA hits in the CODIS system that are relevant to this case to be disclosed to us. The unknown suspect's DNA was found inside two used condoms next to Ms. Hermann's body was entered into CODIS.

The first item we asked to be tested was item #004; a Billy club found under the bed that Ms. Hermann was found lying on top of. The medical examiner noted a large, v-shaped blunt-force wound on the back of Ms. Hermann's head, and the Billy club was the only blunt-force weapon found at the crime scene. MCSO investigators found its context within the crime scene to be an indication of its relevance to Ms. Hermann's murder, preserving it as item of evidence #004. We believed that it should be tested for fingerprints and DNA. The second item that we asked to have tested was item #011, described as a "red plastic gas container, from the victim's house."

A diagram of the crime scene showed this gas can to have been found just outside the front door, where the fire was alleged to have been started. Both sides in this case agreed that it was used in the arson. MCSO deputy Kenneth Martinez said the gas can was not at the scene at 4:15 pm that day, when he was standing at Ms. Hermann's front door knocking, after having found her truck burning on the side of the road. Crime scene investigators arrived after the house fire then found the gas can at the scene.

For those reasons, MCSO Detective Paul Smith not only preserved the gas can as evidence, but also requested that it be tested by the DPS crime lab for DNA in 2008. The tests produced "inconclusive" results, however, there were enough markers to compare the partial profile to my DNA profile, and that comparison demonstrated that it was not my DNA on the gas can. It was an unidentified person.

In my meetings with Lindsey Herf, she explained to me that new testing had been developed in 2011 that could produce a complete profile. This technology was known as mini-str. We asked for that testing.

The next item we asked to have tested was item #071, "section of drywall with blood." In the original discovery and thereafter, this was described as the "bloody palm print." It was sent to the DPS crime lab for a palm print test but was found to be "lacking sufficient ridge detail for comparison." It was never swabbed for DNA, nor was the blood even typed, in order to determine whose blood it was. The victim showed no blood on her hands, so the palm print could not have been left by her.

Additionally, in cases involving multiple stab wounds, it is common for the assailant to injure himself. A common scenario occurs when the knife or stabbing instrument becomes slippery from blood from previous stab wounds and the perpetrator's hand slips from the handle, down the blade, and is cut.

Crime scene investigators seemed to agree that this was a key piece of evidence as shown by their efforts in entering a burning house and cutting this section of drywall out of the wall, carrying it out of the house, and following police protocols in preserving it as evidence. Most notable was the fact that this was one of the few items not only *collected* as evidence, but *tested*, much like the gas can, and the condoms.

To quantify importance of evidence, over 500 pieces of physical evidence was collected. As in any case, trusted investigators viewed and analyzed the crime scene, in an effort to discern which items were relevant to the crimes. In this case there were two crime scenes—Ms. Hermann's home, and the truck fire scene. Then they conducted the same evaluation at my house—and from my dad's green and silver dodge truck, and two other vehicles at our property, my cousin's white Chevy truck, and a tan SUV.

Who knows how many items or objects total, are present in two houses, four vehicles, and a side-of-the-road car fire scene. Five thousand, ten thousand? MCSO crime scene investigators narrowed it down to 500 important pieces of evidence, using their knowledge and experience, and no doubt taking into account each object's context within the crime scene, and blue-star luminal testing results, which are used to indicate the presence of blood.

Once that process had been completed, it was then up to the lead detective to evaluate all of the evidence that was preserved for testing, and decide which items to send to the DPS crime lab for actual testing, which required time and e-mail communicators. In this case, lead detective Paul Smith triaged the evidence, and began sending what he thought were the most important items of evidence in this case, starting with the gas cans, condoms, sex kit from Ms. Hermann's body, and the bloody palm print. That amounts to six items—out of 500. Roughly one percent. This means that any item that was *tested* in this case was deemed by Detective Paul Smith to be in the *top one percentile* of important evidence in solving Ms. Hermann's murder. Therefore, the state and Detective Smith, in July of 2008 and the months thereafter, deemed the gas cans, which had another person's DNA on them, the condoms, which had another person's DNA on them, and swabs from in and on Ms. Hermann's person, which did not have my DNA present, to be in the top one percent of evidence that would identify Ms. Hermann's killer.

We the defense agreed.

After their most relevant evidence tended to indicate that they had focused their investigation on the wrong person, whom they had unfortunately already arrested and paraded to the media, MCSO Detective Paul Smith decided that no further testing should be done on anything.

We the defense did not agree with that.

Going forward in our September of 2013 request for DNA testing we also asked for the "contents from the bathroom sink trap" to be tested, item #87A.

Investigators had removed the sink trap from Ms. Hermann's bathroom because they found blood smear and splatter in the bathroom and on its walls. They theorized that the killer used the bathroom to clean up, and possibly showered. They believed that the killer's DNA would be found in the sink trap. We agreed. Unfortunately Smith changed his mind after the first wave of DNA results and chose not to have it tested. We respectfully petitioned the court to override that.

Despite the fact that Ms. Hermann did share the residence with one other adult, her roommate Allen, and at times his two small kids, a layout of the house showed that Ms. Hermann was the *sole user* of the bathroom. It was *part of* the master bedroom. One could not use this restroom without first being in her bedroom, and there was a separate bathroom halfway down the hallway available for use by others.

The next item which we asked be tested, re-tested actually, was the "red plastic gas can" from Ms. Hermann's truck, item #150.

We knew this was a long shot, since DPS lab tech's had concluded that it was "too charred" for testing, unlike the gas can that was found at the house, untouched by fire, this one was *in* a fire. But we had to ask anyway.

The final two items that we required be tested were items # 213 and 214, left and right hand "fingernail scrapings" from Ms. Hermann.

In our filing we emphasized how important fingernail scrapings were in such an up-close and lengthy assault. Specifically one wherein the trial court, Judge Barton, had found that there were "defensive wounds" in her Chronis ruling. Additionally, Ms. Hermann had a deep gash in one of her fingers, and a broken fingernail.

Though it wasn't disclosed early on, years later a review of color photos revealed abundant evidence of a lengthy hand-to-hand melee' preceding the knife attack. This was probably why crime scene investigators meticulously collected fingernail scrapings and clippings in the first place. They were obviously important.

To bookend our request to test these items, Mr. Haglund and Delozier authored an introduction and statements of facts outlining the situation in the first several pages, and then legal arguments establishing that legal standards had been met for testing in the last several pages, with a bit of common sense evaluation for good measure.

They reminded the court that "no physical evidence links Lunsford to the July 2008 murder in Cave Creek," that "only a few items were submitted to the DPS crime lab for analysis," and that the results of which either "excluded Lunsford or provided inconclusive results." They reminded the court that I looked nothing like the red-haired arsonist that eyewitness Jimmie Larson described, that I had no history with Liz Hermann, no history of violence, that I had an alibi for the whole day in Gerald Coco, and that "Arizona's post-conviction DNA testing statute, A.R.S. 13-4240, is the legal vehicle through which defendants, like Lunsford, can make use of evolving DNA testing technology *in the search for justice*."

Haglund and Delozier also reminded the court that Ms. Hermann's roommate verified that she came home on the night of Monday 7-7-08 to find that an intruder, or intruders, who had never been identified, had been in her house that night leaving the back door open, and finally, that from the day of my interview forward I had always maintained my innocence.

If there was ever a case that warranted DNA testing this was it. If not now, then when.

Jill and the family and I were excited to have this legal document, the request for DNA testing, so persuasive and well written, and we passed it around for multiple friends and family members to see.

We were also excited that it was filed with a new judge, the Honorable Bruce Cohen, rather than Judge Barton, who had orchestrated the railroading. We were certain that this new Judge would be surprised and disturbed by what he saw.

It is a rare situation wherein *the defendant* is demanding testing and thorough investigation rather than the MCSO. In this case, the MCSO seemed to insist on confusion.

Upon the filing, David Gurney told Jill that things should be a lot different for us in six months; that excited us even more. It was the first time, since sentencing two years earlier, that we were given a time frame!

In the meantime I began meeting with Lee Damner and he became surprised and somewhat concerned, as he learned more about the case. Having come into the case

177

thinking a lot about the Parker confessions and finding Krista Racz, his focus now shifted to forensics and other science. He realized that both were completely absent, perhaps intentionally avoided, in this case.

He became further concerned when he learned about how Rick Miller and Marci Kratter used the threat of execution in order to force a plea agreement. Initially, I could see the doubts he had as I explained it to him—it really was unbelievable—but after he'd left, reached out to Ms. Kratter, who he knew personally, spoke to her about it, and heard it from her, he returned to our next meeting shaking his head about it. He said that knowing her personally, he didn't think she would have done something like that.

I would find out over the years that a lot of legal professionals, who had been out there practicing their craft, were in as much disbelief over some of the things that had happened in this case as we the laypeople were.

Lee Damner was also concerned about the coercion of Gerald Coco, which was both psychological and physical. Lee said he wanted to bring in law enforcement expert Dr. Tom Streed for that reason. Lee was perplexed by the M.E.'s report, which was bizarre, and suspiciously avoided time of death. It seemed incomplete, yet consistent with the underlying theme of avoiding specifics. In an investigative report by Wendy Halloran, formerly of local KPNX 12 (NBC), she later detailed routine, grave wrongdoing by this M.E.'s office. More likely in this case, lead Detective Smith simply told Schwartz, the medical examiner to avoid committing to a time of death—especially as he began to realize that I really was 20 miles away in Phoenix all evening.

Arson—Cause and Origin Investigation

Lee was also in disbelief that there was no cause and origin report, detailing the findings of the arson investigators. It seemed like a given. This case involved arson, and a cause and origin report was necessary, he explained, in order to glean details such as a fire speed and fuel load. This would determine actual start time for the fire, and show exactly where I was at that time, in comparison to the fire. This could prove my alibi. Additionally, details produced from the cause and origin investigation could then be compared to witness statements in order to verify whether or not those witnesses had actual information, or just gossip.

The police reports indicated that Phoenix Fire Captain Fred Andes was brought in by MCSO in 2008 to investigate the fire, but bizarrely, his report, if he ever wrote one, was not disclosed.

On November 4th 2013 we drafted and filed a request for funds for an arson investigator, which Damner said should have been done by my public defenders in 2008.

When I inquired of experts in 2010, Rick Miller had told me that the public defender's office could not afford it.

A few days later, when I told him my dad had offered to pay for it, Rick told me that "politics in his office won't allow it.," Then he asked tensely, "nuff said?"

I said no, "not 'nuff said.,"

I didn't understand why I couldn't have a defense. He explained that we didn't need it anyway, because the state's case was so weak. This was the same reason he didn't get all of the DNA testing done back then, and proceeded to change the subject, asking about mitigation interviews. This same conversational maneuver was performed by him numerous times. Later, I took it to be the "pretty good client-control" he boasted of having at sentencing in 2011, and probably the reason he was brought in on this "difficult" case in the first place.

Fifteen days after our request for an arson investigator, on November 19th, 2013, the state filed a continuance, asking for more time to respond to our request for DNA testing. All the while, we were continuing our overall petition for post-conviction relief, in an effort to get the DNA results first in order to incorporate them into our petition, which would ultimately ask that conviction be set aside.

In the weeks and months to come I experienced some good things and some bad things, as I'm sure could be said of every other human on planet earth. I started seeing Garett on TV, every Thursday night on *TNA Smackdown* on *Spile T.V.* His dad had finally brought him into the bizz. It was a small thing, but the familiarity goes a long way when you are stuck in a foreign place. Ninety miles from home might as well have been ninety thousand, a different planet, and a different dimension.

Jill and I went to bed alone every night and woke up alone every morning. Despite the positive legal progress and compelling statements our investigators received, and the hope it created, prison wore on us. The slow but unyielding current of the waters of time, (time apart,) was beginning to wear us down, as is inevitably true. Our weekly visits turned into bi-weekly visits, which turned into me waiting in my visit clothes, but never getting the call because she wasn't coming. It wasn't her fault, she was just busy, and tired, and depressed. Everyone was. My dad, my mom, my brother. But I always acted happy, always projected positivity because I believed it was important.

On the phone, I talked to Garett as if we were at the gym or in some other light-hearted setting. I told granny and grandad that things would change soon, because we all believed they would. The implied promise, which was never spelled-out specifically because it didn't have to be, was that I would get home to be with them while they were still alive. And it *was* a promise, if not to them, then to myself. This was my promise to all of my family members, who I still spoke to every time there was a family gathering at Granny and Grandad's; the hub of all family activities. I would call three or four times in a row and get "passed around" until I had spoken to and updated everyone. When I was there in person it was my custom upon entering to hug every single person in the house, twenty to thirty people, before finding a seat, and an RC Cola. Grandad always made sure that there were two ice chests on the back porch full of RC Cola's.

My cousin Ron said in his letter to Judge Barton in 2011 that I was the "glue" in the family, which took me by surprise, but I really liked hearing it.

Death In The Family

Then on a confusing night in 2013 someone came into my cubicle, waking me up in the middle of the night. I unwrapped the garment around my neck, pulled the blanket down, and saw two female officers at my bunk, telling me to go outside. They informed me that I had been authorized an emergency phone call with my wife.

My mind raced. After what had happened to Noah, I was terrified of what might have happened at home. The two officers would not tell me anything. They offered to escort me to the bank of phones near the chow hall about 200 yards away where I could see a group of inmates by the phones. I wondered what they were doing outside at 2 .a.m. When we got to the phones the two officers stood off to the side about 20 feet away and suggested that I call my wife, which I did.

When she answered, Jill told me that she was beside Granny, who wasn't doing too good. The rest of the family was there. Jill gave the phone to Granny and I spoke to her. She was weak but she was present. I told her it was me, and I loved her and that I knew she was going to pull through and that I would call again tomorrow and check on her. I knew it was supposed to be our last conversation.

The next day I called again and Granny was still alive. The doctors gave her a couple more days. I spoke to my COIII and found out that ADOC had an arrangement that would allow me to be transported for a bedside visit, as long as I paid for it. I explained that Granny was not at a hospital, she was at home, with in-home care. The COIII said that was fine, ADOC would contact local law enforcement (MCSO) and inform them of the transport and they could and would be present. She then did the math, gas mileage and wages, and said it would cost just over $500. I called my dad and told him, he sent the money. Then I called Granny and excitedly told her I was coming to see her. I told her to hang on, for me, because I wanted to hug her and give her a kiss on the cheek like I always did, and she said of course she would. About an hour later my COIII told me never mind, the transport was not approved, it wasn't happening. MCSO denied it.

I was really frustrated because I had just made a promise to Granny and she was waiting for me, and I did not have any more phone calls available for the day. I don't remember what happened in the next day or two that followed or in what order but Granny passed away waiting for me, not knowing why I hadn't shown up, just like my Gramma had four years earlier. Grandad was now my only grandparent left and we were all a bit worried about him. It had been a long time since he'd lived life without Delores. They had been married for sixty-five years, inseparable, and he wasn't getting any younger. I had to get home as soon as I could.

State's Response To Motion For Post-conviction DNA Testing

On January 14th 2014, the state filed its response to our request for DNA testing, authored by Maricopa Deputy County Attorney Catherine Leisch. The claims within it, and the bases for making those claims were so inaccurate that it was impossible to know whether she had not studied the file, or studied it and misrepresented it on purpose.

It started with her statement of facts. Ms. Leisch stated that Liz Hermann and I met at "her workplace." We met at *The Hideaway*. Her workplace was *The Buffalo Chip*. Ms. Leisch then stated we went to "Circle K" to buy beer. Wrong. We went to Chevron. A distinction without a difference maybe, but I had to, just one paragraph into Ms. Leisch's filings, wonder if she'd read *anything* about the case. Maybe she just talked to Gingold, or Detective Paul Smith, who was known for "bullshitting" when on the record, talking about the case.

Ms. Leisch stated that "Lunsford murdered the victim. . . sometime before morning," despite there being no established time of death. First responders had arrived on scene *the next night,* before the blood had even dried, and before lividity, or rigor had set in.

Piggybacking off the imaginary time of death, Leisch said, "Lunsford used the victim's cell phone. There was no evidence connecting me to her phone. Every person who was asked if I called them from that phone said no.

Still using the imaginary time of death, Leisch goes on to say, "Subsequent to the victim's death, some of his friends saw Lunsford driving the victim's white truck." The three "friends" she speaks of, who are always spoken of in this case, were Gerald Coco, Max Piper, and Andrew Phillips. None of them said that.

Coco never said anything about me being in a white truck, even after his coercion. He said he picked me up from the Circle K about midday. We rode in his white Monte Carlo the entire day—including at two p.m. while the red haired arsonist was burning the white truck. Coco dropped me off at home that night at nine p.m.

Max Piper was a guy Gerald and I had seen that day. Detectives, after coercing Coco, tried to pressure Piper to verify some of Coco's coerced statement. They approached him a week after the murder occurred. By then the whole town was saturated in gossip. They told Piper, "We've been told that he told you some things," But no one had even said that. Not even Coco. Piper said in his interview with MSCO, Um, not me directly. . . I was at work all day and um, apparently he stopped by my apartment. I talked to a few people . . . "He [Justin] didn't actually directly tell me anything.

The MCSO interview with Piper should have ended with that. Instead, they try to tickle out of him the rumors he'd heard since the murder occurred, and each time they got him talking about one they then tried to persuade him to say that he'd heard it from me. At this exact time, I was at the hospital with my family, gathered around my 22-month old nephew with my little brother, a single dad who was worried sick about his baby son.

Detective Smith who had coerced Coco Thursday night, and had since spent every minute trying to build an excuse to arrest me. My family and I had no idea what was about to happen the following Monday, when I was arrested. As we sat at the hospital, around little Mason, Smith and his buddies gathered around Max Piper, trying to get him to assign incriminating rumors to me.

Detective Smith asked Piper, "What did he tell you specifically okay?"

Piper answered, "Um, specifically he told me . . . I really don't know man." Detective Smith warned Piper. Because you don't wanna get wrapped up... in not bein' honest with us...let's get through the chase okay, let's stop this get it done, over with and get you back home."

"Right," He said. He had already told them I didn't tell him anything.

Piper was a small time drug addict and dealer. At that point he was guessing at what detectives wanted to hear. He said, "No he [Justin] wasn't with the girl. Well I don't even now. I believe that the girl was with the other party."

Detective Smith said, "We're just trying to confirm the story that [Coco] told us. Okay. I want all the details that he [Coco] told us."] Piper said, "didn't give me much more details"

Smith asked, "So what happens the second time he comes back?

Piper answered, "He said that, you know, there was, there had been a problem that day but nothing to worry about"

This was the point in the day at six or six thirty p.m. on Tuesday, July 7, 2008 when Freddy yelled at me over the payphone and said that he had to move because I'd brought a C.I. to his apartment. Piper is talking about Freddy. Their gut instinct makes them hope he's talking about Liz. They asked him, ""Did he throw a name out at ya?"

Piper said, "Yeah."

Smith asked, "Okay, was it a male or female name?"

"Male."

"Did he specifically tell you that that girl died?"

"Um, no."

Max Piper put a great bit of effort into explaining to the detectives that the only information he had was gossip from his roommate, Andrew Phillips.

"Did he specifically tell you that that girl died?"

"Um, no he took uh, my roommate told me that."

"You've talked to your roommate?"

"Yeah, in passing."

All of this gossip between Piper and Phillips came from brief conversations, "in passing."

MCSO asked, "What'd your roommate tell you?"

Piper answered, "That's where I was getting my information." After lengthy back and forths over different versions of rumors, even the detectives were confused.

"Okay hold on a second. Let me just back you up real fast. So you and your roommate are having this conversation about this girl's death or Justin?"

"Yeah."

"Anything else…that the roommate tells you?"

"No."

"Okay. So now how long is it after you have this conversation that Justin shows back up at your house?"

According to what Piper is saying here, not only was he not getting his information from me, but I was not even present while I was being discussed. I arrived "After this conversation."

They asked what happened when I came to their apartment. Piper said, "Um, we hung out for probably—I don't know it started getting dark, about then, so probably a good two and one-half hours later."

It is unclear to this day, how detectives missed the point of the above quote. I was at Piper's apartment it "started getting dark." That was between 7:30 and 8:00 p.m. in July. We were twenty miles away from the house that was being burnt at that exact same time. It is unclear whether detectives did not think it through, or whether they just assumed no one else would think it through.

Later in the interview, Piper, who should have been drug-tested before and after the interview admits this: "I, I kind of made a connection myself, you know, but I didn't and he [Justin] didn't specifically tell me"

Apparently Piper had, since the day of the murder, heard a version of the gossip that imagined Liz Hermann being killed out in the dessert, from his roommate—which detectives salivated at, in hopes of getting him to assign it to me.

Detective Smith, "Because now I am confused."

"Okay."

"You're talking like he told you the story about this whole desert thing."

"Justin?"

"Yeah."

"Did he?"

"Justin didn't give me most of the story . . . Drew already told me what happened. All I know is did you hurt anybody. And he's like, no you know I didn't do anything."

When the topic of who was driving Liz Hermann's truck was finally broached in Piper's interview—the basis for which Ms. Leisch claims "some of [my] friends" saw me driving it, the exchange between Piper and the detectives went like this:

"So he had the truck?"

"Um, yeah he—he wasn't with him—he didn't have the truck when he was at my apartment."

"Okay. So your roommate [Andrew Phillips] didn't say he drove up in this truck?"

"No. No. he was in the same vehicle that he came to my apartment in later on that day. Uh, older white Buick I believe."

"And your roommate said he was in that car?"

"Yeah."

So not only did I say I was in Gerald's white car that day from noon until 9 p.m. so too said Gerald, Max Piper, and according to Max Piper, his roommate Andrew Phillips.

Also, Kenneth Schaefer, my brother, and Krystal Boughman, and surveillance videos. Deputy County Attorney Catherine Leisch however, disagrees. She said I was driving Liz Hermann's white truck, despite eyewitness Jimmie Larson seeing said truck in the possession of a light-complected red-haired man at 2 p.m. that day. And how would the Judge ever know the difference without reading the actual interviews?

In her crafty response to our begging for DNA testing, Leisch goes on to say that my dad "owned a green and silver dodge truck that "matched the description of the truck that Lunsford drove away from the vehicle fire."

Eyewitness Jimmie Larson said that t the red haired guy got into a "green colored vehicle" and fled. Deputy Kenneth Martinez had said plainly in his on-scene report that Larson was "unable to provide anything further."

Ms. Leisch took it upon herself to provide something further. She pointed out that my court-appointed PCR attorney, Colin Stearns, had already "reviewed" my file and found "no grounds to file for post-conviction relief." Proof that none should be given.

She said that I pled "guilty" and "provided a factual basis for a plea," although the record shows I maintained my innocence adamantly and never provided a factual basis for my Alford plea.

She stated that I had "not suggested any reason why I would not have been convicted" if my DNA were not found on the gas can, or if someone else's DNA was found on them.

She stated that the gas cans were "purchased at a Circle K near the victim's house" and that numerous peoples' DNA might be found on them and so, they were 'immaterial' to guilt."

This was the first time anywhere, wherein someone stated that the gas cans were purchased at a Circle K. Gerald Coco's false statement was that the gas can was retrieved from my garage. Neither house had a garage. She said the gasoline itself was purchased from Circle K. Investigators viewed the Circle K surveillance and found that I was never there.

There was no indication whatsoever that any gas can was purchased anywhere that day. For all we knew, the two gas cans could have had the same owner for twenty ears, with no one else's prints or DNA on them. The only way to know was to test them. But again, Leisch says whatever Leisch needs to say in order to stop testing, fact or fiction.

Leisch also says that both cans are badly "charred" and "untestable." The can in the truck was charred. But the fact that DPS had already tested it proved that it was not untestable. The can at the house was untouched by fire and found outside. The fire was inside—a distinction Ms. Leisch failed to make. It too was already tested, revealing an incomplete profile, which excluded me. We asked for the improved mini-str testing developed in 2011 and suggested by Lindsey Herf of the AZJP. Leisch said no, it shouldn't be tested, arguing that there was "no unresolved issue" that such testing could resolve.

As for the bloody handprint, Leisch states that the claim that it could provide the DNA of Ms. Hermann's killer "is speculative." Then she refers to the "evidence" against me, "including Lunsford's statements to police, his statements to civilian witnesses, and his presence at the scene of the truck burning." She stated it "might show that another person had also been involved," but would not exonerate me.

She goes on to say there is no evidence that the Billy club was used in the murder. It wasn't tested. She said there was "no evidence of blunt force trauma to the victim."

She then lists the injuries but omits the blunt force trauma to the back of Ms. Hermann's head.

She states that the bathroom sink trap might have many peoples' DNA in it, speculating that many people had probably used it. She says, "therefore even if another man's DNA was found in the contents of the sink trap and Lunsford's was not, this would not create a reasonable probability that Lunsford would not have been prosecuted or convicted."

Regarding the nail scrapings, Leisch states that they are irrelevant because "no defensive wounds were found during the autopsy" and that there "was no evidence that the victim scratched her assailant." Judge Barton noted on the record the "presence of defensive wounds" to keep the death penalty on the table in 2010. Ms. Hermann had a deep gash on her finger and a broken nail.

To boot, Leisch gets even more creative and states, "Moreover, the victim's body had been hosed down during the fire and had already decayed before discovery." The body had never been hosed down. The RMFD interviews confirmed that. First responders arrived on scene before the blood had even dried. Besides that, don't they solve cold cases with DNA. On a roll, Leisch then states that if a hit on the condom DNA does ever come up in the CODIS system, no matter who it is, it should not be disclosed to the defense because we are not entitled to that under A.R.S. 13-4240 or under Rule 32. She closes by stating that we had shown no good cause for testing and "no good cause for why the state should be responsible for [the] investigation."

She did everything she could to help Ms. Hermann's killer.

Reading Ms. Leisch's response, opposing all DNA testing, was almost devastating for my family and me. We had gotten our hopes up, thinking that the prosecutor, whichever one happened to be assigned to the argument, would as a human being, recognize the need for DNA testing in this case. We of course hoped that as an individual she would recognize at least the possibility that MCSO had arrested the wrong person, and that even if she didn't, even if she felt certain that I was guilty, she would agree to testing in order to put the case to bed and avoid countless dollars and years of needless appeals.

Seeing that she didn't acknowledge those things made us question the justice system even more. Seeing her willingness to use numerous untruths to "win" her argument was even more disturbing. As a matter of necessity, we carried on our practice of looking for the next thing to have hope in, which is something that all people must learn to do, regardless of circumstances. Ms. Leisch may have opposed testing, but it wasn't up to her. The decision would be up to the Honorable Bruce Cohen, so we now put our hope in his ability to simply order testing.

Back To Eyman

Two weeks later, the first week of February 2014, on a Tuesday night, I was notified to "roll-up." The officers said I was being moved to a different unit, or yard. It was unsettling. I had gotten comfortable at Cook Unit. I had made many friends, some of whom I was really endeared to due to my faith-based activities, workout training, and all of the other little things that come with living, working and eating together for two years. Now I would have to go somewhere where I didn't know anybody. I would have to start all over again.

The officers wouldn't tell me where I was going. They said I would be leaving at 3-4 a.m. the next morning. I had heard rumors about ADOC moving a lot of inmates to different yards due to the prison riots that were taking place at the time. I had seen them move a lot of guys from Cook Unit.

On one morning, Jill and her friend Alley had come to visit, and within an hour all civilian visitors had to leave the unit due to a riot that began in the building I lived in. Jill left worried sick that day.

The next morning at 3 a.m. the graveyard shift officers rounded up about twenty of us and began escorting us to the other end of the yard, towards the back lot, through a gate, and into a chain-link cage. It was freezing cold, and starting to rain. During winter in Florence, AZ, the cold wind blows hard and unyielding, down from the nearby white mountains, south/southwest, removing the prison grounds of all living things. Everyone stays inside. But they left us out there for hours, and would not allow us to wear anything more than a single layer t-shirt, which was quickly saturated with cold February rain, while pre-dawn winter wind pounded away. We begged for relief, begged to be moved inside, into the empty chow hall on the other side of the block wall we huddled against, or to be allowed to wear our D.O.C.-issued jackets. Most officers ignored us, some told us to shut up, and few arguments ensued.

After a couple hours some guys asked to go to the bathroom, but were not allowed. This treatment was normal, but unnecessary. Some inmates began to mutter about "smashing" a "cop." The truth was this was how almost all staff assaults began. Like most other fistfights on planet earth, they were rarely unprovoked. It didn't make it right but it was causative. On this day though, as was usually the case, the inmate population, which by and large and contrary to popular stigma, is actually subservient and docile, just stood around and kept shivering.

The dynamic between staff and inmates was backwards from what I had assumed growing up. The officers went through their training learning ADOC's "keep the foot on their neck" philosophies. Typically, once on a yard, some would create unnecessary conflict. The inmates, most of whom just wanted to get this time over with and get back to their families. They would go out of their way to avoid conflict with staff. I myself would go out of my way to create positive interactions with the staff each day, offering a greeting, treating them like people. I found that usually even a very difficult officer could be nice given the opportunity—just like the most difficult inmate. We were all just people.

Some D.O.C. staff however, were just bullies who could not be reasoned with, especially the brass.

After three hours in the cage, at about 6 am, shift change occurred and all of the officers who had put us in the cage went home. By 7 am the day shift told us that we weren't leaving for a couple of hours anyway so why don't we just go back to our buildings for a while and try to warm up, as they effortlessly opened the gate.

I went to breakfast in the chow hall and saw my friend "Irish, "whose real name was Kevin. Irish was my barber. A good catholic, we had talked about God a little bit. He was also the "head" of the "white boys" on the yard and as such he asked me if I wanted him to talk to SSU and have them cancel my move. I thought about it. But ultimately I decided to go, and see if there was anyone who could use my help where I went. Irish told me to write him if I changed my mind, which I did about 3 months later.

When we finally got onto the bus and pulled out of the cook unit parking lot I knew that there were two possible destinations—the Eloy prison 15 miles away, or Eyman. I wanted to go to Eloy because it was a private prison and had better food. Plus, I had been stuck on the same plot of dirt for over two years and I really wanted to see the open road and new landscape.

We went about 100 yards and pulled into Eyman. My heart sank. They pulled in, put us in a big chain link cage, and we had a three hour re-run of the cage-episode from earlier. Eventually I received my bag, mat, and housing assignment—7D110. As I stepped onto the yard it was empty, a ghost town. I had forgotten how drab Eyman was. Devoid of all life. No color, movement, or noise. With nothing but gravel, grey buildings, razor wire, and an empty feeling. It literally looked like the place where people go to die. And for some people it was. This would be my "home" again. I had done nothing to deserve being moved to a higher custody yard. I had no disciplinary infractions, no write-ups, ever. If there was any fairness in the world it was too far away for me to see it. As the heavy metal door clanked shut behind me, locking me again into a tiny 8x8 cell, I felt like I had officially been wadded up like a piece of paper and thrown away, again.

Thrown Away

Eyman from 2014-2015 is not something I want to revisit. It was miserable, awful. There is nothing worse than being thrown away as a human being, in a place of isolation. The world becomes made up of basically two categories of people—those who believe you should be thrown away like refuse, and those who don't, but don't matter, because they cannot do anything about it. The absolution of the physical separation cuts slowly through the deepest and strongest of loves, and through time, severs the bonds completely that you have had your entire life, suffocating life-long relationships that should have never ended. To the extent that our lives are a beautiful mosaic of the relationships that they are made up of, one sits in isolation, watching his or her own self, losing that life one tile at a time. It guts you of hope. You watch yourself lose your own life, and in the mirror, one day at a time, you watch yourself die, your spirit leaving you, as you get older.

I don't believe in ghosts, I think that when people die, they really die. But if a ghost were a real thing then I would know what it was like to be one, to sit back, held back, just a spectator, as if in another dimension, watching, in your mind's eye, as your loved ones carry on without you, mourning the loss of you.

And like a "ghost," you can't help them. Sometimes all you can do is unsettle them, unnerve them, disturb them when they *were* finally about to find peace without you. You begin to realize that they would actually be happier, objectively happier. If you would just pass away. They could mourn you, mourn you once, and move on. The wife could remarry, the parents could not have to drive to the prison anymore, the brother could get an "RIP" tattoo and none of them would ever have to sit, shifting, through another awkward conversation about Justin. Where's Justin? How's Justin? Is he still appealing his case?

Yes, he's really innocent, holding their breath through that long pause trying to discern if the person believes that Justin is innocent. "He's dead," would be easier, and simpler. Eventually no one would ask. No self-pity, no feelings here, from a strictly pragmatic standpoint, a simple funeral would have allowed some finality, and it would have made a heckava lot more sense than what we were going through. That's why I don't want to write about Eyman. But I'm going to do it anyway because I said I would, I said I would write this book and I believe it's important.

Submersive Emotion

This poem is called, "*Yearning Poem.*"

> *It submits to calm waters*
> *So she lives in a bubble*
> *Since I was taken away*
> *Floating somewhere between*

The presence of my being
And the absence of my presence
Weathering waterfalls, caveats, tidal waves of hope
Leaky blue memories
Crash onto the sand, crawling to us
Fluorescent nostalgia
Intermittent black and whites
The heartbeat of hope, quitter now
But steady
In the distance faint echoes
The ghost of the battle drum
Breathing life from the fog
The heartbeat of hope
Gaining a life of its own
A life of our own
A life dead and gone
But among the remains
My existence remains
Caught in between with her
Till I'm with her again

This is my candid study on a wrongful conviction and on the people involved and affected on all sides. Mostly it is about people; why we do what we do, why we don't do what we don't do. It's about how we do and do not do to affect countless other people and by extension any people who are affected by those peoples' reactions. It is a forum on the human carnage that is left in the wake of cowardly selfish leadership, wherein not a single member of a collective ruling class has the motivation or resolve to swim against the current, to question one's own peers, and do the unpopular thing, at the expense of a family, a culture, that is so friendly and trusting that they've become easy prey.

Within just a couple of days I was called out for legal mail. This should be Judge Cohen's ruling on the DNA petition, I thought, as I walked across the empty yard towards the control tower area. As I got it and opened it I noticed that it *was* the DNA ruling but it was from the Honorable Karen L. O'Connor. It was brief, just two pages. "The court has received and considered defendant's pro per petition for post-conviction deoxyribonucleic acid (DNA) testing pursuant to A.R.S. 13-4240 and request for fingerprint analysis . . . The defendant has failed to set forth any factual or legal basis to support a finding that the requirements of A.R.S. 13-4240 (B) have been met . . . Therefore, it is ordered denying this motion."

I couldn't believe it. My lawyer, Marci, had told me I could go to D.O.C. and get DNA testing. She made it sound so easy. I couldn't understand why so far no Judge or prosecutor who we'd encountered seemed to care about the truth, the facts. And I started to wonder why we, in Arizona, even had a DPS crime lab, staffed with educated, experienced lab technicians, if we were not going to use it.

I found out after the denial of DNA testing that there had been no reply on our part, filed in reply to the state's response. Five days after the court ruled and denied testing, Delozier filed a motion for additional time to reply but it was too late, and his motion was denied.

At about the same time, the court denied our request for an arson investigator. There would be no arson investigation, no fire start time, for me to compare to my whereabouts.

On March 10th we asked for a schedule dictating when our overall petition would be due, and three weeks after that we filed a motion to reconsider the court's denial of our request for DNA testing, along with a proposed reply to the state's response. This was the reply that should've been filed two months earlier, in January. Both were denied.

In the meantime I had more meetings with Lee Damner, as Delozier and his paralegal, Daniel Inserra, another disbarred attorney, worked on the petition for post-conviction relief. Damner brought in Dr. Tom Streed. Damner had told me "get ready, *be ready*, a lot of people want time with Tom but cannot get a meeting with him." He also told me to "get with it" and not to be discouraged over the denials. He said that the courts wanted me to give up, "that is why they deny everything."

So I complied. I got with it. I studied and reviewed documents; I prepared to meet Tom Streed. But I could not speak about him over the phone, because he wanted to stay "off the radar." We started to get excited and feel hopeful.

At about the same time a close friend of mine, Troy Dixon, who was a pilot, caught wind of some of the details of my case and hopped in his plane and flew to Oregon. He met with Sam Parker and asked him if he'd committed the murder. Sam said he thought *I* did it. At the same time David Gurney was looking for Krista Racz. Six months later he found her parents. They said that they had not seen or heard from her in six months, since Troy Dixon flew to Oregon and spoke to Sam.

It was hard to tell what was what, from my prison cell, or if it even mattered. Lee Damner was looking for Gerald Coco. We were afraid that detective Smith would intimidate Coco into staying quiet because of a recent motion that was filed two weeks prior. Lee found an address for the Coco family in Payson, Arizona. Cindy Coco was working at a local grocery store.

Damner made the 2 ½ hour drive right away, went to that grocery store, but she wasn't there. He drove back home to Scottsdale that night, and back to Payson the next day. He found the apartment where the Coco's had lived, but it was vacated. The apartment complex manager said that the Coco's had abruptly left two weeks prior, leaving all of their belongings behind. They were in the wind.

A short time later Lee found an address for Gerald's brother, Kellen, in a low-income south Phoenix apartment. Lee showed up there unannounced and Kellen stood in the doorway telling him that Gerald lived there with him and was home, but that he should come back in a couple of days. So he did, with his secretary. They sat down for an eight a.m. interview. Lee said that Gerald was drinking beer throughout the interview. At one point; he got up and started rifling through a knife door in the kitchen, spooking Lee and his secretary, who both abruptly left. Lee was then convinced that Gerald Coco had killed Liz Hermann.

Lee then called a meeting with Delozier, who had represented Coco. He had accompanied Coco to his 4th interview, with MCSO Detective Smith in November of 2008—four months after my arrest. My Dad and Jill were at the meeting. Probably others, too. Lee told them that he believed Gerald Coco had killed Liz Hermann and that I was "covering" for Coco.

When I called Jill that day, she said, gravely, that something big had come up. She said it wasn't good, and that Tom and Lee had said that when they come back down to see me I'd better be honest with them and we were going to have a "come to Jesus talk."

What now, I thought. And then I just waited.

When they came to visit me they acted like nothing had happened. Jill and I didn't talk about specifics over the phone, so I wasn't aware of their newfound belief, but I was expecting a wrecking ball introduction to whatever topic it was.

When they finally eased into it, they were gentle. When they finally got to specifically stating it, I told them they were wrong. I couldn't believe that they thought I would choose to sit in prison for years while my family and I suffered, in order to cover for someone I hadn't spoken to in years and would probably never speak to again. It made me question how well thought out their ideas were in general.

They told me they had already spoken to higher-ups in AZ law enforcement, and the prosecutor, and that if I would sign an affidavit saying that Gerald committed the murder, I could get released with time-served. They told me that I did not even have to enumerate the details; they would do that, in a way that would "protect" me, and all I would have to do was sign it. I told them no.

They came back two more times in the days afterwards, still trying to talk me into it. "Think about your life," they said, "think about *Jill*." pulling on the heartstrings.

Meanwhile back at home in Cave Creek, grandad had developed dementia, and my dad and his siblings were enduring many emotional difficulties in taking care of him, now that he lived alone. He was playful, albeit forgetful. And he was confused. He would often wake up and ask, "Where is Delores," though Granny had been gone for almost two years now. It was hard for them to see him like that, and it was hard for me to hear about it on the phone each day. It was hard for me to hear my Dad, who had always been a pillar of the family, become so depressed.

We had learned after Granny died that she had written her will in such a way that it dictated that their house be sold upon passing of whichever one of them died second.

We were baffled. We couldn't imagine anyone else living there, at Granny and Granddad's house, right next door to my dad's house.

After Tom and Lee's third attempt at persuading me to sign a declaration to enable Gerald Coco's arrest, and me telling them that Gerald and I never even went to that house, and that they needed to find Krista Racz, they seemed to relent.

I wrote them a letter right afterwards and told them to quit asking me to do it. It was hard to say no to a ticket home, especially at such a pivotal time for our family. I knew that if I finalized my denial of their proposition they would not help me any further. I would have to just file my petition and wait, for a long, long time. I assumed I would lose what little I had left as a result of it, including Jill, my companion.

How long could I expect her to wait? We didn't think it would have taken this long, let alone a couple more years—at least. But I couldn't just lie, at another person's expense. It would violate my beliefs and my identity, and, having been through it myself, there was no way I was going to help them put another innocent man in prison. I thought about Gerald's mom, Cindy, and couldn't imagine getting myself released to start a life out there, knowing what she would be going through. I wanted true freedom, not fraudulent freedom with a bad conscience. Ironically, I was listening to a bible discourse that week, on CD, with my headphones on, sitting out on the yard by myself one evening, when the speaker said, "Someone who does not know the truth [about God] might offer you "freedom," but that's not true freedom…" and I had to marvel, because I knew he meant it as a metaphor, but for me it couldn't have been more literal, or timely.

Rick Porter—Lawyer

A few days after I'd sent the letter to Tom and Lee, Jill and I had a spirited phone conversation. She said that Tom and Lee had gotten another lawyer involved, Rick Porter, who used to be a prosecutor at MCAO and that a deal was back on the table, for time served, (without signing a declaration about Gerald Coco), and that there was to be a meeting at Porter's office on Friday, just two days away.

We were *so* excited. I was finally coming home! For those two days and nights I could hardly sleep. It was the first time in years I had lost sleep over being excited. I lied awake at night picturing all of the fun things we would do together, traveling, camping, visiting family and friends.

There was a Florida/Georgia Line song that had just come out, "Dirt," which mentioned carrying on a generous-long family tradition having to do with the land that was first purchased and excavated by one's own grand-father, and it really hit home with me because grandad was still alive and I believed that I could now go see him and maybe save his house, buy it, keep it in the family, my eyes teared up when I heard that song, it made me feel inspired again.

I could also help my brother, maybe help him get, or stay, on track. At the time, he was going through his own struggles, including depression. I did not have his new phone number. For months I did not see or talk to him, it was really difficult for me. My dad regularly told me that he was concerned about Dewayne going to the bars in Cave Creek, around who knows who and possibly drinking too much. Also he had abruptly walked out of his job, just quit on impulse one day. I was so worried I couldn't sleep, I didn't know where he was headed but he seemed lost, and I couldn't help him. I also worried about his two kids, my niece and nephew. Dewayne had had his heart broken through the revelation of a series of betrayals by my niece's mom and I knew he was in uncharted waters.

If cousin Ron was right and I really was the "glue" of our family, then I couldn't wait to get home and glue everything back together. Additional to my immediate family's struggles, some subtle dissention had begun between some aunts, uncles and cousins regarding the sale of the house and all that went with it. As someone who was always inclined to mediate and help everyone get along it pained me to see the beginning cracks of family fragmentation.

But everything was about to be solved at the upcoming meeting on Friday.

The Thursday night before the meeting I could not sleep, I could not wait to call Jill at 10:30 am, after the 9 am meeting, at which my dad, her dad, Mr. Porter, and Tom and Lee were to be present.

When I called Jill I could hear the absence of life in her voice, "It was a waste of time," she said. The beginning of the meeting was great, "yes we have a deal, yes he can come home," but just after they'd elevated Jill and my Dad's moods they hit them with, "We just need you to help us get Justin to sign the declaration."

It was a setup, just like the meeting that Rick and Marci had had with them and me right before "trial". Now another panel of legal professionals was using emotional extortion on my immediate family members to try to make me sign something. Jill told me that in response to their offer she had "went off on them" and told them that they could not understand our morals.

Hope was gone, again, killed in the blink of an eye. I knew we would never talk to Tom and Lee again, and I knew I was not coming home. Our circumstances had just changed, again, and I was not going to see Grandad again.

Thankfully, I was wrong about not talking to Tom and Lee again. After a couple of months of learning the forensic details of the case and chasing around and trying to sort out the subjective aspects, such as Gerald Coco, Tom and Lee both issued declarations, sworn affidavits of their own, in effect slapping their government issued licenses on the table and insisting that something be done here to solve this case properly. Simultaneously, Delozier and Dan Inserra did the same, drafting a petition for post-conviction relief, which would be much more thorough and all-encompassing than the request for DNA testing, which was limited to forensics. Tom Streed's declaration would mark the first time in this case wherein an investigator did an exhaustive investigation into Ms. Hermann's murder. Buttressed with Lee Damner's declaration, then grafted into the petition, we would finally have a thorough yet easy to understand request before the court to overturn this conviction.

Dr. Tom Streed's Declaration

In June of 2014 Dr. Streed completed his investigation into State v. Lunsford and produced his 17-page declaration, preceded by his 19-page curriculum vitae. His curriculum vitae was impressive. It mentioned his education, training, and experience, which began with his 24-year career with San Diego county sheriff's office (SDSO). While with the SDSO he received dozens of special recognitions, a couple of which read as follows: "One of deputy Streed's many areas of expertise is interviewing and interrogation, a subject he teaches at both San Diego sheriff's academy and San Jose State University... his ability to digest the interview and reach logical conclusions is uncanny...in this area, he is often asked to sit in on interviews or conduct the interview for other teams when special circumstances occur." And, "his reputation has extended to foreign countries such as England and Israel, which have professionally consulted with him on topics such as crime scene interpretation and sadistic death."

Clearly his expertise in interview, interrogations, and crime scene interpretation was much needed in State v. Lunsford. His curriculum vitae went on to list his teaching credentials, as faculty and adjunct professor at San Jose State University, Northern

Arizona University, California State University, and even the Center of Disease Control, among many other colleges and agencies. It mentioned his membership of 15 different professional societies and associations, including the American Academy of Forensic Sciences, United States Association of Professional Investigations, the San Diego Crime Commission, National Sheriff's Association, International Police Association, International Association of Chiefs of Police, and the Fraternal Order of Police.

This gave us confidence that even the MCSO in my case would listen to the high profile Dr. Streed. After all, he himself was a career detective even before his current membership in groups such as the Fraternal Order of Police. he must have even helped to educate some current police and prosecutors while instructing at various colleges. He had even been invited to speak here in Maricopa county, dozens of times, on topics such as coercion, in front of various agencies, including, ironically, the public defender's office where Rick Miller worked.

In Dr. Streed's declaration he outlined his knowledge and experience, how he came to be involved in my case, and then gets right into "State of Arizona v. Justin Wade Lunsford."

He outlines eyewitness Jimmie Larson, seeing a man who looked nothing like me setting the victim's truck on fire, and then driving away in a "green colored vehicle." He illustrates the "tainted identification process" wherein detectives sent Jimmie Larson a single photo of my dad's dodge truck—after my arrest—and *told him* it was connected to the homicide, instead of sending him several photos of several vehicles and *asking* him if he could identify one.

He mentions all of the alleged "evidence" that came from the truck after it was impounded, which according to Detective Kristina Bucaro "tested positive for human blood," but notes that exactly 3 months later, on October 14, 2008, the scientific examination report from the Arizona Department of Public Safety reported "no blood was detected" on any of those items. He mentions that a year later, the truck was returned to the owner because there were "no reports of any evidence from the murder…being found in the vehicle."

Dr. Streed then goes on to explain the huge disparity between the arsonist's appearance and my own, summing up with the composite sketch of the arsonist which "bore [no] resemblance to Justin Lunsford, and Larson's own words when asked if my picture looked like the arsonist he saw that day, "No, I can't say that, no."

Streed mentions that MCSO deputies should have collected or preserved shoe prints and tire impressions from the scene of the truck, explaining, "If shoeprints had been found and properly preserved, such evidence might have been used to (A), identify the footwear of the arsonist, or (B), determine the size of the foot-ware worn by the arsonist."

He mentions that nobody ever checked the "steering wheel, gearshift lever, or either side of the door handles" of Ms. Hermann's truck for fingerprints or DNA, explaining that because those items were metallic, any existing prints would survive the fire.

He mentions MCSO Deputy Kenneth Martinez being at Hermann's house at 4:15pm that day, July 8, 2008, two hours after the vehicle fire. Ms. Hermann was inarguably alive at this time. First responders would not be at the house fire for almost four more hours, at which time her blood had not even dried.

If Deputy Martinez had done a welfare check on the young woman who was already *at least* a victim of arson, it might have changed everything. If at 4:15 p.m. Deputy Martinez would have entered her residence, he may have found her still alive and saved her life. At the very least his findings could have been compared to the Gallagher's surveillance video, which showed that while Deputy Martinez was at Ms. Hermann's residence at 4:15 pm, Gerald Coco and I were sitting at a cocktail table at the sportsbar Gallagher's. Wherever Ms Hermann was, whoever she was with, the video, taken from 3:35 to 4:25 p.m., would show that she was not there and not with us. The question is, where was she, and who was she with? Deputy Martinez had a good opportunity—a good cause—to find out, as he stood at Ms. Hermann's doorstep knocking, but somehow indifference prevailed.

Dr. Streed does not go into the Gallagher's comparison, but he does mention the fact that Deputy Martinez did not see a green and silver dodge truck at her residence, but that detectives did find "several tire tracks that appeared to have been recently made in the dirt in the front yard." They did not process and preserve them for comparison to my dad's truck. Or, if they did, it was never disclosed.

Streed then goes into the examination of the house, after it had become a crime scene. He spends many, many paragraphs explaining the plethora of physical evidence that was preserved for testing, contrary to prosecutor Gingold's fallacious claim at sentencing that "no forensics" could be recovered from the "house." That was his effort to explain to Judge Barton why no "physical evidence linked the defendant (me) to the crime." Streed lists the seven items that we had requested the state have tested, and added to those, "trace evidence from chest, hair and fibers from chest/abdomen, hair and fibers from genital area, combings." He posed "questions why those, and the tested items—including the gas can and used condoms, which *did* yield a complete profile—were never compared to the then-known five other suspects, including, he wrote, Sam Parker, Max Piper, Andrew Phillips, Sandor Polgar, and Paramanathan 'Nate' Renganathan."

He confirmed there is also no trace evidence from any clothes that I owned being connected to any crime. Streed then began discussing the blood evidence in this case, noting that detectives had found blood "inside the master bathroom on the wall next to the shower, on the shower door, the bathtub," adding that, "according to Detective Smith, "this led detectives to believe that after the homicide, the suspect may have taken a shower." Bringing up the bloody palm print, Streed then introduces reference to Ray Krone, another wrongfully convicted Arizona murder defendant who Streed helped exonerate several years earlier.

I had remembered Ray Krone's story, because just after I got to D.O.C. Jill had printed out and sent me some web articles on wrongful convictions, including Ray Krone, and John Watkins, who will be discussed at length later. They had met with Dr. Streed in person numerous times. The Ray Krone exoneration was one of the things we had discussed. Similar to my case, Ray was convicted hastily, due to detectives fixating on him early because of bar-scene gossip and gut hunches, followed by an avoidance of forensics, various manipulations by the State and their expert witness, and a Maricopa County Superior Court Judge eager to run interference for them. They railroaded Ray Krone right onto Arizona's death row, just down the street from the prison yard where Dr. Streed and I were having these conversations.

In highlighting the importance of testing the bloody palm print in Liz Hermann's murder, Dr. Streed explained, "Another case on which I consulted, involved a murderer, Kenneth Phillips, who left a sample of his own blood at a murder scene, which ultimately became a pivotal item of evidence in exonerating the wrongfully convicted Ray Krone. He went on to explain, "the photograph of Mary "Liz" Hermann's hands do not display bloody palms—which supports the suspicion that the piece of wall board with a smeared bloody handprint on it (item 71) that was removed from the master bathroom might have been left by the murder suspect."

He then marvels at why no attempt whatsoever was made in order to determine the donor of the bloody print, either by blood type or by DNA.

Dr. Streed then questions the competence of the investigation into Ms Hermann's murder. "A reasonable, prudent and well-trained homicide detective would have ensured that all of the blood stains, identified as items 42, 45, 53-83 (33 total) with the exception of the pooled blood [near the victim] were typed to determine if any of the blood stains could have been deposited by someone *other* than Mary "Liz" Hermann."

Dr. Streed then specifically mentions a "hair" found on a green and white night gown, identified as item 06a, that was found on a green and white nightgown, identified as item 06, that was found in the master bedroom." He goes on to say "if this was hair intact and properly examined, DNA may have been found on the root of the hair fiber, which might have been able to identify the donor."

Dr. Streed then mentions "a second hair, identified as item 75 and a fiber, identified as item 12 that was found on Mary "Liz" Elizabeth Hermann's head" and goes on to emphasize the importance of testing, just as he did with item 06a.

It becomes perplexing when considering this evidence as thoroughly as Dr. Streed did, why the detectives and crime scene investigators methodically collected and properly preserved so many tiny pieces of evidence, even labeling them, numbering them, and characterizing them in the written discovery as "hairs" and "fibers," even "blood smears," and fingernail "clippings" and "scrapings," if the DPS crime lab was never even going to test any of it. It made no sense.

It is assumed that the crime lab *was* going to test it. After all, that is their role, especially concerning high-profile murder cases. What changed, between the collecting of this evidence and the failure to test it may only be able explained by the lead detective investigating Ms. Hermann's murder; MCSO Detective Paul Smith.

It also makes one wonder why Deputy County Attorney Mike Gingold told Judge Barton at sentencing, that "no forensics" could be saved from the house fire. Did he really not know that it existed, even though it was repeatedly listed and mentioned in the police reports? Was he deliberately misleading Judge Barton? There really wasn't a third option.

Dr. Streed's report then goes on to discuss possibly the two most important pieces of evidence in the whole case, the two used condoms found near Ms. Hermann's body. When one comes upon two used condoms near a woman's nude, murdered body, inside a house that someone attempted to burn down, it is difficult to overstate the importance of identifying the man who wore the two used condoms. This may have been why Detective Smith had the condoms tested at the DPS crime lab, in effect, placing them in the top one percentile of important evidence, necessary in solving Ms. Hermann's murder.

Dr. Streed wrote, "An examination of two used condoms, (identified as items 91 and 92), revealed that DNA profiles (identified as items 91a and 92a) extracted from the insides of both condoms *excluded* Justin Lunsford and were reported as coming from an unidentified male. Criminalist Kelli Raley reported that the DNA profile from the unidentified male was added to the Combined DNA Index System and CODIS searches would be routinely performed. The investigative need for identifying the "unidentified male" that donated the DNA found inside of both used condoms is that the donor could have been identified as being inside the residence at 5536 E. Seven Palms Drive, Cave

Creek, AZ, and engaging in sexual relations with Mary "Liz" Elizabeth Hermann, and may have been involved in her murder."

Steed said, "We have an investigative need. ID him in order to exclude him as a suspect. Cannot rule out a suspect without interviewing him. Cannot interview him w/o ID'ing him!"

For years I had wondered who the "unidentified male" was I wondered if a CODIS match had occurred yet. If so, would DPS would notify me of such a match? Every bit of mental health-related knife violence, and/or arson, that I saw each day on the news, from my prison cell, made me wonder when they put the suspect's face on the screen—is that the guy? I watched the news closely every day.

Dr. Streed goes on to discuss even more untested evidence properly collected and preserved from the crime scene, including "empty condom wrappers—identified as item 93, as well as an empty match book inscribed *Mitchell's Fish Market*, which was identified as item 10.

I wondered where *Mitchell's Fish Market* was. I had lived in the Cave Creek/ Phoenix area my entire life and had never heard of a *Mitchell's Fish Market*. Truth be told, I had never seen *any* fish market in Arizona, as there is no ocean and very little water, period. Finding out where *Mitchell's Fish Market* was could have provided a clue about the killer-arsonist, as the book of matches was found just outside the front door, near the gas can, which had someone else's DNA on the handle, not mine.

I found it incredible that MCSO detectives apparently did not want to know whose fingerprints were left on the book of matches at the house fire murder scene. But of course, they'd gotten everything they needed out of Gerald Coco after threatening his life in the dirt parking lot at 2 a.m., and every attempt they had made to corroborate his eventual story had backfired. Testing the matchbook could have gone *really* bad for their flimsy investigation, but it still should have been tested, as gasoline does not set itself on fire.

Dr. Streed, a 24-year homicide detective himself, who had investigated nearly 3,000 homicides at this point, seemed to agree. He said, "A reasonable, prudent and well-trained homicide detective would have known that an accelerant, such as gasoline, needs something to ignite it. Matches, possibly from the matchbook inscribed "*Mitchell's Fish Market*" could have been the item used to ignite the gasoline at both the arson of Mary "Liz" Elizabeth Hermann's white Chevrolet pickup truck at the intersection of Cave Creek road and New River road, as well as her residence at 5536 E. Seven Palms Drive, Cave Creek, Arizona. While this constitutes a rational for examining the matchbook, no ever did. "

Dr. Streed mentioned that the DNA extracted from the condoms should have been compared to the partial profile from the house fire has can, but never was, probably because Smith knew that the DNA in the condoms was not mine. Matching it to the gas can would have been devastating to Smith's flimsy case.

Dr. Streed did an amazing job of analyzing and evaluating all of the crime scene evidence in Ms. Hermann's murder, detailing each piece's relevance and the importance of testing. Without a doubt it was the first time the forensic evidence in this case was ever given proper attention. And yet, as impressive a job as Dr. Streed did in his crime scene analysis, it was not the primary reason why Dr. Streed was motivated to become involved in the State of Arizona v. Lunsford. Finally getting to his primary reason, Dr. Streed declares, "I have qualified and testified in the superior court, federal court, and military courts martial as an expert in coerced false statements."

Gerald Coco's False Confession

Dr. Streed explains that the scientific research in this area has established six different categories of false confessions or statements. He explains that, "the statements made by Gerald Coco are an accumulation and hodgepodge of Gerald Coco's various statements, which appear to fall under the category of coerced-compliant false statements."

A coerced-compliant false statement, Streed explains, may occur when an individual confesses or makes false statements (a) rather than continuing to endure the *stress* of a continuing interrogation, (b)to obtain some *benefit* pledged by the interrogator, or (C) to escape some measure of threatened or real *harm* or discomfort."

The science, if you will, of coerced statements, be they from a witness, a non-witness transformed into a witness by said coerced statements, or from a suspect, who gives a false confession, was, ten years ago, a very new science. At the time of the Liz Hermann murder in 2008, almost no one in America believed that false confessions or any other types of coercion was real. It was believed to be a mere myth, conjured up by wily defense attorneys whose hypocrisy knew no bounds in trying to get an obviously guilty suspect off the hook.

Therefore in the pre-2008 America, all detectives knew that a confession was gold, and so was any other incriminating or maligning statement given by a witness about the defendant. A detective could glean an inculpatory statement from an interviewee, by any means necessary, even using threats, the threat of violence, or actual violence, as was done by MCSO Detective Paul Smith in the Gerald Coco interrogation. Then he could justify those means internally with the idea that it is done for the "greater good," type-up snippets and soundbites from the interrogation incorporate them into a warrant for arrest, and close the case.

Detectives knew full well that it would almost certainly never be scrutinized at trial, because each arrestee was almost certain not to ever have a trial. Chris Hedges from *Truth/Dig* wrote, "95 percent of all state felony cases are resolved through plea bargaining." He reported, "The reality is that almost no one who is imprisoned in America has gotten a trial."

Detectives also knew that in the very low chance that the case did go to trial, it would almost surely be litigated by a public defender. They believed in holistic advocacy, wherein public defenders work as "full partners with law enforcement." This is according to an article in the Arizona Attorney Magazine in 2015 or 2015. It reported that the Maricopa County Public Defender almost never challenged police conduct. Even if they did, the public wouldn't buy it anyway because nobody believed in false confessions, or false statements from state's witnesses. People thought there was no way a sworn Deputy County Attorney would solicit false info from a witness under oath in a court of law. Most of America believed that nothing bad—no lies, no unnecessary violence—could ever come from police.

It was with that pre-found advantage that police detectives operated pre-2010. Yet, the blame could hardly be placed squarely on their shoulders because the reality of it was that they were simply catering to *we the people*. When an awful crime occurred, we the people *wanted* a hasty arrest. We *needed* a face on the TV screen as soon as possible. If the police had to rough-up a few "bad guys" on the way there, like some of our favorite TV detectives did, so be it. They probably deserved it. What could be more American than that? The hypocrisy lies within all of us, even myself, a wrongfully convicted prisoner.

Even in Liz Hermann's murder in 2008 I wanted a quick arrest; I wanted to know who'd killed the woman I'd just met, who'd created the biggest tragedy in the history of my own small hometown. I supported the idea of a speedy, adrenaline-fueled investigation, just like the rest of society.

Then in the 2010's with the one-two punch of countless DNA exonerations and cell-phone videos, some of which showed police officers actually committing murder, we as a society, as a world, began to realize that something was wrong. We began to realize that a lot of questions needed asking and that the criminal justice system needed a complete renovation.

Some people within the sphere of law enforcement and litigation began to conduct their own re-evaluations, some public, some private, and as they did, even as far back as Miranda in the 1960s, insight, research, and data had begun to pool, eventually accumulating the breadth and depth of a huge information reservoir. Then in the 2010's, with the advent of the tech revolution, information sharing, and hand held devices, the dam broke.

One of the professionals within law enforcement who began to realize—and accept—that change was needed, before the breaking of the dam, was Dr. Streed. Now holding a Ph.D in almost everything criminology related under the sun, he was in a position to make sense of it all. In his declaration he concluded, "A coerced-compliant false statement may occur when an individual . . . makes false statements . . . rather than continuing to endure the *stress* of a continuing interrogation...the continuing stress of the interrogation of Gerald Coco was illustrated in his interview/interrogation session by detective Paul Smith on July 12th, 2008." In this amateurish interview/interrogation session, Gerald Coco was asked by Detective Smith if he was the one who had killed Mary "Liz" Elizabeth Hermann. Coco denied it. Then, he was *accused* of having been at the scene of the murder and helping . . . dispose of her body.

One cannot help but wonder how much stress Gerald Coco felt. He had an anxiety disorder, and a prescription for Xanax. But he had no access to his medication for hours. He was a self-admitted over drinker, and cocaine user. He reached out to detectives at almost midnight that night. Who knows how many substances he might have had in his system *at the time of* this interview? Was he, two hours into it, "coming down" from cocaine, experiencing alcohol withdrawals, or having just a "basic" panic attack? Two things were certain. The interrogation had not gone how Coco had planned; to get the Sinaloans arrested. It did not go like the Max Piper interview. Coco probably should have been drug tested before and after the interrogation. After all, he could have been on hallucinogens for all they knew.

Whatever "stress"that Coco was feeling during the recorded portions of his inter-rogations wherein he was being accused of murder, he must have been relieved when Detective Paul Smith, out of the kindness of his heart, turned the recorders off and invited him outside to the dirt parking lot for a smoke break. What a kind, understanding gesture.

Imagine the dread, and panic, that must have flooded into Coco's mind when detec-tives surrounded him, outside at 2 a.m. in an unfamiliar area, and raised their voices in aggression, yelling at him face-to-face, or face-to-the back of the head, calling him a murderer, a "f---ing murderer," and a "murdering piece of s—t," threatening to give him the death penalty. Imagine the fear that must have paralyzed him when he felt that first shove in his back, as they all simultaneously shoved him. Imagine his primordial terror when he felt the industrial dust and dirt under his palms, against his cheek, in his nostrils, as Detective Smith and company began spitting on him. What would any 24-year-old person do in that moment to escape this measure of threatened or real harm? These were the criteria of a "coerced-compliant false statement," brought to life perfectly in what Streed characterized as Detective Smith's "amateurish interview/ interrogation session with Gerald Coco." Harkening back to an afore-quoted special recognition award earned by Dr. Streed, one can't help but believe that Smith et al could have profited greatly from having a more experienced interrogator with them that night.

One of Deputy Streed's many areas of expertise is interviewing and interrogation, a subject he teaches at both San Diego Sheriff's academy and San Jose State University. His interviewing skill and knowledge are outstanding. His ability to digest the interview and reach logical conclusions is uncanny. Because of his excellent education and street savvy, he was equally comfortable talking to the bank president or the local guttersnipe. In this area, he is often asked to sit in on interviews or conduct the interview for other teams when special circumstances occur.

Thankfully, Dr. Streed was finally given an opportunity to, in a sense, sit in on Gerald Coco's interview/interrogations years later by reading the transcripts of the interviews, watching the videos of the parts that Detective Smith chose to record, reviewing the case file in order to understand their context within the investigation, and then becoming privy to the information regarding what went on when the recorders were off, in the dirt parking lot, as discovered by Lindsey Herf and David Gurney when they interviewed Gerald and his brother in 2012.

Putting all of this together for the court in an easy-to-understand report, Streed declared, "In addition to the inappropriate and coercive content of his interview/interrogation session on July 12th 2008, as well as a second...conducted by detective Kristina Bucaro, Gerald Coco provided an affidavit, and declared under oath:

> Regarding July 8, 2008, I state that Justin never took me to a crime scene.
>
> When I was interrogated by the Maricopa county sheriff's office, I was told that if I did not implicate Justin, I would be tried for murder.
>
> At one time, the investigators questioning me, turned off the recorder, took me outside, pushed me, knocked me down, spit on me, and threatened me.
>
> Justin never asked me to lie for him or to be his alibi.
>
> Justin was with me all day, July 8, 2008, and we never went to either crime scene.
>
> If I gave inconsistent stories, I was scared and the MCSO detectives threatened me if I did not say what the detectives wanted me to say."

Streed read the Affidavit of Gerald Coco's mother Cindy Coco." It confirmed that Gerald and Justin were at her apartment in the early afternoon. That was consistent with her statement to the MCSO that we had arrived at 1 p.m. and stayed for a couple of hours. This is important because the truck fire was at 2 p.m. We arrived and left in Gerald's white Monte Carlo, not a green colored truck, like the one the red-haired arsonist was driving, when he burned the truck, while we were at Gerald's mother's house.

Streed introduced the topic of "suggestibility," wherein individuals who are more gullible, suggestable, or desperate to escape harm), are manipulated or coached into making false statements. He explained that in coerced-compliant false statements, "instructional manipulation" may be used. The person being interrogated is coached and/or given instruction, or guidance, about what they want to say to satisfy the interrogator.

One cannot help but wonder about the perfect storm created during an interrogation, when the interviewee is first threatened into a stressful state, and then told what to say in order to make it appear that the interviewee really is familiar with the crime.

After the male/masculine detectives threatened Gerald Coco into being scared for his life and liberty, dictating to him that he had better incriminate me, the kinder, softer voice of a woman detective, Kristina Bucaro, was brought in. She was there to help Gerald Coco better understand the details that he needs to give.

A key "adjustment" that Bucaro needed Gerald to make was to change his time-line. This was because Gerald and I were not in Cave Creek for the latter part of the day, when the crimes actually occurred. We were in north Phoenix, approximately 20 miles away, which was a 30-minute drive, one hour round trip. Gerald didn't know that. He did not have actual knowledge of a crime when detectives coerced him to say that I told him I burned the house. The detectives basically told Gerald that the fire, the murder, this whole mess, must have occurred in the morning, before we were together. Gerald was operating under the assumption that it all occurred on the morning on July 8th. ., He didn't have actual knowledge of it, because we never had anything to do with it. The coercion of Coco produced a willingness on his part to incriminate me, but his wrong guesses about the time of day that these things occurred produced a need on the detectives part to employ "instructional manipulation." In effect, they told him what to say.

Streed wrote, "an indication of "instructional manipulation" can be seen in Gerald Coco's un-dated interview/interrogation by MCSO Detective Kristina Bucaro, as follows:

Q: Well, here's the problem. When you guys were together, the house wasn't burned down.
A: But he, he told me the house was burned down at Gallagher's. The house couldn't have been burned down while we were at Gallaghers, because MCSO deputy K. Martinez was *at the house* at that time.

Q: I know, it actually, the, the fire was much later.
A: Yeah. *That's what the detectives were telling me.*"

This specific interview ends with Gerald Coco, the state's star witness, saying about me, "Well then, he obviously he didn't do it." But it didn't matter. The detectives were not required to include that in their charging summary, or share it with the grand jury, or the public. They got the soundbites they needed in order to craft the narrative that suited them. Never mind how they got there.

Dr. Streed however, and many advocates of proper interrogation techniques, and champions of constitutional rights, would mind how they got there. Every occupation has a certain set of "tricks of the trade," including investigating and interrogating. In the 1960s it was becoming apparent that police had an unfair advantage over almost anyone they interrogated. Streed told me himself, that many decades ago, he and his colleagues at SDSO could get anyone to confess to anything. He shared a technique or two with me and sad, "get me in a room with Gerald Coco, and I could have him confessing to sinking the Titanic..." and he was right. The difference between Streed and some other detectives though, past and present, was that he would not actually use his authority that way.

The Law

As a result of the not-so-even playing field, and some of the injustices that it gave birth to, the U.S. Supreme Court began handing down a series of rulings. The Powell decision paved the way for Gideon and Betts, which preceded Escobedo, the predecessor to Miranda. Each ruling ensured incrementally more rights for the interrogatee.

Powell v. Alabama in 1932 gave the accused a right to counsel. Three decades later the warren court's rulings in Gideon and Betts re-established the right to counsel by overruling the lower courts' decision in those two cases, which plowed the ground for Escobedo.

Escobedo was a California murder defendant in 1960 who repeatedly asked for a lawyer and wished to not speak with police. Both requests were ignored. In 1965 the California supreme court ruled in Escobedo, "when the process shifts from investigatory to accusatory...our adversary system begins to operate and the accused must be permitted to consult with his lawyer

This phrase "when the process shifts" became the answer to the central question in Miranda. When Miranda was being heard in the U.S. Supreme Court in 1966 most people on both sides had already come to an agreement that suspects should have the right to counsel and the right to remain silent, the only question was—at what point? Opposers of Miranda worried that attorneys for any and all witnesses in all investigations would barge into the police station at the beginning of any and every interview, telling the interviewee to stop talking, and that then the police would never be able to solve crimes ever. Sheer bedlam it would be.

Champions of constitutional rights agreed that the police deserved ample opportunity to interview witnesses in order to solve crimes and so, following Escobedo, the US supreme court decided its Miranda decision and that he or she becomes a "suspect," as Escobedo states, "when the process shifts from investigatory to accusatory."

One could hardly argue that Gerald Coco's interrogation had not become accusatory. Certainly Gerald himself felt that adversarial "shift" as he lie in the dirt parking lot being spat upon and yelled at literally accused of murder.

For this reason Dr. Streed writes, "in spite of the accusatorial format of Gerald Coco's interview/interrogation on July 12th, 2008, he was never advised of his constitutional rights."

Dr. Streed, going further in his declaration regarding Gerald Coco's interrogation, says, "The supreme court ruling in Miranda versus Arizona states, 'the atmosphere and environment of incommunicado interrogation as it exists today is inherently intimidating and works to undermine the privilege against self-incrimination…again we stress that the modern practice of in-custody interrogation is psychologically rather than physically oriented. As we have stated before, since Chambers v. Florida, 309 U.S. 227, this court has recognized that coercion can be mental as well as physical, and that the blood of the accused is not the only hallmark of an unconstitutional inquisition'"

The problem, in my case and so many others, was that for every step that civil rights took forward, there were groups of police detectives inventing new tricks of the trade in order to get around those rights. This can be seen in Missouri v. Seibert wherein police intentionally withheld Miranda rights from a suspect. In an opinion, justice David H. Souter addressed police attempts to circumvent Miranda by stating, "strategists dedicated to draining the substance out of Miranda cannot accomplish by training instructions what Dickerson held congress cannot do by statute." (

Perhaps police strategies such as Detective Paul Smith had given up on trying to "drain the substance" out of Miranda and had gone right to simply ignoring it, in post-Miranda Arizona. How ironic, because Miranda came *out of* Arizona.

The Debra Milke Case

Speaking to the law culture in Arizona, in the case of another wrongfully convicted Arizona murder defendant, Debra Milke, lead detective was Ernesto Saldate of Phoenix Police Department admitted it was his understanding that just because someone invoked their rights it didn't mean he had to stop interrogating them, His position was insulated by Arizona judges for twenty-two years thereafter, as Milke sat on death row. She awaited countless appellate rulings while her case was juggled from one court to another, then another, and back to the prior, and forward again, sometimes with years in between stops. As that process carried on, so did Detective Saldate, who was known for "closing" cases. He became a legend of sorts and younger Arizona Detectives like Paul Smith began to imitate his misconduct, especially when they saw the Arizona judiciary insulate him and prosecutors.

The exculpatory information in Milke's case was known by the trial Judge and prosecutor, who, together decided that the defense need not know about it. Detective Saldate had claimed that Milke confessed to him. He said that he was "not in the practice" of recording confessions, so there was no recording of it. The judge, jury, and prosecutor had to take his word for it. This was in the pre-2010 atmosphere wherein everyone assumed the police officers would never lie. The exculpatory information was eighteen—at least eighteen—documented incidents of Saldate's misconduct, mostly lying under oath, but also including sexually assaulting a woman during a traffic stop. Milke was released after twenty two years, in 2013. Saldate is now an Arizona town constable.

In Milke's suppression hearing, held September 10th, 1990, twenty-four years after Miranda, in front of Judge Cheryl Hendrix, a very telling exchange took place between defense attorney Kenneth Ray and Detective Saldate. It spoke to the culture of investigating and litigating in Arizona, as it pertained to constitutional rights.

Saldate bloviated his seemingly psychic ability to read people, like Detective Paul Smith did in my presentence report. Saldate said he had 21 years of experience and relied heavily on his "gut reaction." Ray asked him, "Sir, as an officer with 20 some-odd years of experience, you know when a suspect invokes his right to remain silent, especially after you have read him his Miranda rights, assuming that was done, that you are to break the interview off immediately, aren't you?"

Saldate answered, "I don't believe it says in any police manual that we have in the police department does it tell me I need to stop listening or asking questions. No."

Maybe it doesn't say that in "any police manual." I don't know, I've never read one. But it says that in the U.S. constitution. While that is supposed to matter, it seemed to have little to no effect on many Arizona cases. One year and three days after Milke's suppression hearing, just across the street from Judge Hendrix's courtroom, in the Madison jail, would sit four other innocent Arizona murder defendants—Michael McGraw, Leo Bruce, Marcus Nunez, and Dante Parker, dubbed "The Tucson Four." They were accused of murdering nine Buddhist monks. And just when we thought the MCSO could not possibly fit any more innocent murder defendants into one building, they hauled in George Peterson three weeks later. They falsely accused him of killing a woman that the actual murderer of the nine monks had killed. MCSO was responsible for all of them.

Milke was also housed in the Madison jail, women's section. All were falsely arrested due to the same Miranda-oriented disregard and improper interrogation techniques that were later employed on Gerald Coco. In between Coco and the previous six examples there was another suspect named Robert Luis Armstrong. MCSO extracted a "confession" from him in 2003, regarding a five-year-old unsolved triple murder that occurred in the Agua Fria river bottom west of Phoenix. Ironically, that was the same remote location wherein Alex Garcia and Jonathan Doody, the real murderers of the nine monks, divided the spoils from the Buddhist temple. Armstrong was later found to be in in Oregon at the time they accused him of the triple murder.

Despite the campaign promises of "the toughest sheriff in America," Joe Arpaio, to end the crisis by overhauling MCSO interrogation practices, the 2003 false arrest of Armstrong showed that the new policy of recording interrogations only forced us to now have to watch the coercion on video afterwards. The techniques hadn't changed. At all.

And why would they have? As author, law professor and longtime practicing Arizona attorney Gary Stuart wrote in *"Anatomy of A Confession: The Debra Milke Case,"* regarding the afore-mentioned Milke suppression hearing from 1990, wherein Saldate as much as thumbed his nose at the United States Supreme Court Miranda opinion.

> "Nothing about Judge Hendrix's judicial career, her prosecutorial favoritism, or her rulings remotely indicated that she might suppress the supposed confession... [the] entire point of the hearing was to create an appellate record" which would not matter anyway because Judge Hendrix's superior in 1990, Presiding Judge Broomfield, would climb the judicial ladder, as it were, essentially keeping pace with Milke's appeals, and as her appeals reached the Arizona Supreme Court in 1992 so did he. *Broomfield authored* the written denial of Milke's claims, and "studiously avoided any discussion...of the state's failure to provide" the voluminous documentation of Saldate's "confession" misconduct.

The Milke case is discussed here, in conjunction with my own, and the others, to illustrate that none of these are isolated incidents. This is still the way things are done in Arizona, even today, and it causes a lot of harm to many people.

So in 2008, as Detective Smith and gang "investigated" Liz Hermann's murder, the Saldate tricks—violating Miranda, lying under oath, etc—had worked, and stuck. The Arizona judiciary was essentially signaling to Arizona police investigators (like Detective Paul Smith) that despite that silly federal ruling in Miranda, and the constitutionality that came with it, they could still do whatever they wanted to. Yee-haw.

For years I had wondered, from a very practical, straightforward standpoint— 'okay, if the police are going to arrest *me* for this, and charge *me*, and it is inarguable that Gerald and I were together that evening, why didn't they also arrest him?' In Arizona, the law states that if an "accomplice" is even present at the scene of a crime, he or she is guilty of the same exact charges as the person who actually committed the crime.

Why didn't they arrest Gerald Coco? Because if he was the defendant, his statements would be inadmissible, and unverifiable.

Question is why are they admissible with *me* as the defendant? Miranda protects the interviewee only if he incriminates himself, it offers no protection in the cases wherein the coerced interviewee, in the spirit of self-preservation, chooses instead to falsely incriminate someone else, which happens quite frequently, and happened to me.

For someone like Detective Smith, he knew that it didn't matter who Gerald Coco incriminated, himself, Ronald McDonald, or me. Once a detective feels he has identified the proper group of "dirt bags," it doesn't matter which dirt bag the handcuffs go on, as long as they go on somebody. Of course the question in my case would become some years later, did he even have the right group of dirt bags? The answer was no.

Perhaps there is still room for, or even a *need* for, shoring up Miranda rights. Perhaps Detective Smith, and many other detectives, have found solace and a resting place within the only gap or hole left in the Miranda doctrine. I would proffer that an interview/interrogation that was coerced, and in violation of Miranda, or any other constitutional rights, and its fruits, should be thrown out, regardless of *who* the terrified interrogatee incriminates. If interviews like those were not usable, it would force investigators to look to other avenues to solve crimes. To more reliable avenues, such as cell-phone records and DNA testing. It would keep innocent people like myself out of prison. It would enable each victim's family to direct their anger at the proper party. It would keep that proper party out of the community so that he can do no more harm. It would save the county and state taxpayers millions of dollars in needless court-appointed appellate costs, and each eventual civil lawsuit for wrongful imprisonment settlement.

Imagine what the county could do with all that money. Red for Ed. V.A. Hospitals. State Parks. Perhaps there is hope.

The fact that professions and fields of science now exist for the sole purpose of addressing criminal justice concerns, such as Dr. Tom Streed in my case and Dr. Richard Leo in Debra Milke's case, may mean that we are turning a corner, however long and slow. Dr. Leo's words are now on the record and in print. He said that Milke's tragic injustice was a result of detective Saldate "too often treat[ing] his gut hunches…as if they are established facts, rather than hypothesis to be tested against the evidence. and Saldate attempting to persuade and influence a perception of Milke's guilt. That is what

Detective did with Gerald Coco in my case. Rather than merely soliciting information. He should not have been and advocate rather than an investigator. In the Milke case, Dr. Leo emphasized that, "Detective Saldate's actions in the Debra Milke interrogation were not isolated. They are clearly part of a pattern and practice

Dr. Leo gave that testimony at the United States District Court for the District of Arizona, which is located in downtown Phoenix, walking distance from the 4th avenue jail that I was housed in. My parents, family, and Jill drove past it on their way to visit me each time, and on the day that Dr. Leo gave his testimony—January 12, 2010. That testimony would eventually end up in front of Judge Rosa Mroz. My case was moved from her court to that of Judge Barton, who was ten days away from removing Rena Glitsos from my case and appointing Rick Miller, to complete the railroading of an innocent man (me), with no evidence.

As the invisible forces that drove the tank-like vehicle that carried the Saldate and Smith way of investigating was carrying on in one direction, the newer, more open-minded way of evaluative truth-seeking was raising its head in Lori Vopel's *coup de grace* argument for ending civilized society's over-reliance on coerced testimony, and Judge Kozinski's response, to it at the United States Circuit Court for the Ninth Circuit, in the Debra Milke case.

Ms. Vopel wrote, "If we as a civilized society have learned anything in recent years, it's that 'confession' evidence is inherently unreliable"

Judge Kozinski said, "No civilized system of justice should move to rely on such flimsy evidence, quite possibly tainted by dishonesty and overzealousness, to decide whether to take someone's life or liberty" which "not only risks convicting the innocent but helps the guilty avoid detection and strike again."

That happened in my case, thanks to, in the face of an obvious injustice, what the Ninth Circuit Court of Appeals branded in Milke as "The state of Arizona's unconstitutional silence."

The examination of a wrongful conviction such as my own, or the many, many others, wherein police boycott forensics and lean on impressionable witnesses, violate rights, abandon common sense and rush to judgement raises a question. Especially now, in 2019, it raises the question—why? Why, with all of the empirical data we now have about wrongful convictions, why do they still happen? why do appellate courts still enable and support them? Why did detective Smith and other actors within the criminal justice system do some of the head-scratching things that were done in my case?

Dr. Streed, touching on the interaction of social science and law, said, "It appears that MCSO investigators in the investigation of the murder of Mary "Liz" Hermann fell prey to the risk of confirmatory bias, or "tunnel vision." In a 2006. two years before the Hermann murder, a study was reported in the Wisconsin Law Review entitled *"The Multiple Dimensions of Tunnel Vision in Criminal Cases."* It detailed the causes of hundreds of cases of wrongful convictions in the last fifteen years.

> The Wisconsin Law Review study stated, "a theme running through almost every case is the problem of tunnel vision. Tunnel vision is a natural human tendency that has particularly pernicious effects on the criminal justice system. By tunnel vision, we mean that "compendium of common heuristics and logical fallacies," to which we are all susceptible, lead on a suspect, select and filter the evidence that will build a case for conviction, while ignoring or suppressing evidence that points away from guilt This process leads investigators, prosecutors, judges, and defense lawyers alike to focus on a particular conclusion and then filter all evidence in a case through the lens provided by that particular conclusion.

Streed's report says, "As reported in the 2006 study by the Wisconsin Law Review, the Ryan commission's report illustrated that in any given investigation, *especially high-pressure investigations,* (emphasis added) the danger exists that rather than keeping an open and objective mind during the investigatory phase, the police may prematurely conclude that a suspect is guilty. Once the police have reached this conclusion, instead of fully investigating other possibilities, their investigation focuses exclusively on assembling facts that will convict the suspect."

Getting more specific, Dr. Streed goes on to say, "Rather than falling prey to tunnel vision, a reasonable, prudent and well-trained homicide detective conducting an investigation of the murder of Mary "Liz" Hermann would have prepared at least six (6) separate photographic lineups, that included a photographic lineup containing a photo of (a) Justin Lunsford, (b) Sam Parker, (c) Max Piper, (d) Andrew Philips, Mary "Liz" Hermann's ex-husband, Sandor Polgar, and (f) Hermann's ex-boyfriend, paramanathan "Nate" Renganathan. These photo lineups could have been shown to eyewitness Jimmie Larson to determine if he could identify the arsonist. "

Why didn't Smith and his colleagues show *the only eyewitness* in this case a photo of the six known suspects? Why didn't they at least show him a photo of their favorite suspect? Why did they avoid showing Jimmie Larson any photos of anyone? They sent him a picture of the Dodge truck and *told him it was* the truck he saw, but they didn't send him a picture of a person. After my arrest, they asked him to make the drive from the east valley to the MCSO GID dirt parking lot, where they had roughed up Coco two weeks earlier, to go inside and help Detective Weege with a composite sketch.

However, 70% of the way through the process the picture looked nothing like me; so they stopped. They never finished the sketch. And despite the fact that they were sitting right there together, in a room at the GID, no doubt with the file on hand, and photos of me readily available, they still didn't show him one. If detectives *really* believed they had arrested the right guy a week earlier wouldn't they be *eager* to show the only eyewitness in the case a picture of their suspect?

This was one of what the Wisconsin Law Review study referred to as the "pernicious affects in the criminal justice system," resulting from tunnel vision. Detectives were "focus[ing] on a particular conclusion and then filter[ing] all evidence...through the lens provided by that conclusion," specifically in the "high pressure" case that the Hermann investigation had become.

Streed points out that, "Rather than falling prey to tunnel vision, Detective Smith and the investigators under him should have compared the DNA found inside the two used condoms near Ms. Hermann's body with the partial DNA profile found on the gas can, and they should have taken DNA samples from the other five known suspects. In the course of their entire investigation, *they never took a DNA sample from anyone* other than Justin Lunsford, *after* his arrest. That despite the DNA from the condoms coming back to an "unidentified male."

Why? Tunnel vision, the leading cause of wrongful convictions. It is as the Ryan commission stated; "once police have reached this conclusion, instead of fully investigating other possibilities, their investigation focuses exclusively on assembling facts that will convict the suspect."

Streed finishes brilliantly. "As a further illustration of "tunnel vision," the MCSO investigators never presented any evidence as to how Justin Lunsford was able to drive Mary "Liz" Hermann's white Chevrolet pickup truck, as well as a green colored vehicle to Cave Creek road and New River road, *at the same time*."

Lee Dammer's Declaration

When I received a copy of Dr. Streed's declaration, my family sent copies of to David Gurney and others. That was also the time I received a copy of private investigator Lee Damner's declaration. It was empowering to have multiple licensed legal professionals reading my file, agreeing that an injustice was done, and producing detailed reports to the court adding their voices to our petition for post-conviction relief.

Damner covered the whole case, in shorter form than Dr. Streed did, yet with added variance, as his role was slightly different. He began by introducing himself to the court and giving his background, having been, as he said, "A licensed private investigator in Arizona since 1955, with a BA in public law. He had also earned the

CLEAR certification and was awarded the designation of national certified investigator/ inspector. He said he had "investigated hundreds of homicides, murders, and wrongful death cases... [and] cases involving police procedures, police liability and arson," and that "the investigative file" (2,000 pages) "served as the basis of [his] declaration."

He began by telling the factual, investigative story, in chronological order, beginning with the truck fire scene at 2:16 p.m. Tuesday July 8th 2008, then the house fire scene 5 ½ hours later at 7:44 p.m., then the events that took place in the days and months to come, from nonsensical states' witness accounts, to forensic testing that points away from the defendant to the avoidance of any further forensic testing.

Regarding the truck fire scene, Damner pointed out Deputy Martinez's complete lack of interest in eyewitness Jimmie Larson explaining to him exactly where the arsonist stood, walked, parked and drove away from, bizarrely choosing to not secure any shoeprints or tire tracks. It is hard for me not to imagine, now six years later, how much a simple set of shoeprints could have cleared up. For years I would never be able to understand how a sincere police officer could find the torched vehicle of a 29-year-old woman and not be immediately determined to find the woman.

Damner also pointed out, "A citizen (Larson) described the white male leaving the vehicle fire scene to be around 200 pounds, six feet tall with blonde/reddish hair. An MCSO sketch artist prepared a partial sketch of the white male identified by witness Larson, which bore no resemblance to the defendant."

To be sure, eyewitness testimony is inherently subjective, and unreliable. We the defense did not wish to keep leaning on this eyewitness testimony or showcasing it. But the MCSO's continued refusal to perform forensic testing forced us and them to staple our arguments with only subjective things. The eyewitness account of Larson, rather than being a basis for drawing a conclusion, we argued, was an example of exculpatory information in this case that proved the need for testing all the mores. Besides, we had to go there, because the state was using it to convict me.

They opened the door for relying on Larson's account when they made it a staple of their narrative. Officer Barnes even relied on it in her presentence report. Judge Barton said in open court she had read the Barnes pre-sentence report before sentencing me. She said that Larson had described a man "fitting the defendant's physical description" while committing the arson.

As Damner went on to explain, nothing could be further from the truth. He confirmed, "At the time of this murder, Detective Paul Smith, reported that defendant Justin Lunsford was 5'10" tall, 225 pounds, with black hair and blue eyes." Later in his report, Damner pointed out "Numerous individuals saw the defendant wearing a black shirt and grey shorts. These witnesses contradicted Larson who said the white male at the scene was wearing a white…t-shirt and pinkish shorts."

Surveillance video of Gallagher's confirmed I was wearing a black shirt and grey shorts, and that I was very dark complected, almost Hispanic looking, with black hair. If Ms. Barnes, or Judge Barton, were not able to connect the dots, Lee Damner connected them for everyone.

Damner mentioned all of the same physical evidence that was properly collected, labeled and preserved for testing, evidence that sworn peace officers literally ran into a burning building to save, and urged the court to please test it. He emphasized the importance of identifying the man who used two condoms found just feet away from the victim's body. One can only assume that it was precisely evidence such as the condoms that the killer intended to destroy by burning the house. Here we had all of this evidence that the killer tried to destroy by setting the house on fire—which sometimes works in the favor of the killer. But here, the house was miraculously preserved, at least the portion where the crime occurred, and yet the state refused to test any of that evidence.

Regarding the fire, Damner emphasizes that "a fire cause and origin investigation may have determined the time of the fire and other evidence that could have led investigators to the murderer(s)."

Laid out here by Damner in simple Terus, I believed that any thinking person could see, that the way to solve this murder was to identify the man who wore the condoms, by collecting DNA analysis from the men in her life, get a fire start time, and a time of death, and find out where the man in the condoms was at that time, along with any other suspects. Pretty straight forward.

Damner points out—and he is the only person to point this out—that "neither the medical examiner nor the police examined the victim's wounds to identify the characteristics of the weapon used in this murder."

I shook my head every time I watched an episode of Dateline. For all of the simple, "automatic" things that detectives did in those cases—identifying what the murder weapon is (or could possibly be), doing DNA testing, eliminating suspects, determining *what time* the crimes occurred, identifying a motive—MCSO detectives did not do any of that. They used coerced statements, even though there were already well-known problems with that here in Arizona, and refused to fact check, and refused to let anyone else fact check, anything, and the courts loved it.

When addressing the coerced statements, PI Damner referred to them as what they were—"preposterous stories"—mentioning as Dr. Streed did that Gerald Coco was interrogated by MCSO "without advising him of his rights," and that "polygraph and common sense evaluations of these preposterous statements coupled with proper forensic testing could have clarified these issues."

Why did common sense evaluations and proper forensic testing not take place in the summer of 2008? There simply wasn't any time for it. The public wanted an arrest. The small-townspeople demanded swift "justice" especially with the hot wind of local media coverage in our sails. Detective Paul Smith simply did not have the resolve to stand up to that pressure, to tell the town, that he lived in, to be patient while forensics were being done. At the moment of my arrest not a single DNA test had been done, and not a single DNA sample had even been taken, not even from me. My sample was given *after* my arrest.

In his conclusion, Damner states, "in summary, the witnesses the police relied upon to charge the defendant did not support the defendant's guilt. Additionally, there appears to be significant forensics evidence, which could lead police to the real murderer."

The only thing left now was to explain to the court why a plea was involuntarily signed. The plea coercion was a process that took place behind the scenes. No court was aware of the details that forced me to accept a plea bargain.

Justin Lunsford Affidavit

After I received the declarations of Lee Damner and Dr. Streed, Delozier asked me to write an affidavit of my own, in letter form, to Judge Barton explaining how a plea came to be signed She would be the Judge analyzing my petition for post-conviction relief and the attachments that went with it.

I was eager to sit down and write candidly to her Honor. It had been almost three years to the day, since the sentencing screenplay. I was really confident that Judge Barton would recognize a coerced plea and injustice when she saw one. I assumed she herself had played the role in other cases that Judge Sherry Stevens had played in my case, blindly coercing a plea in a case she knew little about. I thought about what Judge Jed S. Rakoff had described in an article in the New York review of books titled "*Why Innocent People Plead Guilty.*" Maybe it would help her understand how a "secretive plea system works to thwart justice

There is perhaps no better word to describe our plea system than "secretive." Ninety-nine percent of it goes on behind the scenes, in the secretive environment of attorney-client privileged conversations. I used to assume that it was only the client who had "secrets." By secrets I mean things that they wished to not be made public. Through my experience I realized that the attorneys have secrets too. Some of their secrets they wished to be kept not only from the public but also from the judge. There is something deceptively dangerous about a secretive environment, wherein one party is made to feel safe by the privacy while the other party is easing into an almost predatory role, however politely. The subservient party, who has come to view the secret or private environment as their only safe place in the world, may later realize that it was actually harmful. I was glad to do away with the secretive process and speak to Judge Barton directly, no attorney-mediator, just my words, to the paper, to her eyes.

In my July 1, 2014, letter to Judge Barton, I gave a thorough yet succinct account of the secretive plea process in my case It did not start at the settlement conference wherein I told Gingold I was innocent, but at a private meeting wherein Rick and Marci had led my family members into a room under the pretense of sincerity, only to pounce on them with the ultimate emotional extortion—your son/brother/husband will be executed if you do not do as we say, conveying the iciest of apathies.

Judge Barton had never heard that. She did not know about that meeting, nor was she present at the settlement conference before Judge Stevens. She didn't see me teary-eyed declaring my innocence, begging for help, while my fragile mom looked on just feet away, with the rest of my family.

Surely Judge Barton would be concerned about what had gone on behind the scenes—the deception, the threats, the morbid fear. This was not justice, surely not American justice. Judge Barton's inner sense of right and wrong, her zeal for the law that she had as a law student all those years ago, something authentic inside of her, would be genuinely offended by the way this tax-paying, (mostly) law abiding family had been devoured. Not just me. My whole family was devoured.

I explained to her that, "the first thing I told [my attorney] was that I am innocent and will never consider a plea." I described to her the conversation about residual doubt that took place after our final pretrial conference, in the presence of MCSO Deputy Hoffman, in between her courtroom and her chambers. I wrote about the meeting and preparing the family. I told her how the meeting really went and what they did to me in a legal visit right after it. I explained to her that despite what Rick Miller had said at sentencing, to her face, and on the record, about this being "it," was not true. I wanted to get out of the plea. He had *already advised me* to get out of the plea that by pursuing an "ineffective" claim against him. I also said my 2nd chair Marci Kratter had told me to get DNA testing done from prison, and that a match from the condoms to the boyfriend "Nate" would exonerate me. I told her that we had filed for DNA testing but another court had denied it.

The gist of my letter, whether Marci Kratter had simply lied to me just to get me to sign, or she genuinely thought I would be granted post-conviction testing, whatever the case, was that we needed Judge Barton to help us find justice. I told her that, "I was basically refused a defense and threatened with death at the very last minute." I was in prison for murder even though I had never even thought about murdering someone. At the very least I hoped Judge Barton's own inner curiosity would cause her to want to know who the man was who wore the condoms, found next to the woman's body—the woman in whom my DNA was not present.

Post-Conviction Relief—Arizona Reality—July 10, 2014

Many moons ago the federal government saw the need for an avenue for convicted American citizens to pursue relief from a conviction. This was in the interest of assuring that individual states were honoring the United States Constitution and not imprisoning innocent defendants, or keeping them imprisoned. It was decided that all fifty states would have construct within the framework of their own rules of criminal procedure at least one such avenue, so that no such injustice would occur, and if it did, it could—and should—be quickly remedied.

Arizona, under its previous procedure, had "seven avenues for post-conviction relief: appeal, federal habeas corpus, writ of *coram nobis*, motion for new trial or newly discovered evidence, motion to modify or vacate judgement, and delayed appeal. "

Under current Arizona law, we have now instead, Rule 32, which "consolidates the last five avenues into a single, comprehensive remedy...requires consolidation of all claims in a single petition...permits summary dismissal of frivolous claims...[and] provides for a full-scale evidentiary hearing on the record."

Perhaps amenable to ideas or suggestions, the state of Arizona looked to other states in order to determine how best to write its Rule 32. With well-developed, long-existing state governments such as New-York and Maryland on hand, Arizona instead borrowed from the least developed state in the union, Alaska, known by Americans as "the last frontier." Arizona's Rule 32 is "based upon Rule 35 of the Alaska Rules of Criminal Procedure"

The scope of Rule 32, according to Arizona Rules of Criminal Procedure, states, "*Any person* who has been convicted of, or sentenced for, a criminal offense may, without payment of any fee, institute a proceeding to secure appropriate relief."

The language used here is important because "any person" includes defendants who have signed pleas. At the time of my coerced plea in 2011, other defendants I had spoken to were of the mind that if a defendant signed a plea, all appellate rights were gone. With animated demeanors, they urged that I should go to trial—even if my attorneys were unprepared—just to preserve impressive-sounding appellate rights. But as I watched through my newspaper-lens as Jeffrey Landrigan lie down to what I will always believe was an erroneous death sentence I realized that those appellate rights were not as impressive as the naïve defendants around me made them sound.

At the same time, my second chair attorney Marci Kratter, (an actual attorney, not a jailhouse lawyer), told me that I could, and should, sign the Alford plea, go to D.O.C., get a DNA match to the used condoms found near Ms. Hermann's body, file my Rule 32, and get exonerated. As she said that, my first chair attorney, Rick Miller, told me yes, do that, file a claim of actual innocence in your Rule 32, and also make a claim of ineffective assistance of counsel, alleging that he was ineffective.

I had no way to do any legal research in the maximum custody jail at the 11th hour. Inmates were not allowed to actually go to a library. We filled out a literature order form each week, and if what we requested was available it would be brought to us the following week. But unless you ordered crossword puzzles and Sudoku's you would almost never get what you ordered. So, I had to take my attorneys' word for it, just *hoping* that they were sincere. I had no choice. No indignant defendant does.

After I got to D.O.C. and Jill mailed me copies of the Arizona Rules of Criminal Procedure I finally got to fact-check their legal advice. According to the way the law was written, it appeared that my attorneys had been honest with me. All I needed now was for judges to apply it the way that it was written. Under the scope of remedy, it went on to say "Any person who pled guilty or no contest...shall have the right to file a post-conviction relief proceeding." This was reassuring because it seemed obvious that by including "any person who pled guilty or no contest" the powers-that-be were acknowledging that they were aware that sometimes injustices occurred even when a plea was signed. Later, the innocence project would release statistics stating that *40%* of inmates who were found to be innocent and released from prison had *pled guilty* on their way into prison.

Some grounds for relief under Rule 32, which we intended to use were actual innocence, ineffective assistance of counsel, and if they would permit DNA testing, newly discovered evidence. The standards for proving each ground seemed straightforward. Regarding actual innocence, the rule says, "The defendant demonstrates by clear and convincing evidence that...no *reasonable* fact-finder would have found the defendant guilty...beyond a reasonable doubt, *or* that the court would not have imposed the death penalty."

Regarding ineffective assistance of counsel a defendant must show that counsel's performance must be "below an objective standard of reasonableness" and that the "deficient performance must have prejudiced the defendant." The defendant also has to show a "reasonable probability" that if it weren't for the actions or inactions of the attorney, the result would have been "different."

The result in my case was me signing a piece of paper. So I was in the best position to say yes, if it weren't for Rick Miller's actions and inactions I would not have signed the piece of paper. The result would have been "different," which was essentially what I enumerated in my affidavit/ letter to Judge Barton, which was attached to our petition, along with the affidavits by PI Lee Damner and Dr. Tom Streed.

Even if Judge Barton was reluctant to overturn the conviction outright, we believed that our filings would force Rule 32 to "provide a full-scale evidentiary hearing on the record," as it said it would. An evidentiary hearing was what this case always needed. It would force each side to bring their witnesses to court, under oath, to hold their theories up to the light and scrutinize them, in order to realize what is real and what is not. Up until this point I had been disallowed an evidentiary hearing by way of dysfunctional County judges and lawyers who were influenced by MCSO intimidation. Judge Michael Ryan himself admitted and stood to testify that granting an evidentiary hearing in a capital case was "political suicide." As a result, "the record" in my case ended up consisting of Detective Smith's "misleading" grand jury testimony, Ms. Barnes' head scratching presentence report, rife with Smith's own admitted B.S., and the public forum that my sentencing had become, with people speaking "on the record" whose first and last names were never even verified.

Perhaps we could at least get an evidentiary hearing and straighten-out the record.

My petition for Rule 32 post-conviction relief was filed on July 10th 2014. Finally. It was field pro-per, as if I was representing myself, although it was completely written by my father-in-law David Delozier, with the help of some of his colleagues. Jill, his daughter and my wife, was present and involved throughout the whole process, and was actually the person who physically delivered it to the court, in person.

The well-written petition was seventeen pages long. It incorporated some facts from the investigation into Liz Hermann's death from MCSO reports, Dr. Streed's affidavit, and PI Damner's affidavit However it was as it should be, a document designed for the purpose of inserting those facts into the properly applicable laws relevant to the case. Whereas Dr. Streed's affidavit was an investigative report by nature, the petition is a *legal* document. It is the vehicle in which those facts travel through the appellate landscape, replete with countless references to relevant case law, citing cases that had already been overturned for the same justifications that were present here.

Highlighting the complexion of not only this case, but also this situation, the author emphasized that, "the state did not offer a shred of physical evidence linking Mr. Lunsford to either the burning pickup truck or the burned house."

Regarding counsel, the author states, "Throughout the many years that Mr. Lunsford's criminal case languished, Mr. Lunsford made clear to his attorneys that he was innocent of the charges against him, and that it was not simply his objective to defeat the death penalty, but to be absolved at the liability phase of the trial. His attorneys acknowledged his wishes in this regard."

We said in our Rule 32 petition that, On Tuesday February 1, 2011, approximately one week prior to the start of trial, defense counsel changed their tune, advised Mr. Lunsford that he would be "executed" if he did not take a plea. Notably, throughout the settlement conference, defendant continued to maintain his innocence. Given his defense counsel's ineffectiveness, Mr. Lunsford had little choice but to plead no contest to the capital charges against him. His defense counsel had failed to investigate the numerous other individuals who had both motive and opportunity to murder Ms Hermann including, most notably, one person, Sam Parker, who had repeatedly indicated his own culpability in Ms. Hermann's murder. Several individuals interviewed by Leland Damner said that Sam Parker admitted to them that he killed Ms. Hermann."

The petition goes on to mention that counsel "Refused to test any of the physical evidence around both the burnt pickup and house crime scenes, including numerous incidents of bodily tissue that would have provided exculpating DNA evidence." Emphasizing the importance of DNA testing in this case, the author lists the items that need to be tested and why; the bloody handprint, the gas can at the house, multiple hairs and fibers, and he finishes the paragraph with this. "Notably, two used condoms found in Ms. Hermann's bedroom were analyzed for DNA, *excluding Mr. Lunsford as the contributor*. The person whose DNA was found on the condoms has never been identified."

Surely, when Judge Barton read this, seeing this detail again, she would want to know, would *have to* know, what man was wearing the two used condoms found near Ms. Hermann's nude body. Certainly she would demand to know, who wouldn't?

The petition emphasized the importance of DNA in *all* cases, the author pulling a quote from Arizona's own supreme court:

"Indeed, even the Arizona Supreme Court has recognized the importance of DNA testing, having recently declared, We have previously noted that 'science' is often accepted in our society as synonymous with truth. This is particularly so in the case of DNA evidence, which has potential to dominate a factfinder's thinking." The petition touched on the red-haired arsonist, and the fact that still, no one knows who he is, as he is clearly not the defendant. The conclusion succinctly states, "For the reasons set forth herein, defendant Justin Lunsford respectfully requests that this court set an evidentiary hearing to explore the issues set forth in this petition and, following the receipt of the relevant evidence, to set aside Mr. Lunsford's conviction and set a new trial."

Surely now the court would *have* to do something.

Second Request For DNA Testing—July 23, 2014

Thirteen days after we filed the petition, we filed another motion requesting DNA testing to be done on the physical evidence, as we had before. We hoped that now that the court had the petition in front of them, the full pictures, that she, Judge Barton, would be inclined to order the testing, applying its full truth within the context of the situation. We also filed a "stay," asking the court to postpone ruling on our petition until the DNA was brought forth, so that a more informed decision could be made. Two months later, on Oct. 6, 2014, the state filed a continuance, asking for more time to respond to our new request for DNA. Again, we hoped the prosecutor, being a living, breathing, thinking person, who walks around in society with the rest of us, would actually want testing now.

On November 5th Ms. Leisch filed a response, again opposing all testing using the same non-factual arguments that she used in the first one. Some day, I would like to sit down with Ms. Hermann's killer and show him the lengths to which Catherine Leisch went in order to prevent him from being investigated. I'm sure he would thank her.

About a week after that, on Nov 13th 2014, we filed a motion asking the court to appoint an attorney for me, since the situation was gaining momentum and becoming complex. Though Jill's dad could, and would continue to help as much as he could, very few Americans can afford to work for free. Having a paid attorney join us would help a lot, and I definitely could not do all of this litigating myself, pro-per.

Instead of ruling on our request for DNA testing, Judge Bruce Cohen passed the buck and referred our request to another division and another judge, M. Scott McCoy. Judge McCoy had no familiarity with this case, nor would he, because the PCR petition itself stayed in front of Judge Cohen, who wouldn't rule on that either. He was simply preparing to send it back to Judge Barton. By splitting the two filings and sending them in different directions, Judge Cohen made sure that neither Judge would have the full picture.

Less than a month later Ms. Leisch responded and opposed testing, Judge McCoy, who probably assumed Leisch was both accurate and genuine, denied testing with little to no reasoning to support his decision. In his December 3, 2014 ruling, Judge McCoy said, "Defendant waived all of his defenses—including any claim that someone else committed the homicide and arson at issue here—when he pled no contest to the charges." This, despite the Arizona Rules of Criminal Procedure stating in plain English that any defendant who "pled guilty or no contest" was entitled to a Rule 32 proceeding.

Judge Cohen did not cite any legal authority when expressing his opinion. Most judges and prosecutors will, when asserting themselves, cite legal authority in order to validate their position. Judge Cohen did not do that here because it wasn't a legal truth that he was stating, it was his own philosophical or political opinion, despite what the Arizona Rules of Criminal Procedure states, and the law be damned.

That was his first February 6, 2014 justification. In a second opinion, he said, "The court denied the first motion requesting DNA testing." In short, Judge McCoy was not familiar with the case, but he assumed the first court was, so he just did what they did. A safe move.

Next, and probably the most unprofessional thing he said, which came at great disappointment to myself and my family was, "Dendant's second DNA motion offers only unsupported and wild speculation." I presume he means that it speculation to think that DNA testing would solve the case. All speculation is "unsupported" until testing is done. It was becoming clear that as long as they denied testing, or allowing us to get a match to the used condoms, the government's go-to response would be that our position was speculative. They leaned heavily on this circular argument: we couldn't prove that I was innocent because we didn't have a DNA match and we didn't have a right to get a DNA match because we couldn't prove that I was innocent. They held all of the evidence in their possession and wouldn't allow us to use any of it.

Judge McCoy finished by adding, "This division will not rule on defendant's motion to appoint attorney for defendant, filed November 13, 2014." The sands of time could weveal that no Judge would rule on our motion to appoint an attorney, it was never even addressed by a judge.

In late 2014 it was becoming apparent that our situation was different than we thought it was. My 2nd chair attorney, Marci Kratter, whether she was sincere or not, was wrong. I could not just go to D.O.C. and get DNA testing and a match to the condoms. She had made it sound so easy, so simple. I began to wonder if she knew all along that I would get no fairness from appellate judges, or if she had really believed what she had said, and would thus be as disappointed as we were when she found out what was happening. Later I would write her, and tell her what was happening, only to get no response.

Lunsford Reply in Post-Conviction Relief

The state's response to our Rule 32 was filed by Ms. Leisch, using the same inaccuracies and blanket statements previously employed. "Despite a badly mutilated body and a burned out structure, the state has never found—and could not find—any physical evidence linking defendant Justin Lunsford to the murder of Mary Polgar. As part of this reply, Mr. Lunsford re-urges his motion for DNA testing in fact, once the physical evidence is, for the first time, actually evaluated and tested, the physical evidence will show that Mr. Lunsford is actually innocent of the charges against him."

In the state's response, they argued that I "plead guilty" and therefore was not entitled to Rule 32 relief, despite Judge Barton advising me at sentencing that I had 90 days to
file a Rule 32. As mentioned before, defendants who pleaded guilty are entitled to a Rule
32 proceeding, but perhaps the bigger point that was lost on the state was the fact that I
did not even plead guilty, I pled no contest and adamantly maintained my innocence the
whole time. Being falsely accused of pleading guilty over and over became frustrating.

Our reply said, "A plea of no contest is distinctly different than a plea of guilty.
The state misses the central arguments of defendant's case: defendant pled no contest;
he never pled guilty. When a defendant has pled no contest instead of guilty . . . the
strength of the state's case becomes all-important as the primary inducement for the
plea. All of the state's arguments center on a defendant that pled guilty. The state ignores
the fact that defendant pled no contest."

Stepping aside from the legal hair-splitting, and harkening back to the critical issue
of actually solving Ms. Hermann's murder, the evidence, we argued, "It seems circular
that the state argues that defendant cannot have the evidence tested until a petition is
filed, and [now that] a petition is filed, the state argues that because the testing is not
done defendant's position is speculative. Aside from the state's fear of the truth, there
is no reason not to test and evaluate the existing physical evidence."

To drive the point home we filed another motion to reconsider DNA testing shortly
after the reply on March 19th 2015 it reasserted the same points. "A bloody handprint.
A used condom. A victim who had recently engaged in sexual intercourse. This case
has every hallmark of a case that should rise or fall on DNA testing. Yet, none was ever
performed. The state's theory in this case was that Mr. Lunsford was the last person
to see Ms. Polgar alive—a theory that DNA evidence from the bloody handprint and
the used condoms would clearly dispel. The investigating officers found a plethora of
physical evidence at the crime scene. Two used condoms were located in the bedroom. A
bloody handprint was found on the wall. Various hairs were found in the bedroom, tissue
samples were taken from Ms. Polgar's body. Nonetheless, of the foregoing physical
evidence, *only* the used condoms were tested for DNA. And, *the results of these tests
excluded Mr. Lunsford as the contributor*. In short, the only DNA testing conducted was
exculpatory. Apparently fearing that further DNA testing would dismantle its highly
circumstantial case against Mr. Lunsford, the state conducted no further DNA testing;
neither did his public defender. h=However, under section 13-4240, Mr. Lunsford is
entitled to further DNA testing."

This would be the first request for DNA testing that Judge Barton would see. We
wanted to be thorough—especially since she now had the entire Rule 32 proceeding in
front of her, including Dr. Streed's affidavit.

We explained that "at the evidentiary hearing in this matter Mr. Lunsford will demonstrate that (1) he is actually innocent of the charges against him, and (2) that his appointed counsel was ineffective for failing to investigate and explore the evidence demonstrating his innocence. Specifically, Mr. Lunsford will show (1) He has an alibi demonstrating that he was not near the murder scene on the day of the murder. (2) Most likely an individual known as Sam Parker was the real killer, and (3) The physical evidence excludes him as the murderer.

We addressed the erroneous Judge Cohen had made in his ruling, denying our previous requests for DNA testing: "The defendant waived all of his defenses...when he pled no contest." Our filing pointed out that "The law is well-settled that his claim of actual innocence is not waived by his plea of "no contest." The plain language of Rule 32 demonstrates that Mr. Lunsford did not waive any such right by pleading no contest."

Of course the plain language of Rule 32 said that—otherwise why would Judge Barton have advised me to *file* a rule 32? Additionally, we cited an Arizona Supreme Court's holding, that "DNA results need not be completely exonerating in order to be considered favorable, and that "evidence is exculpatory...if it is generally favorable to the accused's defense, or, if it simply contradicts the government's evidence against the accused." We established that we had "not only met, but far satisfied, the requirements of the statute."

Taking it even a step further, Judge Barton would read in our filing that, "Ms. Polgar did not associate with a particularly savory crowd, specifically, Sam Parker. He will be shown to be the most likely perpetrator. Mr. Parker had prior encounters with Ms. Polgar. Mr. Parker is a "patch holder" with the Hell's Angels, and has a reputation for violence among Cave Creek residents. Purportedly, one week prior to Ms. Polgar's death, Ms. Polgar had Mr. Parker removed from the bar she worked at, the *Buffalo Chip* bar, a known hangout for Hell's Angels. This would have been a very humiliating incident for Parker.

"Since Ms. Polgar's death and Mr. Lunsford's arrest, Parker has told various individuals that he should be in jail rather than Lunsford, and that he was the person who killed Ms. Polgar.

It seemed like I had everything I needed now, right in front of Judge Barton. An alibi for the whole day, an exculpatory DNA match from the condoms, and a guy who confessed to the murder. What more could Judge Barton want? What more could there possibly be? The filing finished with a sentiment shared by all who were familiar with the case—save for Ms. Leisch. "Given the plethora of physical evidence available, it would be a tragedy if the evidence was not tested to determine the truth of what occurred on July 8, 2008."

Post-Conviction Relief—Denied—August 13, 2015

On August 13th 2015, Judge Barton issued her ruling. It started, in all caps, center justified, with the words: "PCR DISMISSED" She wouldn't even grant an evidentiary hearing, wouldn't allow us to test any of the evidence. Her ruling was brief—seven pages long, beginning with a robotic recitation of the case's history, dates of settlement conferences and continuances for PCR, then a parroting of the police narrative, rife with the same misleading mischaracterizations originally given by Detective Smith. She stated that I was not forced or threatened to sign the plea, and implied that the plea was my idea.

In the end, she references her own opinion in the first half of her ruling, instead of case law, to justify her opinion in the second half. "This court has already found, however, that counsel's alleged lack of preparation had nothing to do with defendant's decision to plead." He said this even though I had said in plain English, in my letter/affidavit to her that was exactly why I pled.

▌▌ Chapter 9

A World Apart

∙∙

Jill too was realizing that our situation was different than we had expected. By now, I had been in prison for 3 years, after having been in county jail for 3 years, so she had already spent 6 years of her life, in her late 20's and early 30's, alone waiting at home for me. There were no Friday visits at Eyman, so she had a good reason to not come to visit as often, and I could tell that this was welcomed by her, but I never complained about it. I became really frustrated after getting ready for visits and waiting for the call to go to visit, sitting there in crispy new oranges, shiny black boots, fresh haircut, waiting, waiting, waiting…everyone asking me, "Oh, all cleaned-up? Going to visit?" "Yeah" "Nice, who's coming" "Wife." "Awesome!" yeah. In the back of my mind I knew she was probably not coming, but I had to get ready anyway just in case she did. And when she did not, all those same guys would ask me later, "What happened, she didn't come?" over and over, I had to have the same conversation until eventually, I became "the guy" who often got ready for visits with his wife, who wasn't showing up anymore.

The progressive feeling of being wadded-up and thrown away was becoming complete. Everyone—the judiciary, my old friends, my wife and best friend, it seemed like everyone had thrown me away, except my Dad. He never slowed down, never missed a visit, always answered the phone, and often he would bring other people with him when he came to visit. Those other people probably would have visited more if they knew that my visits had slowed down but I never let on about that. I never complained to others that Jill was no-showing a lot of times.

227

It wasn't Jill's fault. She was hurt too, and tired, and she was doing the best she could. We all were. I believed that too much unnecessary conflict existed within families due to a lack of empathy, usually, if we put ourselves in our spouse's shoes, we can appreciate and relate to them, maybe even help them, help the situation, rather than destroy it, regretting it later. Jill was one of the best friends I had ever had, one of the most important people in my life, and I knew that no matter what happened at this juncture I would always want her in my life, so I just supported her. Even when I was frustrated, I was polite; I always put her up on a pedestal every time we spoke. And she never outwardly complained either.

Knowing how trapped she was beginning to feel, and seeing as how she was too sweet to say it out loud, I brought it up one day at visit. I told that I had begun to know for months that we were going to have this talk. But I had to get myself ready to have it in a mature and sincere way, because she would have to know that I really meant what I was saying.

I told her that she didn't have to stay with me, that I would truly understand if she wanted to go in a different direction with her life. I told her that I would support her, and that no matter what she did I would always be her friend. I wouldn't punish her with the threat of resentment, and I reminded her that I didn't even have the capacity for resentment; I naturally forgive everyone, which she knew. I reminded her of times when we were younger and she had gotten angry with someone, then frustrated at me for not getting angry at them too, and she let out a laugh of relief, because she could now see that I really wouldn't be angry with her and I loved her and would let her go with genuine support. I told her she could leave that day and never come back, and she would still go down in my life story as the person who'd done the most for me, just for what she'd already done in the previous six or seven years. I told her she could go out there and get married to someone else, have a family and a whole life and if she found herself alone, a widow at seventy, she could call me and I'd be right there for her.

Jill had been through enough, I felt. I definitely was not going to add further emotional trauma to her. Going forward we had our visits and phone calls, Smalltalk, and I didn't bring this back up or force her into any conversations about it. I wanted her to know that she was free, and if she was driving the ninety miles out to the Florence prison complex to visit me it was because she wanted to.

Anders v. California—The Right To Counsel

Still waiting on a ruling regarding my request to have an attorney in late 2014, we filed another motion on December 28th asking the court to please issue a ruling. As an indigent, pro-per defendant, it seemed like the courts did not take seriously the claims of defendants who did not have an attorney representing them. Some of my filings just seemed to get "lost" and were never ruled upon.

Under *Anders* (Anders v. California), I was supposed to have the right to be represented by an attorney. "Anders guarantees that an individual who is appointed counsel enjoys that right equally with those who can afford private counsel." Put simply, if I'd had a million dollars in my bank account in 2014 I would have hired an attorney to get me out of prison. Any defendant who did have a million dollars would have done that. Anders dictated that there should be equality among defendants. I shouldn't be left in prison with unjust and nonsensical rulings just because I was from a working class family. But I was.

By 2014, Arizona had taken up the practice of making it look like defendants such as myself had an attorney, when we actually didn't. The attorney who was trying to get Into my case in 2014, per OPDS funding was Rick Poster. Poster was a prosecutor at MCAO, then a defense attorney. PI Lee Damner had had a series of conversations with him about my case and Poster agreed he was "all-in" if OPDS would appoint him. All we needed was for the court to order OPDS to appoint him—but they wouldn't even rule on the motion, because I filed it pro-per they basically acted like they had never received it, and because I was trapped in a prison cell, I couldn't prove otherwise.

Poster and Delozier assumed, as an alternative, that since Colin Stearns was still listed on the computer as my "advisory" counsel, maybe that was why the court had not appointed an attorney to my case. Colin Stearns, who David Gurney had referred to as "a joke" had never even read my file. He never withdrew from my case. As a result, a computer search of the electronic index of record made it appear that I still did have an attorney, even though I hadn't spoken to him in over two years.

Sadly, this was not an accident. The state of Arizona had adopted this as a practice in order to make it appear that Anders rights were being satisfied, when in reality, thousands of defendants were sitting in Arizona prisons (like me), after being "represented" by Arizona public defenders, perhaps unjustly convicted or sentenced, with no recourse.

This was addressed in Pacheco v. Ryan two years later in 2016, when United States District Court Judge David G. Campbell said, "There is no indication in the record of when the superior court accepted the motion to withdraw made by petitioner's counsel, triggering his Anders rights...it is not clear when the trial court permitted counsel to withdraw and petitioner's Anders claims became cognizable." Ultimately Pacheco was granted relief, despite the fact that he pled guilty—not no contest—guilty, because, additionally, while a guilty plea does waive many claims, it does not waive all. A defendant's right to allege that his plea was involuntary, as I had, due to ineffective assistance of counsel, survives any guilty plea.

When I was trying to get untangled from Colin Stearns' phantom representation in 2014, Pacheco had yet to be decided by Judge Campbell. So I wrote Colin Stearns and politely asked him to officially withdraw, so that OPDS could justify paying and appointing Rick Poster. Colin Stearns never responded, or withdrew. Eventually, on December 15th, 2015, I wrote him a letter wherein I was more direct and explained to him that we had a serious situation wherein we were trying to move forward with another attorney who agreed to help, and I asked him to "step aside" and file a motion to withdraw.

Less than two weeks later he responded, saying, in part, "I no longer represent you in this matter...I cannot withdraw from your case because I do not represent you in this matter." Then, in a comment that seemed quite extra, as if rubbing it in, he said, "Further, it appears that your pro-per petition was summarily dismissed on August 29th, 2015."

Give up, was his message to me. I would receive that message many times while facing adversity, as many people do. Colin Stearns would never withdraw. To this day, my electronic index does not show a withdrawal from him, and an argument could be made that he is still my lawyer. After all, the computer screen says so. It must be true.

The amount of frustration my family and I dealt with as a result of these injustices and brazen disregard for the law and common sense exhibited by Arizona judges and prosecutors was hard to deal with. Nobody feels more betrayed by these things than those who previously centered their simple lives around believing in "justice for all," patriotic and hailing from a small town. When I mentioned earlier that nobody embodied or personified what America is, the American dream, better than my dad, who started his own business and successfully raised two good boys in a small town, I was wrong.

His dad, my grandad, did it a little better than all of us. Grandad sat with me at visit at Eyman unit while I was dealing with Colin Stearns, Catherine Leisch, and prison in general. Grandad believed in the American justice system so much that he put his life on the line to protect it, and our rights, while stationed in Japan, serving in the US. Army on the tail end of world war two. We found it difficult to accept that these rights, and these laws, so thoughtfully designed to create fairness and a peaceful society would, after being defended by life and limb overseas, come to be so skillfully disregarded by the suits back home. It pained me that visiting his wrongfully convicted grandson in prison had to become a part of the last years of his life. It should have never been. It was unnecessary and easy to remedy. The lawyers weren't perfect, the filings weren't perfect, but Leisch and Judge Barton had everything in front of them that they needed in order to do the right thing here. It would have been easy to quietly begin testing, effortless.

Three weeks after we filed our final, thorough request for DNA testing in front of Judge Barton, my dad, his brother, two sisters, and other family members gathered around my grandad's in-home hospital bed in the family room of his house. I had spent many family functions there. They saw him off, into the great unknown as he passed away at 88 years old. After going from a high school football captain, to soldier, to "powder monkey" in the pot-ash mines in New Mexico in the 1940's, where he met his Delores in '49, he built his business and family in Arizona, leaving behind four kids, eleven grandchildren, and 17 great grandchildren, 32 progeny in all, good people.

I held it in when I was told on the prison phone the day he died. But it came out that night; the first time I'd ever cried in my sleep. It was the first time I'd cried since Noah died. During a dream I had in my prison cell, I was crying with my head on Grandad's chest, telling him that I was so sorry I wasn't there for him when Granny died.

Grandad's passing was the last real corner that our family rounded together. Him and Granny were what held our sprawling family together, at the end of that half-mile long dirt country road in Cave Creek, shooting north off of Carefree Highway, where my whole world had happened.

Their house would be sold, an entire generation of my family had now passed away while I was gone. My dad was getting older and now I'd lost both of his parents. I was feeling lost in the world. *My* world, that I had left in 2008, was gone.

Adverse Family Impacts

The adverse court rulings had a cumulative negative impact on my father-in-law, David Delozier. Aside from myself, no one put more time, thought, and mental and emotional energy, into the specific arguments taking place and the case in general, than David did. As much as my grandad had believed in the justice system, and made sacrifices for it, so too did David. Perhaps no group of professionals cares more about the law than lawyers and other legal professionals. The law is worthy of adoration, it is something to marvel at, complex yet consistent. Law students learn this well as they earn their degrees. Many are told by their professors that they will be the saviors of our society. These wide-eyed law students are our future judges, senators, congresswomen, and even presidents. Indeed they are our collective future, period.

Like his classmates, David believed this. The law is perfect, as it is written on paper, and like many religious ideologies it then inspires profound adulation and loyalty, sentimentality and even love—love for the law, love for the people it is designed to protect. But also like some religions, the doctrine of the law, albeit perfect on paper, is only as perfect in real life as the people who interpret it and enforce it are. Regardless of objectivity or clarity, with *us*, the human family, everything is subjective. There is no topic under the sun that all humans agree upon, be it global warming, religion, or who is going to win the Super Bowl. We argue.

Reading the adverse rulings and their apparent disregard for our interpretation of the law gutted David's peace of mind. He had watched this tragedy unfold in his own small town, had become personally involved early on through professional representations of Gerald Coco and Dwayne Rucker, who shot Sam Parker. He became more involved as he learned more about the case through his own work on it. But perhaps nothing affected him more than watching it impact his daughter's life, changing her trajectory altogether. Just like my dad, he raised her to believe in the American justice system, but also just like my dad, nothing he could do would protect her from it when it became predatory. He had more than one meltdown and crisis over this, and like my grandad, he simply should not have had to spend the latter part of his life like this. The message, that I hope people will understand through this case, is that a wrongful conviction does not just ruin the life of the defendant, it pulls the entire family under, as if trapped under water, disoriented and panicked, trapped, dying for air, hoping that some kind of unimaginable help will come and that by the time it does few or none of us will have actually drowned. That was what it was like for our whole family, as if lost at sea, and it was all unnecessary.

All Detective Smith had to do in 2008 to prevent this was to test the evidence and tell the truth. All Judge Barton had to do to stop our family from drowning was to be fair, to honor Rule 32 and uphold "justice for all." But I guess it didn't really affect their families.

After Judge Barton dismissed our PCR and disallowed DNA testing, or an evidentiary hearing, David drafted and filed a petition for review with the Arizona Court of Appeals and I was moved back to Cook unit. This started a new chapter. The Court of Appeals was notorious for sitting on cases for two years at a time and then rubber-stamping whatever decision the lower state court had already made.

Well-known attorney, Mark Barrett, stated, in a book titled *Journey Toward Justice*, "the truth is that when an Oklahoma prisoner gets past his first appeal (and his conviction is presumed to be a valid conviction even in the first appeal), his claims are generally considered to be unworthy of even being analyzed" and that "as harsh as this sounds, most states have similar provisions of law."

Senior United States district Judge Neil V. Wake, when speaking of Arizona specifically, said, "The best indication of this is the reasoning of the state courts and where such reasoning is summarily affirmed, or review denied by a higher state court. Silence implies consent, not the opposite—and courts generally behave accordingly, affirming without further discussion when they agree"

The points that Mark Barrett and Judge Neil Wake articulated were concepts that I had begun to learn through the slow process of life experience. Because of this I was entering a chapter of my life in which it became more difficult to cultivate optimism. I was always good at talking myself into being positive because I would use objective reasons, and objective reasons are easier to hold onto than vague reasons. But I was running out of objective reasons at this point, and the case for pessimism and doom was growing.

Jill had stayed, for the time being, but I knew she couldn't stay much longer. I began to question the value or definition of "staying" or "waiting" anyway because due to the physical separation neither one of us could be much tangible help to the other. She needed help at the house, and with her equine business. She had thirty horses to feed and fence lines to mend. I couldn't do it. There were helpful people around who could though; some men, some women, and even though it was emasculating at times—many times—to have other men at my house working with my wife on things I should've been doing, I trusted that they were all good people and understood that it was neces- sary. Sometimes you just have to trust your spouse's judgement, and cultivate enough respect for them to keep it that way.

But the most difficult thing was the unanswered calls. She would go five days at a time without answering. Due to the fact that I had planned my future around her, I began to feel that I didn't have one anymore. She'd had her own chapter of suicidal ideation in 2011 and 2012. This would be mine. I would never do it, I knew, but sometimes I found great comfort in fantasizing about it. The cold steel of a gun barrel against my warm scalp, the power to easily conclude this nightmare right under my finder tip. It gave me comfort. Not panic, not anger or grief, comfort, and the ability to finally rest. That was the scary part. The only thing that brought me comfort was the thought of sleeping, forever.

At that same time, from 2015 through 2017, Liz Hermann's killer was on the streets of Phoenix, having the time of his life, enjoying the full insulation given him by MCSO, the Phoenix police department, and the prosecutors in the Maricopa County Attorney's office. They excused him from sexual assault, multiple armed robberies, multiple arsons, wielding a machete' upon a young woman, and even a two million dollar bank robbery attempt. He didn't do a day in prison for any of them. Phoenix PD admitted, collectively, that they knew he was "a daily meth user," that he had a penchant for knives, and that they alone arrested him thirty-seven times between 2015 and 2019.

My family and I did not know any of this, or that there was now a DNA match from him to Liz's murder. We were depressed. We'd lost all hope. All the while he was hiding behind dumpsters smoking meth, looking for his next stabbing victim. MCAO thought it best that no one knew about it.

The only question was who was he?

▌▌ Chapter 10

DNA Results and New Suspects

∙∙

A t my lowest lows I languished behind prison walls in an unre-
markable day in April of 2017. I had prayed to Jehovah to help
me get back to my family every day and night for almost ten years. Literally, every day
and night. But I began to realize that I needed help from someone on the government's
side. I remembered a scripture that says that God can affect even the hearts of Kings.
I became more specific in my prayers, asking him to soften the heart of someone in
the county attorney's office. I had been praying specifically about this for a couple of
months when the officer in my building told me I was being called for legal mail.

As I walked to another building to pick up the legal mail I became curious. I was
waiting on a ruling from the Court of Appeals but I knew that it was still a long way off,
months, or even a year probably. I stepped inside the building, found the officer who was
handing out legal mail, found the clipboard, located my name, signed for it, and noticed
on the ledger that the large manila envelope was from the county attorney's office.

Bizarre, I thought. There was no reason why they should be sending me anything,
because both sides had completed filings and were awaiting a ruling. I signed for it and
began to open the envelope while walking out of the building and as I slid the packet
upwards I began to see, from top down. I saw the words—DNA results. And I began
running to the phone, I had to call Jill right away.

Jill answered with something like "ye—ess?" because we had just spoke, and she
wasn't expecting me to call again until the next day.

I said, "Honey, I just got something in the mail from the prosecutor's office, are
you sitting down for this?"

235

Jill, used to nothing but hate mail from the prosecutor's office, sat down, saying, "Okay.

I told her, "It's DNA results!"

"What!" she said, jumping right back up, shouting, "Joey, Leah, Mom! We got DNA results in Justin's case!"

There was a full-on track meet in the house. Sprints, hurdles, pole-vaulting, over who could find the pen first. Sheer pandemonium. Then we both sat down, and read it together, me reading, her and her mom taking notes, all of us with glossy eyes.

Written by Detective Paul Smith, the report, starting with the first paragraph said, "On Thursday, November 17, 2016 I received an email from the Maricopa County Sheriff's Office, Property and Evidence Custodian. In the email was a copy of the Department of Public Safety, Crime lab DNA Report, a copy of which is attached to this supplement. The DPS Lab Examination Report, #2008-731008, reads that on November 7, 2016 the DNA generated was run through the Combined DNA Index System (CODIS) and a match came back to Nathaniel Noble, 05/01/1980. Attached to this supplement is a copy of the DPS Examination Report."

Almost in unison Jill and I both exclaimed incredulously, "*who*?!"

We had been buried in the case file for years, read every document, spoken to investigators who'd gone to the ground and interviewed witnesses, thought we knew who all the characters were, what the possibilities were, and yet one of us had ever even heard of the person, Nathaniel Noble.

At this point in his day, Detective Smith, upon receiving this e-mail from the MCSO evidence custodian, could have just dismissed it and gone about his day. After all, his position was that the case had been solved years ago, and he specifically told officer Kim Barnes, on the record, that he believed only one person was involved in the murder. Ms. Barnes included that in her presentence report. But perhaps Detective Smith's curiosity got the best of him, because the second paragraph reads,

"I reviewed the case file for the name Nathanael Noble, and discovered that he had never come up during this investigation. I had no information in reference to this subject linked to our victim, Mary Polgar."

Nathanael Noble

I was impressed that Detective Smith reviewed the case file, looking for this guy. It would have taken a lot of time and thought to do that, and I was sure he was busy. But since that netted no information, he took it a step further. His third paragraph, as I read it to Jill over the phone, said, "In running an intelligence report it showed that Nathanael did live in the Cave Creek area at the time of this homicide. I also located that in 2011 there was an expired Order of Protection from a female subject, Teresa Otte. When researching Teresa, I found a connection between Nathanael and Teresa lived in Cave Creek in 2008, around the time of the homicide."

Jill and I, and everyone in the house with her that night, were ecstatic. It sounded like Detective Smith was beginning to see that he might have been wrong in 2008. We couldn't wait to tell her dad. This was just the positive development our family needed, like a lifeboat, finally.

As I read on and skimmed the 19-page stack of documents it appeared that Detective Smith had even left the office and conducted interviews in light of this new information. There was even a hand-drawn map in the back. This was going to be good. By the end of our allotted 15-minute phone call Jill's mom had done an internet search and found that several months earlier, in July of 2016, Nathaniel Noble had been arrested for wielding a machete' upon a young woman and charged with aggravated assault and armed robbery. We hung up the phone on a great note; I would go "home" for the night to read all nineteen pages and call them back the following morning.

The second page said briefly that Detective Smith conducted a telephone interview with Theresa Otte. 'Good' I thought. The next four pages revealed that the specific items, from the horrendous crime scene, which Noble's DNA came back to, were the used condoms found near Ms. Hermann's nude, stabbed, body. We now had the identity of the man wearing the condoms found near the female stabbing victim, and had found quickly in a basic internet search, that he had a propensity for knife violence against women. Big surprise.

It gets even better.

Theresa Otte

Pages 7-10 revealed that the interview Smith conducted with Theresa Otte took place exactly three months *after* he'd received the DNA results. I wondered why he waited three months to call her. Did he experience some indecisiveness as to whether he should go forward with this inquiry? Was he afraid of what he might find? He didn't have to do anything. He could just ignore it, bury it, and leave it hidden in the darkness behind the computer screen. Nobody would be the wiser. I assumed he spoke to a trusted colleague about it. He did not have to disclose it. The case was closed, according to the state. Judge McCoy had opined that I had waived all defenses by pleading no contest, even though every thinking person knew better.

On Thursday February 16th at about 10 a.m. Smith called Theresa Otte. He told her he was calling in reference to Nathaniel Noble, and asked if she would be willing to meet with him in person. Theresa, standoffish, preferred to do the interview over the phone.

The interview revealed that Noble was a Michigan transplant and that he worked at "*Hammerhead Jack's*" in 2008. It was new bar and restaurant located across the street from the *Buffalo Chip*, where Liz Hermann had worked. Theresa had met Noble in 2006 when he lived in Michigan, but had come to Arizona to visit his mother. She lived up the street from Sam Parker's condo. After a telephone relationship it was decided that Noble should move to Arizona in early 2008 to live with Theresa at her parents' home in an up-scale Carefree neighborhood. Carefree was on the east side of Black Mountain, a stone's throw from the Parker mansion. Theresa said Noble seemed "normal" at first, especially during their telephone-only chapter, but that when she actually lived with him she began to realize that he was "sick." She said, "he was bipolar and had an episode when he was 18 years old while living in Michigan [and] at that time had to seek professional help. She said Nathaniel became a patient at the Southwest Network located at 32nd street and Bell Road The audio recording reveals significant differences with Smith's typed summary of it.

She said Noble "hid his bipolarness [sic]" from her but that once she "knew what happened in Detroit she made an agreement with Nathaniel that if they were going to be in a relationship he would have to be under the care of a doctor for his illness."

Court documents would later reveal that Noble's actual diagnosis was paranoid schizophrenia. When Smith asked Theresa if Noble had a violent side she said, "Yes, especially when he got really drunk. She said he had "hit" her, spawning a "situation in court." She told Detective Smith in this interview that there were actually two orders of protection she had gotten against Noble, in 2009 and 2011, due to his violence toward her and obsession with knives.

When Smith asked her specifically if Noble had ever threatened her with a knife she stated "yes" and that he "destroyed" her house. To be even more specific, Detective Smith asked her if Noble threatened her *while* having a knife in his hand, and she said "yes". Despite the audio recording of the interview stating this unequiv-ocally, Smith typed in his own summary, "Teresa [sic] said he has never pulled a knife on her."

Theresa stated that Nathaniel Noble used "cocaine, meth, and heroin," and that "he hid his usage" from her parents by doing it in the bathroom. Noble would later say in his own interview that Theresa used with him in the bathroom.

Theresa stated that she and Nathaniel's relationship "started to go bad in the middle of 2008." Hermann was murdered in July of 2008. And she said they moved out of Cave Creek, in August of 2008, several weeks after the murder, to an "apartment at Tatum and Bell, close to his mental health facility at 32nd street and Bell.

That was a stone's throw from where Jill lived at the time of the plea coercion. And it happened on the day that she came home to find our Boston Terrier massacred in our backyard.

Theresa stated that, "in 2008 Nathaniel "had a guilty conscience" and told her he had cheated on her with "a girl from one of the bars in Cave Creek." When Detective Smith asked her if she was familiar with a homicide and house fire in 2008, she said, "He cheated with someone from Cave Creek." She denied any knowledge of the murder. It was unclear why she thought of the cheating when asked of the house fire, but it was interesting.

Theresa said that Noble had repeated "episodes" and "bouts with his bipolar." When Smith asked her if she noticed "any changes in Nathaniel in 2008," her first answer, given without hesitation, was, "Yes, he was getting sick in 2008 with his bipolar, he stopped taking his meds, and was having episodes." Inexplicably though, Detective Smith's written summary states that Theresa "did not see any changes in Nathaniel during 2008."

Once I listened to the audio of the interview, it became clear that Detective Smith was mischaracterizing key points within the interview. This illustrates the need for defense attorneys and defendants alike to put forth the time and effort to listen to the audio recordings of what witnesses actually say, rather than only reading a detective's versions of it.

Theresa told detective Smith that she knew she was not safe around Nathaniel and that the more he avoided his prescribed drugs, and consumed street drugs, the more "paranoid" and knife-oriented he became. She said she had to hide all of her kitchen knives from him. One day she came home and he was sitting in the backyard with a shrine of her photo albums around him along with every knife from the kitchen, countless photos and knives all over the backyard. She said he had "knives on him all the time and would carry knives in his car."

Detective Smith asked Theresa, "Do you think he could kill somebody?" She responded, "I don't know…if he was under the influence and with certain people he definitely could have done it."

Detective Smith's written summary says the opposite: "She said he would not harm anybody in 2008."

Theresa said he was "Just a hateful person when bipolar," and that "when he got really paranoid, he liked huge kitchen knives." Detective Smith asked her if Nathaniel was "capable of hurting someone.," She said "yeah" without hesitation, adding that he was "hanging out with the wrong friends.," This begs the question who did he socialize with? Who was Theresa talking about?

As Detective Smith wrapped up their interview, Theresa interjected something. This is the only part of Smith's summary wherein he was accurate . "I'm always scared of him as I don't know that person anymore."

She said that she also felt that "As long as he was in jail that she would know she was safe."

MCSO Interviews Nathaniel Noble—February 22, 2017

Six days later, on Wednesday, February 22, 2017, Detective Smith, accompanied by a detective R. Lopez S1835, entered the twilight zone environment of the Maricopa County Lower Buckeye jail psychiatric unit. They were there to interview Nathaniel Noble. He was in in custody for the machete incident. A detention officer, T. Sanford A6398, checked on Noble, said he "appeared to be capable of being interviewed." Then he escorted Smith and Lopez to a round table in the jail pod, in front of the control room. He left them there and left to retrieve Noble.

When the officer brought Noble in, we can only assume from the slurring, jumbled statements he gave that day, that he must have been very well medicated, droopy-eyed and slouching. When he sat down, the first thing he asked, before Smith had said anything, was:

"Are you here about the murder in 2008 where a girl was murdered and the house was burnt?"

An *amazing* question, considering that everyone from the small town of Cave Creek had assumed that that case was closed ten years ago. They'd seen the arrest on the news, the sentencing three years later. It was all they'd talked about back then. Now the question was why did this Nathaniel Noble think that it was *not* solved?

But Detective Smith never asked him that question Smith never asked Noble if he killed Liz Hermann, He didn't ask Noble where he was that day, what he did, or who he was with on July 8,2008. It became clear quickly that Detective Smith wasn't trying to find out if Noble killed Hermann. —He was trying to find out if his conviction of me was in jeopardy.

He asked peripheral questions, danced around the central issues, yet netted a lot of insight, along with some really bizarre claims. Noble told Smith that he and Theresa had to move out of her parents' home in August of 2008 because it was "a good Christian home" and that him and Theresa were "being irresponsible" and doing "coke and meth in the bathroom." Smith asked Noble if he hung out with other women, Noble said he "cheated on her a few times," Smith asked with who, and Noble said, "Do you want me to make a real serious analogy. because I'm going to tell you some things I need to know who you're going after. Are you going after someone I know or are you going after me?"

240

Smith said, "We're just talking."

Then Noble begins to rant. He talks around in circles about Liz and Theresa and mentions that he gave his phone "to a drug dealer for some rocks and they had access to his Facebook account and they could be the Facebook killer."

He said he could "go on for 8 hours" and that they should because he had "a lot of info." He said he could identify Hermann's killer if he was shown a photo. He asked Detective Smith to bring photos of Cave Creek drug dealers so he could identify them and provide information to police.

Detective Smith tried to redirect Noble's focus to the murder and said, "I want to talk to you about the murder." Noble responded, "*Which one?*"

Detective Smith asked him if he knew of other murders. Noble said, "My family has been murdered." Then he leaned in and began whispering to Smith that his sister leaves the back door of her house open, in Mesa, that the guy next door was a "kookou," and that her house was burned down and that Smith should go check on her.

This had become a theme in Noble's life, revealed in his other arrest reports, wherein he expresses anger towards police officers, stating this his family was murdered and that their house was burned down and that no one will listen to him. He also said the "pale skinned" guy on "Spur Cross Road" killed his mom. His mom's home, and Sam Parker's condo were on Spur Cross Road.

Smith asked him if he'd ever started any fires.

Noble said, "Yes."

Smith asked him if he ever carried any weapons.

Noble said, "Yes, a folding knife and on one occasion a butcher knife." He omitted talking about the machete' that he threatened the young woman with, which got him in jail and made this interview possible.

He said he had been "seeing" Liz Hermann for three months, had sex with her several times, and would visit her at her workplace, the *Buffalo Chip*. When Detective Smith asked him what he did with the last condom he used at Liz's house, Noble claimed that he put it in his brown leather coat pocket and took it with him, claiming that this was a normal practice. It seemed unlikely that anyone would carry used condoms in their coat pocket—or wear a leather coat on a 109-degree day. Maybe he assumed he had successfully destroyed the condoms in the house fire.

Smith kept asking Noble who his drug dealers were in Cave Creek. Noble had said he was a thick guy with pale skin and that he needed to see pictures. He said that he was fired from *Hammerheads* then got a job at *Lowes* on Carefree Highway and Cave Creek Road. While there he was told by a "paint guy" named "Josh or Jason" that there were "3 or 4 dangerous drug dealers who would rape and kill woman.," He aid that he would not do that, he'd only tried to rape one woman, while she was half-asleep, but was unsuccessful.

Forty-five minutes into the interview Detective Smith asked Noble if he'd ever stabbed anyone. Noble started to describe a situation involving himself and a knife, and his dad, in the kitchen at his dad's house in Michigan in 1998. Detective Smith cut him off mid-sentence, abruptly ending the interview. Smith didn't want to hear any more.

On the hand-drawn map that Noble created he drew the Cave Creek loop around Black Mountain, marking Theresa's parents' house, *Hammerheads'*, Liz Hermann' house, the *Buffalo Chip*, the MCSO substation, his mom's house, near Parker's condo, then an "X" at Parker's house, writing the word "drug dealer" next to it.

When I called Jill back the following morning we shared a happy, celebratory mood. I filled her in on all the details and she sent e-mails to David Gurney, PI Lee Damner, Dr. Streed, and even my former public defenders Rick Miller and Marci Kratter, telling everyone the news. Meanwhile, my excited mother-in-law began making plans for Jill and I to give her some grandchildren. Who knows, I thought, maybe we *will* have a family of our own now.

David Delozier—Notice of Appearance—State v. Lunsford

David, Jill's dad, filed a notice of appearance, becoming my attorney-of-record. Meetings were held at his office, between him and Dr. Streed, Damner, Evan Haglund, Jill, my dad, my brother, and my sister-in-law Ashely. We filed a notice of intent to file a new petition for post-conviction review under Rule 32). We began filing transcripts from status conferences we had attended from 2008-2011, illustrating the theme of postponed DNA testing, or a lack of DNA disclosure on the part of prosecutor Michael Gingold who blamed it on lab technician Kelli Raley.

We wondered who had sent me the new DNA evidence. The handwritten return address read "Maricopa County Attorney's Office" but in the dozens of pieces of mail that I had received from them over the years their envelopes were always addressed with typed, computer-printed letterheads. This one was hand-written, hastily, with black permanent marker, in a man's handwriting. My prosecutor was a woman. Truth be told, we did not even know for sure if it came from that office. It could have been a whistleblower from my agency.

But assuming that it was from that office, why did they send it? Did they want me to hurry up and file it so they could charge Noble—the clearly better suspect—with the murder? We hoped they did. With Noble sitting in the Maricopa county jail now for another serious knife crime committed upon a young woman, we waited every day to see if they would charge him—especially since his first words to Detective Smith were "Are you guys here about the murder from 2008?"

I thought I could get called to "roll-up" at any time, with D.O.C. staff telling me "Lunsford you're going home." When I told other inmates about the DNA match they started asking me who was getting my TV and other belongings. Could they have them when I leave?

Dr. Streed and Lee Damner came in to visit me and we had a celebratory meeting. Dr. Streed talked a lot about the similarities my situation now had to Ray Krone, we now had a DNA match to a new suspect with the proper M.O. Streed asked how long, exactly, had I been in prison, and then comparing financial settlement numbers to Krone. He said that I had "so much" to offer "this field" and that I could become a public speaker.

Damner said that he hoped to get a confession from Noble but that even if he didn't, we already had an established pattern of behavior on his part. Damner said that he had spoken to an ex-girlfriend of Noble, Krystal Weaver. She said, "Noble had 'help' committing the murder." Apparently, she talked to *Hideaway* bartender Rebecca Harding, who said Liz did not leave the *Hideaway* with me that night—she'd left with another man, "Nate." And she said that Liz couldn't have died Monday night because she saw Liz the next day at the *Hideaway*, with "Nate," alive and well.

The MCSO assumed that they were correct in ruling out "Nate" (Paramanathan Renganathan) in 2008, but were unaware that Hermann was actually sleeping with two "Nate's" at the time. So, no one looked for Nate Noble back then, despite Hermann's roommate Allen Bauer telling Detective Bucaro that he assumed the person who was with Hermann the night she was murdered was "Nate," a "white male." Nate Renganathan was Indonesian.

Damner also went to Theresa's parents home. He interviewed them. They were terrified of Nate Noble, saying that he was still leaving incoherent messages on their phone about wanting to marry Theresa, despite Theresa being five years into a new relationship. They began to worry for her safety if Noble were released—a worry the Otte family had lived with for years. They played the messages for Damner, who recorded them.

Theresa's dad spoke at length about Noble's partner-in-crime back then, a kid who'd grown up down the street from Theresa, riding the bus and attending school with her, but growing up in his dad's mansion to become a drug dealer. He was a light-complected man named Sam Parker. Sam had moved into a condo two miles away on Spur Cross Road, near Noble's mother. Theresa's dad said that Noble spoke "all the time" about the Parker family drug operation "south of the border"

Damner called Detective Paul Smith and arranged a meeting with him to discuss the case. Smith never showed up and quit answering his phone.

Damner spoke to Liz Hermann's employer, Ret. MCSO Chief Deputy Larry Wendt, owner of the *Buffalo Chip*. Ironically, the *Buffalo Chip* had since been burned down by an unknown suspect, a clear arson, yet no one was ever prosecuted.

Upon Damner's first contact with Wendt, he claimed to not remember anything about a woman named Liz Hermann or a murder/arson in Cave Creek in 2008. This, despite the fact that he worked side-by-side with her at the *Buffalo Chip*, held a huge memorial for her at the bar five days after her death, and lived and worked in the small town that couldn't stop talking about the murder.

Now, in light of our new situation, Wendt finally told Damner that he would speak to him. But he would not help us, because he believed that all people who were in prison deserve to stay in prison, even if they are innocent.

I began to wonder how many other keystone authorities in Arizona, not just cops, judges and lawyers held that belief. It seemed like it was almost a religion to them, as if trying to reason with them in a legitimate claim of actual innocence was like trying to persuade someone to change or alter their religious beliefs, or lack thereof. It was exactly the same.

Intent on filing a new Rule 32 petition, and open to making it even stronger, Dr. Streed went down to the DPS crime lab to request additional testing in person. Dr. Streed had done this before. He still works in conjunction with the Department of Homeland Security, and even caries a badge. So, it should be no problem, especially in light of the new DNA match and obvious botched investigation by MCSO. But when he met Kelli Raley and told her he wanted items tested in the Liz Hermann murder case, Raley became aggressive, unprofessional, and belligerent, even sending an e-mail to a supervisor accusing Dr. Streed of wrongdoing. Thankfully, and unbeknownst to Raley, Dr. Streed had audio-recorded the entire interaction.

It seemed bizarre that Raley so vehemently opposed further testing. Streed, and the rest of us, began to wonder if they were hiding something.

New Appointments—State v Lunsford

Seeing that our request for OPDS funding and court appointments of Damner and Streed had been successful, we filed requests for the court to appoint an arson investigator, a second attorney, and eventually a DNA expert. Seeing good cause, new DNA evidence, the court appointed all three. As my father-in-law along with Evan Haglund, perfected and finished our Rule 32 petition, the court, thanks to Lee Damner, appointed a premier fire investigation firm, *Andler and Associates* out of Scottsdale, Arizona. They would assign arson investigator Dave Smith, who turned out to be an outstanding investigator and person.

The court appointed attorney, Kerrie Droban Zhivago, who was also a best-selling true crime author, writing books about, among other things, motorcycle gangs such as the Hell's Angels, Mongols, and Outlaws.

Dr. George Schiro—DNA Expert

Kerrie petitioned the court to appoint DNA expert Dr. George Schiro, whose credentials in biological research and forensic sciences were too many to mention. The court granted her motion. Dr. Schiro's seven-page declaration was succinct and powerful. The first two and one-half pages explain who he is and his experience. He had worked for eighteen years with police crime labs in Louisiana, and an additional twelve years working for private labs. His current positions were as DNA-technical leader, and forensic scientist, and lab director at Scales Biological laboratory, Inc, in Mississippi. He had consulted on over 4,000 cases.

In my case, Dr. Schiro reviewed not only the police reports but also Dr. Streed's declaration, and MCAO Deputy County Attorney Catherine Leisch's counter arguments, opposing DNA testing. Leisch was not a DNA expert. Schiro said simply that everything should be tested—everything that detectives deemed important enough to enter a burning building to save, in some cases preserve for testing. He noted that both used condoms that Noble had left at the crime scene, and thankfully failed to burn, were "deemed significant enough by the crime scene investigators to be collected, and a request was made by Detective Smith on 12-10-08 to specifically test these condoms."

Schiro addressed Leisch's claim that Ms Hermann did not scratch her assailant, pointing out that if Mr. Noble was the perpetrator, no one knows what his face or body looked like after the crime," because police did not contact him. He added that sometimes microscopic examination and DNA analysis of the fingernails is the only way to tell if a victim scratched the assailant.

Addressing Leisch's head scratching claim that the fingernails should not be tested because the "body had already decayed to an extent before discovery," Schiro stated "Ms. Polgar's body had not already decayed to an extent before discovery. The autopsy photographs and autopsy results show very little post-mortem changes had occurred. There was no lividity or rigor mortis present in the body. The hands were in good condition and DNA results would be obtainable."

Schiro's last two paragraph's addressed Leisch's blanket-statement claim that no new DNA evidence could ever exonerate a suspect She had argued that new DNA matches only mean there were accomplices. Schiro said, "The state and law enforcement's position has been that only one person committed this crime. No other resources have been committed to finding...accomplices. In this case, the potential "accomplice" would be Nathaniel Noble; however, Mr. Noble's name never came up in the investigation and there is no evidence that he was an associate of Mr. Lunsford."

Arson Investigations—Dave Smith—Andler & Associates

Dave Smith, arson investigator with Andler and Associates, had an interest-piquing background, both professionally and personally. Dave Smith was a retired police officer, having worked for the Phoenix police department for twenty-three years. In between his employment at PPD and Andler & Associates, he worked as a livestock broker and provided bulls to Ret. MCSO Chief Deputy Larry Wendt in order to facilitate the bull riding that took place at the *Buffalo Chip* every Friday night. His opinion of Wendt was not overwhelmingly positive. His opinion of MCSO was not overwhelmingly positive. He told Jill, at a meeting at our house, which he did not want to have in public in Cave Creek, that if he ever wanted to get away with a crime he would commit it in Maricopa county, because MCSO had a reputation for terrible lazy investigations. Most agencies in Arizona felt that way.

In 2008 while Dave was providing bulls to Larry Wednt he got a close look into the Cave Creek dynamic, the dysfunction, the coexistence and apparent closeness of characters with different lifestyles. He was friends with Joy Gorski, the *Buffalo Chip* bartender who identified herself as Liz Hermann's best friend at the crime scene. Dave had even met Liz herself, while she was still alive. Being assigned to this case, remembering how its controversies affected the small town in 2008, Dave was very eager to now have access to the actual file, my eight banker's boxes, and investigate our case.

Much to our encouragement, Dave did not limit the scope of his investigation to the house fire; he investigated everything. After establishing credentials and professional standards he goes right into the truck fire scene, laying out the detailed descriptions at length. "This description is crucial, in that the person witness Jimmie Larson described is clearly not Justin Lunsford."

In reference to a follow-up interview conducted with Larson, wherein Larson stated that I do not look like the suspect he witnessed, Dave Smith states, "this funeral solidifies the idea that there was one person at the scene of this truck fire and was an individual with reddish or orange bushy hair and not Justin Lunsford."

Telephone Records—Trap and Trace Cell Phone Data

Dave Smith then incorporated trap and trace cell phone data into his declaration, because a crucial part to solving an arson, is knowing where the suspect was at the time the arson was committed. As a defendant, I had explored different ways to establish my whereabouts. In pretrial posture I had assumed that multiple witnesses placing me in

Phoenix at the time of the arson was enough. After the conviction I never quite let it go. I'd had Gerald Coco's cell phone records, and my own, the whole time, along with Liz Hermann's and Max Piper's. Max Piper's did not establish anything, except that he was at his apartment the evening of the house fire, 30 minutes away from the scene, where he said I also was at "around sunset," which is almost 8 p.m. Liz's records showed her phone leaving the Cave Creek area Tuesday morning and being in north Phoenix until 11 a.m., With no evidence of whose possession her phone was in, it was our position that either she or the real killer had it, while the state theorized that I had it. Her phone was never recovered. My phone records showed zeroes across all columns because I had just purchased it from Target the night before and didn't activate it until I woke up on Wednesday.

Gerald's phone however *was* activated, on, with us, and established by various witnesses to have been used by me—specifically at 4:10 pm, 6:45 pm, and 7:54 pm. It was crucial in determining my whereabouts on the evening of the house fire. Especially so since Detective Smith had coerced Kenneth Schaefer to change the time in his statement. Schaefer went from saying that he saw Gerald and I after 8 pm, to saying he saw us at his house at 6:30 pm, in order for Detective Smith to put us in Cave Creek early enough to commit the arson. Since I made the 6:45 pm phone call from Gerald's phone, to Kenneth's son, Zach, it was crucial to know where his phone pinged at that time.

The problem was Gerald's phone records were incomplete. Detective Stephen Fax stated in his sworn affidavit to a judge, requesting a subpoena for Coco's phone records, "By obtaining these records detectives will be able to obtain historical cell site information, and this will allow detectives to determine Justin and Gerald's *location* throughout the day of Tuesday July 8th, 2008." This was the affidavit for a warrant that Detective Fax left the July 7, 2008 Gerald Coco interview to type up. Detective Kristina Bucaro stayed behind yelling at Coco "he's a monster!" over and over, trying to get Gerald to incriminate me. Gerald had told her repeatedly that we never went to that house.

These actual phone records, including the locations, would not be ready for three weeks and Detective Smith couldn't wait that long. So he had arrested me that night. By the time he put Gerald's phone records in the discovery, which would be given to the defense, a year later, the locations were missing.

The locations on the other phone records were present and easy to read—mine, Hermann's, and Piper's, so I knew it was deliberate. Still, for years, I could do nothing about it. And I could do nothing with the three-page document for the next ten years.

I watched an episode of Dateline wherein a woman was accused of shooting her husband's mistress on the side of a lonely road at nighttime, with her pink handgun, which she had recently posted a picture of on her Facebook page. Detectives found flakes of the pink paint on the victim's driver's side window, very damning. The woman's phone was not activated at the time so it couldn't be used to prove her whereabouts, like myself. But also like myself, she was with someone—her toddler son, who had a tech device with GPS. In this TV version, a year after her arrest the D.A. used it to show that she was not on the road in question that night, released her, held a press conference declaring her innocent, then used her as a "consultant" to build a case against who they believed was the real killer—her husband, who planned to get rid of both women by killing one and framing the other.

When I saw that TV show, I knew I had to do *something* with Gerald's phone records. This woman had gotten exonerated solely on exculpatory cell phone records, which I knew I also had. I had the knowledge of where I was. I knew I was not in Cave Creek--I just had to prove it. We already had the DNA to the real killer. If I could prove that I wasn't there it would be a clean sweep. I rummaged through my 30,000-page file and found the three pages of Coco's phone records. Then I found and pulled the others as well. For three days I stared at them.

With Dave Smith now involved and a new window of activity, I had to solve the riddle quickly. Each phone company used a different numeric language and labeled their columns with different acronyms. I looked for tendencies in clusters or digits within larger numbers and began hilting similarities. Once I established a couple of common clusters I began comparing them to time stamps from the Gallagher's surveillance videos in order to determine which cluster, at which time, was associated with that location. Then I applied the same cluster to different times in order to establish locations at those times. I also used different witness statements. When I knew I was onto something I networked, and found a friend of a friend who used to work on T-Mobile towers in Phoenix. T-Mobile was Gerald's provider! He verified my hunches and told us what the acronyms stood for. He explained that the actual cell towers he worked on were fenced-in, and that on the gate at each location, the tower number was posted. The tower numbers were on my document. But the addresses were what was missing from my document. Therefore, all we had to do now was match our tower numbers to addresses.

I created an elaborate chart, snuck it out to a visit with my dad and stepmom. I explained it to them so they could understand it. They left the prison with it, pulled up Google Earth, and literally drove around the streets of Phoenix physically locating each tower and writing down its number and address. I called them that night, added the addresses to the document. I was right. It showed that Gerald and I could not have been present at the arson.

After passing this information along to Dave Smith, he was able to go out and physically drive the drive times and distances, proving that I could not have committed the crimes. He included this in his report, after establishing a fire start time. Later an active police detective would also drive the route, confirming Dave Smith's findings.

Dave Smith's report states that "from 6:35:48 p.m. until 6:45:31 p.m., Justin Lunsford and Gerald Coco's phone was in the area of 26th St. and Greenway Road. From 7:01:59 p .m. until 7:17:37pm. Justin Lunsford and Gerald Coco's phone was in the area of Cave Creek Road and Union Hills Drive in Phoenix." That was thirty minutes away from the house fire.

Using fuel load calculations, Dave Smith was able to determine that the house fire was started at 7:30pm, and would be noticed by onlookers at about 7:40. He opined that even if Gerald and I hurried straight to the house, we would not have gotten there until the fire had begun to manifest itself to the outside. This would not even include or allow for time to stop, purchase gas, fill a gas can, etc. It would also not allow for time to do what the actual arsonist did inside the house before he lit the fire. Dave Smith found by way of crime scene photos and fuel load calculations from nationally recognized expert Dr. Kimble Clark that the arsonist disconnected the "gas flex line behind the dryer" in order to accelerate the fire. This, combined with the fact that the burner knob on the natural gas stove was in the fully "on" position, indicated that the arsonist tried to blow up the house, not just burn it. The reason that the state's "witnesses" never mentioned the gas flex line, or blowing up the house, was because they never spoke to the real arsonist. Dave Smith ascertained that gasoline was not even used in the fire.

The fire start time, combined with the cell phone data, combined with the lack of lividity and rigor mortis established by Dr. Schiro, also proved that Gerald, and most importantly myself, could not have participated in the murder.

Lividity and rigor mortis appear in a decedent within two to three hours. The fire started at 7:30 p.m. Obviously Hermann was killed before the fire started. Her dog died of smoke inhalation, obviously after the fire. Deputy Kenneth Martinez was at Hermann's house at 4:15 pm, three hours and fifteen minutes before the fire started. She and the dog were still alive, yet he heard no dog barking and saw no one at home. Gerald and I were on video at Gallagher's at this time, watching ESPN, leaving at 4:24 p.m. and going straight into north Phoenix as shown by phone records. We couldn't have had anything to do with any of it. And now we had Noble, Sam Parkers buddy, who loved knives and hated women.

Where was *he* that evening?

Arson Investigator Capt. Fred Andes

To understand why such a poor job was done with the arson investigation in this case, Dave Smith explained:

"This investigator, MCSO Detective Steadman, utilized and seemingly relied upon the work performed by, and conclusions offered by Phoenix Fire Captain and K9 accelerant handler, Fred Andes. This individual, Captain Fred Andes, was summoned to the scene by Detective Steadman, the individual responsible for investigating the origin and cause of the fire. Since this fire has occurred, Captain Andes has had a complaint filed against him. As a result of this complaint, the Phoenix fire department utilized the investigative resources of the Arizona Department of Public Safety. The results of that comprehensive investigation performed by DPS were that DPS submitted and requested a criminal charge of false swearing against Captain Fred Andes. The Maricopa County Attorney's Office stated in a letter to the chief of the fire department dated October 8th 2014. "Effective immediately, MCAO will decline for prosecution any cases previously investigated by Captain Andes. These decisions are made in the interest of justice and to prevent any further damage to the Phoenix Fire Department's arson investigation program."

Dave Smith's report goes on to say, "Since then, Captain Fred Andes has also been disciplined and permanently removed from the Phoenix fire department's fire investigation unit. Captain Fred Andes has also been placed on the "Brady" list by the MCAO as stated in the previously mentioned letter to the Fire Department Chief. Furthermore, Captain Andes has also had his certification and membership revoked permanently by the IAAI, International Association of Arson Investigators."

In other words, Fred Andes is not allowed anywhere near a crime scene again, ever. In finishing up his declaration Dave Smith harkens back to the cell phone data, stating, "In fact, the exculpatory information they did obtain from the phone records of Gerald Coco was never explored and applied to this case because the information did in fact show that the opportunity for Justin Lunsford to have been involved in the ignition of this fire was highly unlikely." It was actually impossible.

Arizona Court of Appeals—First Try—Another Rubber-Stamp Ruling--2018

During our ongoing investigation and preparation of our second petition, the Arizona Court of Appeals issued its ruling on our first petition. They were unaware of the new evidence. So, their ruling was almost irrelevant. Almost. True to their form, the appellate judges leaned on "the record," a tightly scripted narrative carefully molded by the government and rife with errors, stigma, and mischaracterizations, in order rubber-stamp the Superior Court's ruling. The appellate judges stated, "We will only reverse the Superior Court's ruling if petitioner proves an abuse of discretion or an error of law." And then, "On this record, we find no error." They even go so far as to say, "the record supports the superior court's findings that Lunsford initiated plea discussions."

They said, "The superior court reviewed the record and identified the evidence the state would have presented at a trial—evidence Lunsford does not dispute."

My family and I could not understand how these appellate judges could write that I do "not dispute" the so-called "evidence." There was no evidence, and I disputed *everything*. That was why we were filing a petition of *actual innocence*. We could not believe how absurd some of their claims were. It wasn't even intelligent.

Perhaps borrowing from Ms. Leisch's creative suppositions, their ruling also stated that I "met the victim at a bar the evening of the murder." glossing over the fact that I met her on Monday night, she died Tuesday night—almost a full 24 hours later. It was concerning, how careless the appellate judges were with the facts, assuming it was accidental.

Second Petition for Post-Conviction Review—
Kerrie Droban—October 11, 2017

In October 2017, we filed our second petition. Once that was filed, Kerrie submitted her supplemental petition on my behalf, in support of the petition crafted by David Delozier and Evan Haglund. On February 26th 2019 prosecutor Andrea L. Kever filed her response to our petition, after a continuance. It was brief. "Lackluster," according to one Kerrie. "Poorly written," according to another. It looked like Kever wasn't even trying. It was the first time I'd ever been happy *after* reading a state's response.

She stated, "The fact that the DNA contained in the condoms now has a name attached to it, does not make the evidence newly discovered" She then cited an over-reaching interpretation of the law, claiming that I was "precluded" from raising any claims. She did not address the new cell phone data, or Dave Smith's report, including the timeline he constructed showing that I could not have committed the arson. She did not even mention Dave Smith's report, as if it did not exist. She stated that under Rule 32.2(A) (2), I was "precluded from raising [any] issues again... and any issues that [I] did *not* raise in [my] previous petition have been waived." In other words, if I did not bring up actual innocence in my first petition, which I did, I cannot bring it up in this one, and even if I did bring it up, I still can't. It seemed like a "nanny-nanny-boo-boo" argument. While some complain defendants "get off on technicalities," she was arguing to keep me in on a technicality, despite the gravity of the situation, as if I were a game.

Kever stated that "Rule 32 is a safe guard...but it may not be abused," implying that we were abusing the privilege of being heard. She even went on to state that we were "abusing its purpose by filing multiple petitions presenting fanciful theories about rights."

On March 22, 2019, Kerrie fired back in her reply to Kever's response. She outlined the situation. "Petitioner, now represented by counsel, filed a *second* petition for post-conviction relief alleging actual innocence, newly discovered evidence, and ineffective assistance of counsel based in large part on newly tested DNA results that disclosed a never before identified perpetrator." She said That police *always* knew of the used condoms by the victim's bed on the night of the murder does not negate the import of having now learned the *source* of that DNA. The state's suggestion that the "new name" makes no difference is disingenuous." She also argued, "Petitioner…received *additional* support for his claims for relief after arson investigators evaluated the origin of the fire started in this case and reconstructed a timeline using Gerald Coco's cellular phone records obtained by the Maricopa County Sheriff's Office pursuant to a search warrant [which stated] said documents *will* allow detectives to determine Lunsford's location throughout the day of Tuesday July 8, 2008."

Creating the appropriate nexus between the cell phone records and the ineffectiveness of trial counsel, Droban states, "Significantly, petitioner's trial counsel never reviewed the cell phone records obtained by MCSO though it was clearly exculpatory."

After going into detail about Dave Smith's findings and laying it out in a clear and easy to understand format, she summarizes with, "In short, according to the arson investigation, petitioner could *not* have committed these crimes."

At the risk of being redundant, she restates it for emphasis two paragraphs later—"Trial counsel failed to challenge the fire in this case, or explore the phone records of Gerald Coco, data in its possession that *confirmed* petitioner *could not* have ignited the fires."

In conclusion, Kerrie asked Judge Barton again, to overturn my conviction, or set a new trial, or at the *very least*, to finally set an evidentiary hearing in this case so we could bring all parties into a courtroom.

The more I read about the phone records within the filings, the more I became glad that I had watched the episode of Dateline some months earlier. This had to get Judge Barton's attention even though I was aware of her bias towards me, and perhaps all post-conviction defendants. I knew that she was a person, and now she would know that I could not have done these crimes. To boot, we handed her the real killer on a silver platter, thanks to MCSO's own supplemental report and DPS's forensic testing results. Judge Barton had seen me in court every month for years, had seen my family, knew what I was like, heard all about me at sentencing, even said herself that she saw no violence or evil in me whatsoever. Now, here we are, along with MCSO and DPS, handed her a DNA match to the meth-smoking-schizophrenic-knife-violence-guy who asked Detective Smith, "Are you here about the murder in 2008?" Judge Barton would *have to* do something now.

Judge Barton Denies Petition for Post-Conviction Review—May 14, 2019

Judge Barton did something all right. On May 14, 2019, she issued her ruling on my petition for relief, my petition for actual justice, by stating at the top, "The court finds that none of the defendant's arguments are colorable." She spoke very little about the facts of the case, omitting any mention of the phone records or Dave Smith's report, and leaned heavily on the letter of the law, or her interpretation of it, that is. She cited the rule of preclusion, just as Andrea Kever did, yet admitted that it "Does not apply to two of the claims raised by defendant herein, newly discovered material facts and actual innocence. So long as defendant explains the reason for not raising these claims in a previous notice or petition." This implies that she would have granted relief if we'd given "the reasons" for not raising it before. She states that "Rule 32.2(b) goes on to provide that, "If the notice does not identify a specific exception or provide reasons why defendant did not raise the claim in a previous petition or in a timely manner, the court may summarily dismiss the notice,"

What Judge Barton was stating here, was that she took issue with the fact that we did not explain, in enough detail, why we "did not identify a specific exception or provide reasons" why we "did not raise the claim (new evidence) in a previous petition."

We did not raise the claim of new evidence in the first petition because we did not have the new DNA evidence in 2014. That was why it was "new." We were clear about the dates, and the dates were already printed on the DNA reports, which we attached to our petition. The fact that Judge Barton was avoiding the central issue of who tragically ended Ms. Hermann's life, way too early, and creating her own side issues where there really weren't any spoke volumes about her intentions.

Even Andrea Kever, for all of her indifference, did not raise this "issue." But that didn't matter because Judge Barton, leaning on another misapplied technicality, states in her ruling, "A court may determine that an issue is precluded *even if* the state does not raise preclusion." In other words, a prosecutor does not even need to make the proper arguments in Arizona. The prosecutor knows that he or she can issue a brief, "lackluster" document, "poorly written," because Arizona judges will make the arguments for them, as Judge Barton was doing here for Ms. Kever. Judge Barton explains why judges do this, by emphasizing "avoiding piece mail litigation and fostering judicial efficiency."

Judicial efficiency is important. The courts are busy, overwhelmed, and too many defendants are filing too many documents, they say. Understandable, but since I was denied justice here, again, and so brazenly, I would *have to* refile with another court, and another, and another, if the denials continued. I would have to appeal this conviction for the rest of my life, even after my release. That is not efficient. On the other hand, if I were to get justice here I would never need to file anything again. *That* would be efficient.

And since when is a game-changing DNA match and exonerating cell phone records "piece mail litigation?' Prosecutors convict defendants every day based on DNA and cell phone records; there is nothing more impactful in a courtroom.

Judge Barton went on to use the fact that she herself denied us the first time, as a good reason to deny us this time. She said, "The claims referenced above were each raised by the defendant in his first petition for post-conviction relief and rejected by this court.," And with a flair that bordered on the pedantic she added, "Even if they had not been raised, defendant would be precluded from raising them." She talked about everything *but* Nathaniel Noble.

Avoiding consideration of the new DNA match and the disturbing details of Noble's history of knife violence towards women, his meth use, his schizophrenic meltdowns, or his "Are you here about the murder" way of greeting Detective Smith, Judge Barton instead focuses on a clerical error in Dr. Streed's report-it had the wrong date typed onto it. Judge Barton said, "Defendant's claim of actual innocence seems to be based in large part on the declaration of Thomas Streed. SIGNIFICANTLY, that declaration is dated June 30, 2014, which is approximately 45 days *BEFORE* (emphasis, hers) defendant filed his first petition for post-conviction relief."

"Significantly…" she said.

Judge Barton piggybacked off the court of appeals' blanket statement that, "Given the nature of the evidence" nothing could exonerate me anyway. This ended up being a vague characterization, or cliché, commonly used by Arizona appellate judges who wished to sway the opinion of the courts above them, but found it difficult to produce specifics. The same was done in State v. Milke and State v. May; both cases were overturned.

When she did attempt to be specific, Judge Barton stated, "He was with the victim the night she was killed." I was not. Then she stated that, "I was acting strangely the next morning." That in itself is not at all specific—nor does it equate to murder, or evidence. It is not found anywhere else in this case. But when a court does not have any hard evidence to point to, they are forced to support their position with speculation.

Petition For Review—Arizona Court of Appeals—2019

In light of Judge Barton's denial, Kerrie drafted and filed an impactful and well-written thirteen-page petition for review, which she added to the stack of documents that had been in front of Judge Barton, and sent the entire sum of it up the chain to the Arizona Court of appeals. They would finally get a chance to see the new evidence and to learn about their new suspect.

Under the boldface heading that read: "Reasons why this court should grant review," Kerrie wrote:

"This court should grant Lunsford review because the court's denial of his claims of newly discovered evidence and actual innocence are short-sighted and do *not* adequately address the additional findings of DNA belonging to Nathaniel Noble, or the declarations of George Schiro, a forensic scientist and DNA analyst who opined that further testing should have been conducted on the bloody handprint found on the wall in the victim's bedroom as well as testing of the victim's fingernail clippings. Additionally, the court's rulings failed to comment at all on the arson expert, Dave Smith's findings and declaration that, according to the timeline he constructed, Lunsford could not have committed the arson because he was *NOT AT THE SCENE.* (emphasis in the original) This court should give due consideration to the additional findings in the context of the previously submitted evidence and arguments."

Right, including Dr. Streed's backdated declaration.

Kerrie pointed out that, "Police concluded Lunsford was the prime suspect and the "last person" to see Ms. Polgar alive that day" (in 2008), and yet now, (in 2019,) "the Maricopa county sheriff's office issued a report that *refutes* the state's supposition that Lunsford was the "last person" to see the victim alive."

She gave context by explaining, "Lunsford was advised he would be "executed" if he did not accept the state's plea offer," and that during that "settlement conference…Lunsford continued to assert his innocence…when no physical evidence linked Lunsford to either [crime scene]" and by contrast "Noble suffered from bipolar disorder with sometimes violent outcomes. Noble abused drugs and alcohol at the time of the murder. He was violent and paranoid, carried "knives on him all the time…and in his car" Noble's name never surfaced during the MCSO investigation despite that "*vital evidence linked*" him to the victim—he had sex with Ms. Polgar the night of her murder. Additionally, Noble was at least an acquaintance of Sam Parker, an investigative lead in this murder case."

In an effort to make sure that the appellate judges would not lump me in with Noble, Kerrie pointed out, "Petitioner received additional support for his claims for relief after arson investigators evaluated the origin of the fire started in this case and reconstructed a timeline using Gerald Coco's cellular phone records," which, even according to MCSO "*WILL* allow detectives to determine petitioner's location," and that "*in short, according to the arson investigation, petitioner could not have committed these crimes.*"

255

She mentions that the state's fire investigator, Captain Fred Andes, was basically a fraud and was since banished by the prosecutor's office, for repeatedly lying under oath, and "training his canine to implicate innocent people."

Getting into the law of it, she states, "Trial judges have inherent authority to grant discovery requests in PCR proceedings upon showing of good cause, and that "Rule 32 not only provides a procedure through which a defendant may be heard, but also ensures a record from which reviewing courts can determine whether the facts "support petitioner's claim for relief."

Citing State v. Schrock she then stated, "This court must conduct an evidentiary hearing when a petitioner presents a colorable claim which, if true, might have changed the outcome…accordingly [Lunsford] is entitled to *at least* an evidentiary hearing and, at most [having his conviction overturned.]"

She mentions Dr. Streed's findings, asking the court to at least order DNA testing on the bloody handprint, stating, "Dr. Streed stressed that similar evidence became "pivotal" in exonerating the wrongfully convicted Ray Krone, a case he worked wherein the *REAL* [emphasis hers] murderer, Kenneth Philips, left a sample of his own blood at the murder scene."

Judge Barton had pointed out in her ruling, that I trusted my public defender. She argued that it meant that what happened in this case was appropriate. I did trust him. I had to. Every indigent defendant has to trust his public defender, just like every cancer patients has to trust their oncologist. The alternative is too scary. You don't want to think that the person whose hands your life is in might willfully devastate your whole family. Trust is justified sometimes, and well placed. Unfortunately though, it is also in some other cases simply a pre-requisite for betrayal. Kerrie mentions in her petition for review, He relied on his lawyer's counsel, trusted his lawyer to thoroughly investigate his case and exhaust all possible avenues. Clearly his lawyer did not do this and to Lunsford's detriment. Had defense counsel insisted on additional testing, sought his own DNA expert, demanded thorough crime scene analysis, he would have discovered Noble."

Building off of that, and simplifying this supposedly complex situation down to what it really was, an innocent man begging for help, Kerrie finishes by quoting a statement made by me to the prosecutor many years ago, at the settlement conference; in the presence of my mom, dad, Jill, and my little brother:

"First of all, I didn't do it. Second of all it's not fair, I'm in a difficult situation, its terrible what happened to her but I didn't do it. What happened to me was getting kidnapped by MCSO and held hostage [for years] being psychologically and emotionally tortured for the past 2 ½ years with you guys pointing a…gun to my head saying you need to sign, compromise, whatever, or you're going [to die] because that's what happens to people in your situation."

Reading the petition for review made us hopeful, but after what we had already been through, we knew that "hopeful" didn't really mean anything anymore. At times we despised hope, became annoyed at the mention of it, remembering that "hope" had simply become a precursor to angst and dangerously low depression. We now had no illusions about Arizona's judges and prosecutor's caring about justice, or facts, or evidence, or people. They prioritized the appearance of propriety over actual propriety and valued technicality and affirmation over humility. It began to appear that the Arizona appellate process was little more than an elaborate fraud, a process put into place that would keep defendants quiet, waiting years in between rulings, while their sentences would run out, almost like a complex misdirection, with a defendant getting relief once in a blue moon to make it look fair, not dissimilar to Stalin's gulags. The judges, politicians, and even court-appointed defense attorneys were complacent. They had created an unyielding framework designed to constrict and smother, and like a Chinese finger trap it could not be reasoned with. The farther in you went, the more impossible it was to get out. We had to find a way around it.

I wrote a lot of letters to people outside of the Arizona dynamic, and in some cases outside of the justice system altogether. After Noble's machete robbery upon the young woman at the Circle K in north Phoenix, and, simultaneously, his DNA coming back to this 2008 murder, the Maricopa County Superior court and prosecutor's office, inexplicably released him, back into the north Phoenix neighborhood. No prison time, no murder charges. We couldn't believe it. I was in prison with guys who were serving 10-20 years for the same offense. We became concerned that MCAO was almost covering for him, so we did a background check and found half a dozen other prison-worthy arrests by Noble, for which he had still never been to prison, including, additional to the machete' incident, multiple possessions of dangerous drugs, threatening and intimidating, arsons, and numerous petty crimes, from theft to trespassing to still stalking his ex, Teresa. Now we really felt that they were running interference for him, trying to keep him out of sight.

The help I had gotten from MCAO, in the form of the DNA reports, was not enough. So I kept praying for more help from the other side—someone, anyone. I had to. I had almost given up hope; I began to feel that if God wanted me home, I would have already been there. But I had to pray and meditate to keep my sanity, and I just couldn't give up, it was not in me. So I kept on. When you are innocent you cannot accept imprisonment.

My court-appointed attorney, Kerrie, was submissive to the process and therefore very limited in her helpfulness. She said to Jill, in a text, that she believed I was innocent. But in real life, her court-appointment was over, she didn't really care what happened to us, and she was onto the next paycheck. This ended up representing one of the most hurtful elements we encountered, the complacency of court-appointed attorneys. The system is broken, everyone with a television or twitter feed knows that now—certainly attorneys like Kerrie know that. They know that their B+ filings are never going to help their clients, even the innocent ones, but they carry on anyway, silent, because the system works for them—they get paid every time. We needed an attorney who cared about what was right who, as a human being, simply refused to accept wrongdoing.

The Advent of Joy Riddle

"I…wanted to reach out to you with some concerns. Recently I was contacted by a criminal defense attorney named Joy Riddle. Apparently she is a friend of your wife's and wanted to offer her services…unfortunately, there is a finite conclusion to this process [and] all investigation [is] completed. If you have spoken to Joy, I need to be "kept in the loop"…she should not be communicating with you…when she inserts herself into your case, schedules meetings with my investigators having read none of the materials much less the petition or expert reports it becomes concerning."

Joy Riddle *had* read all of those reports, and the petition, and I *had* spoken to her, at length, because as an adult human being I had a right to consult with as many attorneys as I wished. The experts and investigators did not belong to Kerrie. They had been brought on by my father-in-law, before she was involved. The investigation was not even near complete, and Kerrie's off-the-mark statements spoke to how detached she was from the case. She simply did not want anyone else poking around.

There was a three-way texting conversation that took place leading up to Kerrie's letter that day, and it was not a peaceful one. But there was a much more important three way conversation that led up to all of this, and it took place at Jill & I's house one evening between Jill and some of the good people who I'd mentioned earlier that had been helping her at home with the horses.

In 2008 when I was indicted by the tag-team duo of prosecutor Jeanette Gallagher and MCSO Detective Paul Smith, wherein Gallagher solicited and coached his "misleading" grand jury testimony, there was a young prosecutor back at the office who Gallagher was mentoring. This young prosecutor had gotten her law degree and become a prosecutor because she wanted to make a difference in the world, wanted to help people. But after a few years of finding out what the MCAO was doing under Andrew

Thomas, then Bill Montgomery administrations, she realized it was going to be difficult to help people from there. Eventually, she went into private practice, and her and her husband, a detective at DPS, moved their large blended family to Cave Creek. As I said in the beginning, everyone wants to live in Cave Creek, from Sonny Barger, to DMX, to Sheriff Arpaio, and everyone else. This prosecutor-detective combo had, among many other children, a daughter who was at the age of needing a hobby, who really loved horses. After shopping around for an equine teacher they naturally chose the best one in all of Arizona (2019 Best Trainer Award), Jill Lunsford. As a result, Joy, Larry and Jill found themselves standing around together at our house one evening when Joy said, "Oh, I've got some stories," in reference to her adventures as an attorney. To which Jill responded, "Yeah, I've got some too…" Joy said, "Right, cause your dad's an attorney?"

They hadn't spoken about me yet, even though they had known each other for about two years at this point. And, with her woman's intuition telling her that it was a safe enough and appropriate setting, Jill told Joy and Larry, "No, my husbands in prison for murder and he had nothing to do with it. He's innocent."

And their jaws dropped.

Jill and I can both now tell you from experience that nobody believes that statement at face value. For that reason we almost never bring it out, it is too private. But after Jill elaborated, Joy went home and got on the computer. She was up all night. She could not believe what she found. We arranged a conference call, spoke at length, and she made an introductory call to Kerrie which went well. It was the second call that Kerrie chaffed at. Joy and I met in person I answered all of her questions—even though she was a prosecutor at MCAO while they were trying to give me the death penalty, and even though her husband was a cop. I'm sure any defense attorney would have told me not to talk to them, but I was done taking advice from court-appointed defense attorneys ten years ago. Besides, I was sitting down with Joy *in* person, and she treated me *like* a person, like an equal. I couldn't even get Kerrie to meet me in person; the court-appointment doesn't fund that type of thing.

Joy also went to see Nathaniel Noble in person, attending several of his court appointments. He was now in custody for yet another offense, in this case trying to break in and stab two young woman at a north Phoenix Jack-in-the-Box, up the street from the Circle K machete robbery scene, in the pre-dawn hours, before a construction vehicle scared him off.

A series of meetings was held, an unlikely combination of the family members of a convicted murder defendant, with a former prosecutor, and some current law enforcement, speaking freely, nothing was off limits. With that, Joy was determined to *really* help, which prompted the second call to Kerrie, who, upon realizing that someone was really trying to get involved, became defensive, and then aggressive towards Jill, via text message, prompting the afore-quoted letter, and a threat from Kerrie to Joy, that she was going to file an ethics complaint against Joy if she continued to talk to me.

We were surprised at Kerrie's reaction. We thought that any sincere attorney would be glad to have more people on our side and more people helping. We would always be left to speculate about the intentions or sincerity of some of the people who had worked on my case. Kerrie fought tooth-and-nail to keep the exculpatory phone records *out* of the petition, even though they proved that I was not in Cave Creek when the crimes occurred. I had to use family members to go back and forth with her via e-mail because I could not get her to meet with me. Ultimately she wouldn't include the phone records, but I happened to call Jill one day at the exact time that Dave Smith of Andler and Associates was at our house discussing the case with her, and she put me on the phone so I could explain it to him. Looking at the documents as I explained it, he then went out and drove the route, constructed a timeline, and concluded it in his report, which forced Kerrie to address it in her filings. In her filings she leaned heavily on it, because it was completely exonerating. Eventually Joy and Larry drove the route as well, to double check, but if it had been left up to Kerrie the phone records would still be hidden.

Eight days after the text message standoff between three and four of the most important women in my life, Kerrie sent Jill another text that essentially said, "Judge Barton denied Justin's PCR, my appointment is over, come get your stuff." She meant the file. We never heard from her again.

Joy filed her Notice Of Appearance shortly thereafter and drew up a contract for us, that she would now represent me, do everything she could to get me home to Jill and the family, for a grand total of one dollar.

We put together our camp, which still included David Gurney, Dr. Streed, Damner, Delozier, and some who cannot be mentioned. It also included a zealous young law student turned attorney, Ashton Coleman. Ashton was in the fifth grade the day that I was riding around with Gerald Coco, a week before my arrest. When I was standing in my cell at 4th avenue in 2008 I knew that *someone* out there would help me, I just had no idea she was only ten years old at the time.

With genuine representation came a lot of digging, a lot of networking, and some new information. Since my family members were dignified with helping they came up with new ideas and felt empowered.

We started making public records requests and were finally able to read Noah Todd's death investigation report, which created more questions than answers, such as, why was the safe in his bedroom left open with its door obstructing the walkway?

Whose marijuana was on his coffee table? Why did he drive around all day that day telling people he'd finally found proof that I was innocent? What was the proof? What did he and the Parkers talk about at dinner that night? What were the "documents" on his coffee table that Scottsdale PD impounded as evidence? And who shot him in the head?

We also started making public records requests on Nathaniel Noble.

The World of Noble

Nathaniel Noble lives in his own world, an alternate reality wherein the rules do not apply, a world governed by schizophrenic disillusions and the impulses they inspire, fueled by fleshly cravings and primordial instances, free of all consequences, a world the most deranged criminals can only dream of.

A records custodian at MCSO said that all she could tell us over the phone, regarding the public records request for Nathaniel Noble, was that he is connected to 2008 homicide, (Liz Hermann) A request at Phoenix PD however told a much more elaborate story about Noble, detailing his activities over a 4-year span.

After Noble's Cave Creek chapter had run its course, and he and Teresa moved away 3 weeks after Liz Hermann's murder, he found himself living in north Phoenix, closer to his mental health facility, but even that would not help him. After 2008, due to his lack of cooperation with his treatment program, continued use of street drugs, and perhaps guilt from what he had done to Liz Hermann, his condition deteriorated drastically. In order to appreciate the other side of a wrongful conviction, not just the details about the guy who shouldn't have been in prison, rather, the details about the guy who got away, and what he did after, we catch up with Noble in the spring of 2015, while I was thrown away at Eyman unit, mourning the loss of my grandad.

Already having gotten in trouble with the law, Noble was on court order to attend Southwest Behavioral Health for mental evaluation on March 27th, 2015, where, instead of cooperating with the evaluation he began punching people "in the face." Eventually the facility had to call the police because they could not contain him. When Phoenix Police Officer Theresa Chapman arrived, Noble told her that he wanted to file a report because "Several members of his family were killed and that monsters who live in the drains outside of his window took gold and money from his inheritance." The officer had to cut off her interview with Noble because, according to Officer Chapman, "All he wanted to talk about was the monsters outside of his old house."

Victim Andrew Gannon told officers, "Nathaniel thinks he is God and has problems with everyone," and then he (Gannon) began ranting "about Jesus and the devil" and so "due to the mental instability of *all* parties" no further statements were taken and no charges were filed.

Nathaniel Noble was then moved from Southwest Behavioral Hospital to a half-way house on 27th ave and Portland, where a woman, Shawna Bartman had to deal with him a week later. Police had seen Noble at 11 am walking on the side of the road with a woman's purse and jewelry. Liz Hermann's purse and jewelry were also taken. Bartman called police at about the same time. She stated that Noble had come up behind her and grabbed her private areas saying that he "Wanted to have sex with her." When she rebuffed him, he took her purse and jewelry. They were physically pulling back and forth on the items, but he overpowered her, and broke a "glass object which was a memorial to Shawna's deceased son."

The people at the halfway house did not know what to do with Noble. He could not take sex by force that day, so he took her possessions, to sell them for more drugs. She said she "has had many problems" with him, but did not wish to press charges for sexual assault. They just wanted him gone.

A month later he tricked a taxi driver into giving him a ride to treatment center Community Bridges, which would be the closest thing to a home that Noble would have for the next few years, until they too no longer wanted him around. Noble stiffed this taxi driver, who then called police, who noted that Noble was "currently suffering from schizophrenia."

After a five-month hiatus Noble called police to say he'd been harmed on the light-rail but left before they arrived, and two days later, outside of Community Bridges police responded to a "disturbance" caused by Noble. They said he "is a heavy drinker...had not taken his medication [and] thought he worked for the C.I.A." The report goes on to say that Noble was "verbally abusing everyone" at the facility (LARC), that "staff restrained him" and he knocked a computer off of a desk. Police then transported him to UPC (Urgent Psych Care).

Two weeks later police give Noble a ride *back* to LARC, on November 13, 2015 at 6:00 p.m. He had already told police they (LARC) did not know what to do with him, and by 11:00 p.m., five hours later, they had to call police to come back and arrest him again. The responding officers refer to it as a "hot call at the church ministry" because Noble was "lighting" things "on fire.. The officer reported, "S1 (Noble) very 390 and had already left LARC. Booked on 10-52."

Three weeks later, on November 15, 2015, police responded to a bus stop where Noble was lighting more things on fire. When bus driver Aaron Hanton, at 6'4" and 280 pounds saw the fire in a trash can and tried to put it out, Noble, who had left the scene, saw him, ran back to the scene and knocked him to the ground and yelled "Don't you put out the fire, I'm the fire starter, I'm gonna be on the news!" Noble fled from police who caught him in a nearby field and said that they "recognized Nathaniel as a subject [they] had dealt with in the past." He "has known psychiatric issues." When they apprehended him "he started to rant about being "the fire starter" and reciting, "bible verses."

Eleven days later officer Derald Rine was sitting in his patrol car outside a Circle K when, according to Rine, he "Observed Nathaniel Noble enter the Circle K at this location, [then] he left the store with a drink and walked to me (Rine) and said he didn't pay for it." It was becoming apparent that Noble was really comfortable committing crimes, yet somehow also comfortable with police. Officer Rine stated that, "he had him pay for the drink," and added of Noble, "he is a known 918 and uses meth on a daily basis." Police knew him well, and did not want to take him off the street.

Five days later, on New Year's Eve 2015 at 4:39 a.m. officer James Blanco responded to a Circle K on north 7th street where Noble had barricaded himself inside a Circle K bathroom, "with a cross made out of a broken baseball bat and a wooden stake." Circle K then had Noble trespassed. One more place that was not comfortable with having him around.

Three and a half hours later, at 7:54 a.m., officer Bobby Madeira responded to a Jack-in-the-Box where Noble, who was "paranoid schizophrenic, [and] off his meds," was "seeing things that were not there," "believing that everyone was out to kill him," "scaring the clerk as he screamed out his delusions in the Jack-in-the-Box" with "a knife on his person." Noble told the officer that he was "drunk" and "on drugs in the past 24 hours," and the officer gave him a ride to UPC to get some meds and sleep it off. No jail.

Nine days later officer John Sticca was sitting in his patrol car watching Noble walk alongside 4th ave, close to 4th ave jail. He reported that Noble "appeared to be talking to himself" and that he then observed Noble light "a couch" on fire, and as it "began to burn" Noble then "walked over to a roadside memorial and appeared to light it on fire as well."

Three days later 55-year-old Marvin Mcclain was driving west bound on Van Buren street at 4 a.m., near community bridges, when Noble ran out into the roadway and threw a fist-sized rock through his windshield, almost causing him to crash, and then took off running westbound down the middle of the street yelling. Noble, who was lying in the street when police arrived, yelled, "Yeah, I threw a rock at his car, I had to stop him because I'm going to die tonight!" Noble was booked into 4th avenue jail for criminal damage and had a pair of pliers in his pocket.

Two days later officer Matt Johnson responded to St. Luke's Hospital at 7 a.m. "In reference to a male that was rambling about a gun." It was Noble. The officer stated that Noble was having "delusions that he was in the FBI" and that the night before, a woman "named Tammy" was shot at Circle K.

On June 8th 2016 Noble was issued a citation by PHX PD for drinking alcohol at a bus stop near Community Bridges. Two days later he called police and reported that he had been shot, on the light rail. But when they responded he "said he had not been shot, he only told security that to get a free ride to the hospital." So they gave him a ride. Two days after that, on June 12, 2016, officer Don Liona responded to an arson call at 3 a.m. at community bridges where Noble had barricaded himself in a bathroom with a 6" fillet knife, and lit the bathroom on fire, scaring everyone. When the officer got the door unlocked and open, he reports, "Nathaniel ran out yelling, "I just smoked G" (meth) and left the property." When the officer caught Noble, he said, "if you get me on camera, I'll do 24 years, I don't care." The officer reported, "he was not arrested, rather taken to urgent psychiatric care"

Maybe he should've been arrested, because two days after that, on 6-14-16 at 12:43 a.m., 19-year-old Madison Rentz was working at Circle K when Nathaniel Noble walked in with a machete' that he "Threatened to use [the] machete" on her as he robbed her. Madison said she "Hit the silent panic button" and thankfully, police arrived quickly, arresting Noble and booking him. This time he received serious charges, and so a DNA sample was take from him and entered into CODIS.

On November 16th, CODIS identified a match between Noble's DNA and two used condoms found next to female stabbing victim Liz Hermann, in her burned down house.

On March 22nd Detective Smith went to interview Noble, whereupon Noble asked, "Are you here about the murder in 2008?" Maybe Noble was smarter than he let on.

Noble was obviously a danger to the community, dangerous toward everyone he interacted with, including the two knife-oriented orders of protection filed against him by Theresa Otte in 2009 and 2011, and trying to stab his dad in Michigan in 1998. And now he was implicated in a murder, wherein a woman was stabbed. This, additional to wielding a machete' upon 19-year-old Madison Rentz. Even the treatment centers routinely called the police on him. Here, the Maricopa County Attorney's office, under the leadership of Bill Montgomery, along with MCSO, had a chance to put him away for a long time.

Instead, they court-ordered him to another mental hospital, which he escaped from, and was caught at 10 p.m. on June 20, 2017, high on meth, still wearing his "hospital bracelet" "setting fires…in front of the family dollar store." Again, he was not arrested. The Phoenix PC gave him a ride to UPC to sleep it off and get more prescription pills. Schizophrenics get the good stuff. Hospital staff who likely do not know what to do with him would likely just feed him *a lot* of pills, "downers," which is exactly what he would want for a "come-down" off meth—every meth-addicts dream)

Three weeks later, July 15, 2017, Noble called Phoenix PC from a payphone near Community Bridges "stating that he is FBI and was requesting PD to respond." He said that he was "Undercover FBI agent" and that if they didn't respond he was "Going to burn the city down." They gave him a ride to UPC.

On October 18, 2017, PHX police responded to a group home, where two women had called them because Noble was "walking around outside of his group home apartment nude" "throwing apples" at people. They drove him to UPC.

Thirteen days later, knowing that he can use PPD as his own personal taxi service, Noble approached two officers, Meyers and Daniel Miller, outside Community Bridges and asked them for a ride to UPC to get his pills. They took him. When they "Arrived at UPC they advised Nathaniel [SIC] was there two days prior and once PD leaves he tears up the place." Noble would play the "sick" card on police, manipulate them into driving him to different parts of town, to treatment centers, and once police left he would threaten treatment center staff and "tear up the place" in an effort to get more prescription drugs. In this case the officers, after driving him to UPC and finding out UPC didn't want him, then drove to his original treatment center that Theresa Otte, his girlfriend from 2008, made him go to, at 32nd Street and Bell Road. Sometimes it seemed like police would take him anywhere but jail.

A month later he was trespassed from Wal-Mart for stealing, but not arrested.

Eleven days after that, on December 12, 2017 he pretended to have a gun and attempted an armed robbery at Circle K at 6649 W. Thomas, in southwest Phoenix. He was not arrested, taken to a "facility" instead. He was trespassed from Circle K. There were becoming fewer and fewer places Noble was allowed to go.

Perhaps benefiting from a free ride two days earlier, now, on December 12, 2019, Noble was trespassed from Circle K on 56th street and Bell, in *northeast* Phoenix, for "loitering, bothering customers, and stealing."

Nine days later, after escaping from another mental hospital, Noble, while still wearing his hospital scrubs, was driving a motorized shopping cart that he had stolen from Target earlier that morning. You can't make this stuff up. He had driven it across the street to Wal-Mart and was driving along the front of Walmart setting all of the trashcans on fire. He then drove *into* the Wal-Mart and filled the motorized shopping cart with merchandise, cruising at leisure around the store, up one aisle and down the other, in his hospital scrubs, picking out whatever he wanted, including a lot of hunting knives—some of which went into the basket, one he removed from the package and stuffed into his waist line. He then drove into the checkout line, let the clerk scan everything, didn't pay for any of it, and drove away, into the in-store McDonald's and ordered a coffee.

As you can imagine, the police who responded had fun with this. It was all on camera. Police noted that Noble was "schizophrenic...and using methamphetamine on a daily basis." He was trespassed from Wal-Mart and booked for trespassing, shoplifting and arson.

Four days later police responded to "an emergency traffic welfare check" and booked him on a warrant.

Three weeks after that, police responded to "an emergency call for service of a male threatening to light Baptist Hospital on fire." Upon arrival they saw that it was Noble, "a little insane." They gave him a ride to UPC.

I've watched a few episodes of "Cops," and I've never seen this many cops be this nice to a meth-user with a rap sheet.

Two weeks later, March 3, 2018, Noble was booked for possession of dangerous drugs—meth. He did a few months in County, then failed at a treatment center and chose drugs and homelessness again. On January 20, 2019 he approached two police officers who reported, "Nathanael stated he was homeless and...had not been taking his medication for the past few days." They gave him a ride to UPC. Three days later on 1-23-19, Theresa Otte, Noble's ex-girlfriend, who he cheated on with Liz Hermann, called police because he was at her house ringing her doorbell. After *ten years*, he still remembered exactly where she lived. She said in her interview with MCSO Detective Paul Smith that in 2013, She saw what she thought was a "homeless person" peeking over her back wall and called police, who caught him, and identified him as Noble. It must have been scary for her, after the whole Liz Hermann murder ordeal, then the knives, and restraining orders, and multiple calls to police since then, that none of it helped, and he was still showing up at her house in 2019, apparently stalking her.

But they didn't arrest him that day either. Six days later he was caught red-handed in an attempted two-million-dollar bank robbery at the Chase bank on North 19th avenue, where he pretended to have a gun and threatened the 4'11" female teller. Police responded mid-robbery, it was all on video, and he gave a full confession. The report stated, "He stated that he worked undercover for the FBI [and] he was trying to buy 500 pounds of meth." Perhaps playing the mental illness card, he also told this officer that, "he is diagnosed bipolar, schizoaffective and he has not taken his medications in a week." It goes on to say "Nathanael asked on numerous occasions to be taken to UPC due to not taking his medication for the last week."

Nathanael's attempt at getting an easy-out to the UPC didn't work this time, because after taking DNA and prints from the check station and counters he touched, these Phoenix officers booked him for robbery and took him to jail. They did their job.

But *something* worked, because *three days later*—not even long enough to review the case, or wait for results on the prints and DNA or do a Rule 11 psych evaluation, prosecutor Douglas Self of MCAO had Noble released, again, citing as his reason: "No reasonable likelihood of a conviction," despite the confession and video.

Noble probably couldn't believe it; they kicked him out of the jail, again, back into the free world. Maybe he did work for the FBI, or just the police, as an informant. Maybe they needed him out there.

Eleven days later he was trespassed from another Walmart and driven to LARC by police.

Five days after that a Phoenix police officer, Katrina Morales, was dropping off another male subject at Community Bridges when Noble "flagged [her] down [and] asked if he could be transported to UPC," so she gave him a ride. Two days after that he assaulted someone on a light rail and was trespassed from all light-rails in the valley.

And why wouldn't he beat somebody up in public? He could do whatever he wanted to do., He knew that now. He was caught red-handed in a bank robbery...didn't matter. Walked around lighting things on fire, as police watched, police knew he was on meth every day...didn't matter, machete' at Circle K, whatever. Sure, now he was banned from every Circle K, Wal-Mart, Target, Chase bank, Jack-in-the-box, all the light rails, so what. Two days after the light rail assault, on February 2, 2019, he went to another Jack-in-the-box, up the street, and tried to stab two young women at 4:45 am, one a minor.

17-year-old Ariana Velia Valisuzuewa was getting the restaurant ready for the day in the February pre-dawn hours, Noble's most active time. She glanced out the drive-thru window and saw a disturbed man staring at her through the glass, with a knife in his hand. You can't make this stuff up. She panicked and stepped behind a machine to hide, while her manager, Guadalupe, just 20 years old, ran down the hall to hide in the office. This infuriated Noble. He picked up a fist-sized rock, similar to the one he'd thrown through Marvin McClain's windshield, and began smashing the window. He then used his knife to pry the frame apart and slide it open, whereupon he began crawling into the window head first, swinging his knife at Ariana, yelling at Ariana, who was crying and shaking now, yelling, "Do you want to die?! Do you want to die!" over and over as he tried to crawl in. Suddenly, a construction vehicle pulled up and spooked Noble, who then climbed out of the window and ran with his knife, like a wild animal. Police apprehended him in a hotel parking lot nearby. They said 17-year-old Ariana was "still shaking and crying" when they interviewed her. If the construction vehicle hadn't happened to pull up, he would have massacred those two young women.

While he was doing that, Judge Barton was trying to figure out how to justify denying my petition and ignoring the DNA connection to Noble, leaving him for the young women of north Phoenix to deal with. While he, Noble, was right on the *cusp*, of viciously attacking 17-year-old Ariana with a knife, Judge Barton was honing in on the fact that Dr. Streed's report was backdated, and our lack of explanation as to why we didn't bring up Noble's DNA connection to the stabbing victim Liz Hermann in 2014, before the DNA match existed. A real service to the community, and honorable way to "earn" her taxpayer-funded salary.

II Chapter **11**

Actual Innocence

••

So, "what now?" is the looming question? Any logical layperson would think that there must be an avenue in place to remedy this situation. There is, it is Rule 32, and we have exercised it, but the appellate courts do not sincerely evaluate claims of actual innocence in Arizona, not anymore.

You've seen the evidence, the arguments, and the rulings. So, if an evidentiary hearing is not to be held in light of this situation, then when? If this case is not a claim for actual innocence that even warrants being orally examined in a courtroom, then what is?

The advent of DNA technology and its exceptional maturation in the 1990's and early 2000's led to a barrage of exonerations so extensive, so many and so vast, that it created a crisis of mistrust in our jury system. How could they convict innocent people, we asked, pragmatically, literally, *how* can it happen? And with each DNA exoneration we learned how as each case was disassembled and dissected. We learned about things like coercion and inappropriate suppression on the State's behalf. We learned about prosecutorial misconduct, lying jailhouse "snitches," and some bad-apple police detectives who were more than willing to commit perjury right along with them. We learned that the DNA issues were only a fraction of what was wrong with the "justice" system.

Simultaneously, a society-changing development took place—the cell phone video. This, along with social media and information sharing placed the power of exposure into the hands of the masses. Local news networks no longer had monopolistic decision-making power over what became public. Everything became public. And we, *the*

269

public, began seeing with our own eyes some police officers shoot people, which we already knew they did, they had to, in order to protect themselves. But some of the videos we watched, to our disbelief, showed some police officers committing *murder*, and then lying about it, with a straight face. The presence of other police officers at each scene, who did not stop the killings or protest them, led us to *really* worry that rather than a matter of a few rogue police officers this might actually be the culture in some police circles.

As a result of inappropriate police shootings, and countless other types of police misconduct now having video evidence, along with the DNA exonerations, state and county governments across the United States had to shell-out enormous amounts of money, for an "expense" that was certainly not figured into the budget.

The goings-on from the mid-1990's to the 2010's cost agencies and offices a lot. Both in the form of money and public distrust.

At first, local governments welcomed DNA technology, worshiped it. Even conservative states like Arizona assembled "justice projects" to look for opportunities to exonerate people, paid for by the government. But perhaps they found too many. After exonerating someone basically every year until 2013 it just stopped. It was John Watkins, then Ray Krone, Bill Macumber, Debra Milke...there was at least one in the newsfeed year-round, until Milke. Milke delivered an especially heavy blow to the pristine image of the Arizona justice system. With a series of other exonerations becoming the collective precursor, and bringing peoples' concerns about the justice system into focus, we all got to watch as one of the most predatory, dishonest individuals we had become familiar with, detective Ernesto Saldate, pled the fifth and refused to testify in Milke's exoneration proceedings for fear that he would incriminate himself, now that the cat was out of the bag. He lawyered up. Most Arizona citizens had spent the last quarter of a century believing Milke was guilty, a monster, who had killed her own son. I spent almost my whole life believing she was guilty, as did my fad, and it stayed with both of us as we drove past the tall white cross that was erected in a desert sand wash next to 99th avenue where the boy was shot, on our way to Litchfield to build houses each summer. The Milke exoneration changed everything.

There is a lot of pressure now on local governments to end these crises. I fear now that the ruling classes in Arizona, leading up to now, have found the problems to be so big, so complex, that they have instead decided to hide them—hide cases like mine, like Jeffrey Landrigan's, and bury my family and I along with their secrets, in order to make it look like the problem has been fixed. Why else would they not test the bloody handprint found near Ms. Hermann's body?

They can't afford to let the public find out that they convicted the wrong person in yet *another* high-profile death penalty case. Can't afford to let the public find out about the methods that MCSO Detective Paul Smith used for years—beating up alibi witnesses, hiding cell phone data, altering interviews. Can't afford to let the public find out about the monster they've created through enabling Nathaniel Noble, D*efinitely* can't afford to financially compensate me, or Liz Hermann's family, or the other women who were terrorized by Noble since then. They can't afford to give justice in this case, and they don't have to, because there is no cell phone video of it.

I have Joy Riddle. She is amazing. She has dedicated her life to the law and to justice. She put in the exhausting years at law school, earned her degree, her license, and worked for years as a prosecutor. She is assertive, smart, and likeable. She is loved and respected by her peers and by her family. She takes her continuing legal education seriously, focusing on PCR and appellate issues just because of my case. She is a networking ninja, small yet powerful, like wonder woman or mighty mouse. She will do anything she has to for the hearing and reunification of my family, the saving of our future, and none of it matters.

The Arizona appellate courts have conveyed to her, as they've conveyed to all defense attorneys, that their role as defense attorneys is no good here. They are welcome to earn an income but are not permitted to exonerate anyone.

I have an amazing wife, Jill. My best friend. I talk to her every day. She keeps our household intact and makes sure the bills are paid, and the puppies are coddled. She is still waiting for me, even after twelve years. She is intelligent and independent, and advocates for me, as does my mom, my dad, my brother, my father-in-law, and many others, all exceptional people.

We have active police officers on our side, exculpatory evidence, a real "bad guy," and none of it matters, because the appellate judges and county prosecutors are only interested in justice when it is convenient for them, when it is easy. The MCAO, under Andrew Thomas and then Bill Montgomery, who Gov. Ducey appointed to the AZ Supreme court, despite Montgomery having no experience as a judge, only as a prosecutor. have, in our experience, prioritized their desires over what is truly justice. To us it seems that when it does result in true justice, it is just a coincidence. Arpaio did the same at MCSO, as did Paul Smith, Judge Barton, and Catherine Leisch, Detective Ernesto Saldate, many U.S. Presidents, and most politicians. The villains are too many, to name, the heroes too few to matter, and for that reason alone my family and I, and many we know, believe that the system is incorrigible. It will never be fixed.

You disagree. Prove it.

If my attackers on the prison yard in Yuma all those years ago had succeeded in taking my life, no one would have ever heard any of this. Certainly no one will ever hear what Noah Todd had to say in May of 2010.

Going forward Jill and I will continue to get older, and older, and we will eventually die alone because we will never have children or grandchildren. She was 28 when I was taken, now she is 40.

Closing Thoughts

I will be forty-nine at my release date in 2030, if I live that long. I will get home just in time to prepare my own dad for his own passing away. My mom, who was in and out of hospitals all of 2019, even on life support in August during her cancer treatments, will likely not live to see me home again, because of Judge Barton's ruling.

I will be unemployable and stigmatized. Being attached to me and having to pay for everything from my vehicle to my shoes and toothbrush will make that portion of Jill's life even worse than this one. Judge Barton will enjoy her retirement, feeling proud and justified of her career, as will Detective Paul Smith, and Rick Miller, and people will believe in them.

Liz Hermann will never get justice. Her family will never know who killed her, they will never know about Nathaniel Noble. Noble, when he plays the schizo-card and gets out of jail for trying to stab the two girls at Jack-in-the-box, for the 100th time, will hit the ground running. He will re-up on anti-psychotics at the nearest mental hospital and then escape from it, while still wearing his hospital scrubs, acquiring as quickly as possible a lighter, a knife, or machete, and a meth pipe, and get loose, again, like a tiger out of a zoo exhibit, and he will be the young women of north Phoenix's problem to deal with—not Judge Barton's.

This is the world you live in, not the one you saw on T.V. This is not the America of law and under SVU. This is America the not so beautiful. There is no true liberty, save for the privileged, and there never was *justice for all*. The rights the soldiers die for overseas, from Miranda, to competent counsel and a phone call the night you are arrested, they are not real, and no matter how thoughtfully written the marvelous law has come to be, major components of it, from due process to the plain language of Rule 32, are continually ignored by Arizona judges, much to the suffering of good American men like my dad, grandad, and father-in-law. If you are an idealistic young law student, strong in your ambition, or a more mature and distinguished titan of the law, and you insist that the system works, perhaps personally offended by the attacks that come upon it, and you insist that indeed, here in *these* modern United States of

America, so pure and sophisticated, that guilty people go to prison and innocent people go home...prove it. Fix this.

In the meantime I'll just be sitting here.

Justin Lunsford

The End

The End

Milton Keynes UK
Ingram Content Group UK Ltd.
UKHW010642100823
426647UK00006B/203

9 780578 979670